Also by Edith Fiore, Ph.D.

You Have Been Here Before
The Unquiet Dead

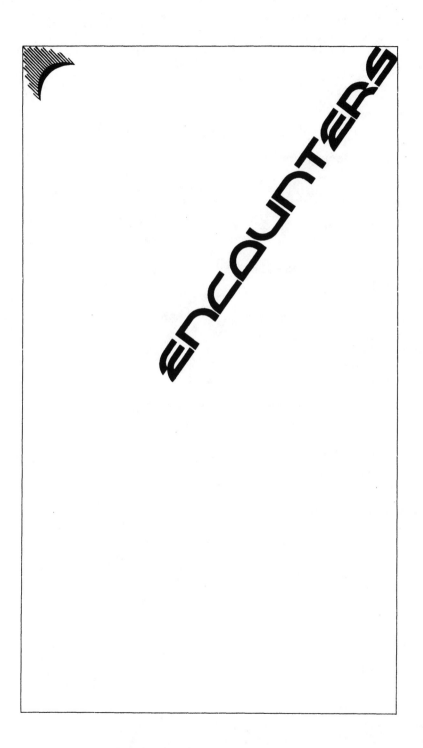

ENCOUNTERS

The Ten Most Common Signs of Abductions
by Extraterrestrials

- Inability to account for periods of time
- Persistent nightmares and/or dreams of UFOs and/or aliens
- Sleep disorders
- Waking up with unusual bodily sensations
- Appearance of mysterious marks on the body
- Feeling monitored, watched, and/or communicated with
- Repeated sightings of UFOs
- Vague recollections of a close encounter
- Unexplained healing of ailments or afflictions
- Reacting with fear of and/or anxiety about UFOs and/or ETs

ENCOUNTERS

A Psychologist Reveals Case Studies of Abductions by Extraterrestrials

Edith Fiore, Ph.D.

Ballantine Books • New York

http://www.randomhouse.com

Library of Congress Catalog Card Number: 97-93871

ISBN 9-780-345-42020-6

Designed by Karin Batten

This edition published by arrangement with Doubleday, a division of Bantam Doubleday Dell Publishing Group, Inc.

Manufactured in the United States of America

144912319

This book is dedicated to Mary Damroth, whose love, friendship, help and patience made writing *Encounters* a joy.

Contents

	Foreword	xi
	Preface	xv
1	"Empty Your Mind. Think of Nothing."	1
2	"They Put Something in My Rectum."	8
3	". . . They're Coming Down Here, Wanting to Mix with Our Race . . ."	34
4	"I Wouldn't Let Them Make Me Forget."	51
5	"They Can Come and Take Me Any Time They Want!"	67
6	"They Said I Had Cancer!"	89
7	"I've Let Those People Touch Me!"	115
8	" 'We Need You as a Contact.' "	132
9	"Oh My God! They Already Know How to Incorporate."	146
10	"They Go in There and Dissolve the Damn Clot!"	166
11	"They Take My Eggs!"	198
12	"To Be Back . . . Would Be Fabulous!"	230
13	"They Call Themselves the Planters."	274
14	"I Went Through Those Venetian Blinds!"	295
15	". . . The Signs and Symptoms That Are Indicators."	319
16	"You Can Discover Your Own Close Encounters."	325
17	". . . The Evidence Can No Longer Be Squelched."	332
	Appendix	335
	Suggested Reading	341

Foreword

It is my pleasure to introduce you to Edith Fiore, Ph.D. Dr. Fiore, a clinical psychologist, has demonstrated her skills not only as a master therapist, but as a master teacher as well. She has contributed her professional experience and knowledge to complex and difficult areas of research.

I am so pleased that Dr. Fiore has turned her writing skills to the timely and controversial topic of UFO encounters. Once again, she shows her ability to identify and formalize basic procedures for personal investigation; she instructs and encourages readers to explore their own UFO memories. Also, she provides information for those who wish further reading and for those who may need additional assistance from professional hypnotists and experienced UFO investigators.

I enjoy Dr. Fiore as a colleague, mentor, and friend because she shares with others her qualities of curiosity, courage and compassion. She is willing to explore paranormal phenomena, which takes curiosity. She is willing to deal with uncertain knowledge, which takes courage. She is willing to listen to the angers, anxieties and fears of others, which takes compassion.

Dr. Fiore is aware of the orthodox scientific paradigm for evaluating UFO reports: Physical evidence is the only basis for "truth"; without physical evidence, there can be no biological evidence, no psychological evidence and no spiritual or psychic evidence! Thus, she knows that she must emphasize her role as a therapist rather than her role as a researcher.

However, in my opinion, the modern scientific paradigm is shifting. Many scientists (e.g., Willis Harman, Ph.D., author of *Global Mind Change)* are considering the hierarchy of physical sciences, life sciences, human sciences and transpersonal sciences, including meditation and spirituality.

My bias, of course, is to regard Dr. Fiore as a true scientist: She follows the trail of the phenomena—regardless of the fears and criticisms of orthodox scientists. She is willing to *explore* (not necessarily *explain)* the ABCs (absurd, bizarre, crazy aspects) of UFO encounters.

The ABCs of UFO reports indicate, over and over, that controversy and ambiguity are the "earmarks" of UFO experiences. Also, UFO experiences indicate repeatedly that there are personal as well as transpersonal aspects in every UFO encounter.

Dr. Fiore knows that paranormal and spiritual aspects of UFO encounters are puzzling but important phenomena. Her case studies reveal the variety of claims about psychic experiences. These same descriptions occur in reports by investigators from all over the planet Earth, from Africa and Australia to the USA and USSR.

Any UFO researcher who has read thousands of reports and listened to hundreds of UFO experiences, as I have, knows that UFO encounters are awesome events. Persons can experience joy and happiness, but they also can experience anxiety, pain, panic, rage and/or terror. The bodily marks and scars of UFO abductees are reminders of their examinations at the hands (or claws) of alien beings. The psychic "gifts" of UFO contactees are a reminder to them of their tasks or missions to assist others around them.

Yes, in my opinion, the evidence for UFO encounters is "real," at several levels. Further, the evidence for a "cover-up" of UFO evidence is impressive. Some writers (e.g., Timothy Good, *Above Top Secret)*, have provided analyses of military and political documents that demonstrate the governmental cover-up of UFO evidence. Others (e.g., Jacques Vallée, *Dimensions* and other UFO books) have emphasized the cover-up by the alien visitors. Other authors, of course, dispute the claims of cover-up either by ETs (extraterrestrials) and/or EDs (extradimensionals), or by governmental agencies.

But there is cover-up at one level of which I am personally aware—the level of individual UFO contactees. I have talked with hundreds and hundreds of UFO experiencers, including many professional persons, who refuse to talk openly about their UFO encounters. Thus, we as individuals are part of the cover-up

—indirectly or directly—if we fail to disclose our own experience(s) or if we fail to listen.

As a counseling psychologist, I understand and respect the wish of any person who requests that I maintain confidentiality of her or his UFO report. However, I claim to be a UFO contactee as well as a UFO observer. (See the 1985 book by Ruth Montgomery, *Aliens Among Us*). As a UFO researcher, I encourage any willing individual to talk to interested persons about his or her UFO encounter. Disclosure is important for three reasons: First, additional information can assist the scientific community to investigate the dimensions of UFO phenomena; second, even if the human community never solves the UFO puzzle, we shall increase our sense of human compassion and social cooperation by sharing our UFO experiences; third, as Dr. Fiore shows in her case histories, most people feel better about themselves if they explore and accept the reality of their UFO encounters.

Dr. Edith Fiore provides competent and compassionate assistance to participants in hypnotherapeutic sessions; also, she provides useful instruction and enlightenment through her perceptive and persistent examination of UFO experiences. Thus, I am pleased to introduce you to a master therapist, a master teacher and an author whose research now provides us all with a clearer vision of the personal and transpersonal significance of UFO encounters.

R. Leo Sprinkle, Ph.D.

Preface

The sun streamed in my window and onto my face, waking me earlier than I wanted on a Saturday morning in 1950. I stretched sleepily in my four-poster antique walnut bed in the very room where George Washington had slept almost two hundred years before. This was to be a day that would affect my whole life and eventually lead to this book.

"Here's a present for you, Edee," Keith said with a mischievous smile, handing me a hardcover book. Keith Winter had been my family's houseguest at Headquarters Farm for months, preferring it and the fresh, clean air and ambience of Bucks County, Pennsylvania, to his apartment in New York City's Greenwich Village. Keith was a writer and had delighted us on many happy occasions by reading his work, taking the various parts and beautifully changing his voice for each character. My favorite was *The Red Shoes*, the classic film about a ballerina obsessed with dancing.

"What's this, Keith?" I asked, turning the book over and reading the material on the back. "What are flying saucers?"

Keith had introduced me to a subject that would become a lifelong interest. *Flying Saucers Are Real!* was the first book on the topic of UFOs (unidentified flying objects). My reaction to it, having read it that very day, was total acceptance of Major Donald Keyhoe's premise that we were being visited by beings from other planets. I believed that the spacecraft were real and that intelligent "people" were flying here in them. From that time on, I have spent hours scouring the night skies, hoping to see a UFO. I have seen lights doing strange things high among the stars, but nothing so convincing that it couldn't be explained as a natural phenomenon.

In 1979, I joined a UFO study group and became intensely interested in extraterrestrial visitations. I lay in my wine-barrel hot tub many a night at my Light Ranch in Lake County in northern California, delighting in the star-studded sky, occasionally sending messages, even "pleas," to our space brothers to make themselves visible or to give me a message. They never did. However, it was during that period that I awoke one morning, feeling particularly good, and remembered a fragment of a dream. It was vague and fuzzy, but I did recall being shown around a "room" in a UFO. My hosts treated me as an honored guest and colleague. I sensed that they were humanoid, not the least bit frightening or strange. I also felt that they were males. I didn't remember any other details. The dream did not particularly impress me at the time. I passed it off as just wishful thinking.

After a few years, my focus shifted, and UFOs and extraterrestrials assumed a background position, along with many other interests and hobbies.

I have been a psychotherapist in private practice, first in Miami, Florida, and later in Saratoga, California, since 1969. I stumbled onto hypnosis accidentally in 1973 by agreeing to join my brother, Frank Fiore, at a weekend seminar at Esalen Institute at Big Sur, California. We took a self-hypnosis workshop, and I experienced going into an hypnotic trance for the first time. The following Monday, in my office, I tried it out with a courageous patient and have been using hypnosis ever since.

Hypnotic age regression is an extremely effective therapeutic technique. It gets to the cause of symptoms and problems of all sorts and results in immediate and lasting cures. I have come to believe that a great majority of symptoms are due to repressed trauma. Sigmund Freud stated that making the subconscious, conscious, in other words, bringing repressed material hidden in the dark recesses of the mind to its surface, results in a cure. I had accepted this for many years but now question the process somewhat. For example, many other hypnotherapists and I have found that symptoms could be completely eliminated when, under hypnosis, a patient regressed to the age at which causative events occurred and recalled or relived them. On occasion it was found that when a patient came out of the trance, he or she did not remember the work that had just so painfully been done. This was due to the patient's having been in a very deep, somnambulistic state, in which amnesia upon awakening is frequently experienced. I have also found some patients who had been in light trances were later unable to recall the traumas they had just "re-

membered." They may have mentally given themselves a suggestion, while still hypnotized, to forget because the events were
threatening to their self-concepts.

Even though I don't understand how the cure takes place, I do
know that it is important for the repressed event, buried in the
subconscious mind, to be recalled, remembered, relived or dealt
with in whatever way the person will allow.

During the fifteen years that I have been using hypnotic age
regression, I have found many of my patients "remembering"
what appeared to have been contacts with and abductions by
extraterrestrials in spacecraft. Once the repressed traumas had
been brought to light, any symptoms or problems caused by them
were immediately eliminated. Generally the patients were surprised, even shocked, to find that they had had close encounters.

In 1987 I was invited to speak at the California Society of
Psychical Research by its president, my good friend and colleague,
Jeffrey Mishlove, Ph.D., author of *Roots of Consciousness*. When
I had finished my talk, I met James Harder, Ph.D., a professor at
the University of California at Berkeley. We had a quick chat
about his work with abductees and planned to get together as
soon as possible to pursue our mutual interest.

Meeting Jim Harder the night of the lecture in Berkeley gave
me a person to work with to explore my one and only (remembered) dream of a UFO. My patients' regressions in which
dreams played a dominant role and the many accounts of abductions and contacts with repeated references to dreams I had read
about made me wonder if my dream could possibly have been the
remnant of a remembered experience. I called Jim and set up an
appointment for a Saturday. Several weeks later, after a delightful
cable car ride up the steep hillside to his house overlooking San
Francisco Bay, we met for several very pleasant hours.

Jim offered me some of his home-baked, low cholesterol brown-
ies, and after we settled ourselves in his living room, he asked me,
"When did you have the dream?"

"Years ago, and even then it was very vague. I have a sneaking
suspicion that it's not a dream."

"Dreams are very commonly the tip of the iceberg of a meeting with ETs," he said, picking up his notepad. "Let's get started and we'll soon find out about yours."

Jim did a gentle, almost whispered hypnotic induction. I could feel my body becoming very relaxed and heavy, sinking down into the cushions of his couch. He had my inner (subconscious) mind select and lift one finger to designate "yes" and another for "no." My conscious mind was not to interfere in any way with the lifting and lowering of the finger. I had used this technique for years with my patients and had already established the responses in myself and had used them during many sessions of self-hypnosis.

Jim questioned my subconscious mind, having it respond through my fingers, which flipped up readily. We quickly discovered that indeed I had been contacted. I had been floated out of the bedroom in my condominium in Los Gatos into a spaceship. Once there, I was treated with respect and kindness and much was explained to me that I was not to remember until later. Then it would filter into my mind, more as memories than as knowledge, and would be very helpful for me. Jim got a description of the aliens and the room. I was in a very light trance and found myself doing exactly what I urge my patients not to do—trying to analyze and critique the material as it came forth. To this day, I am not convinced that I "remembered" an actual happening. I had read a great deal on the subject and had done so many regressions with my patients that I could not separate fact from fiction.

"Edee, most people find it hard to convince themselves that what they bring up in hypnosis is real. We can't really know for sure," Jim explained patiently. "Let's work on it another time. I'll see if I can get you to go deeper." Since then, however, we've both been exceedingly busy, and because it wasn't a top priority for me, we haven't met again.

Several weeks later, a young woman came for a consultation, having been in the audience for my talk that night. I had mentioned a case of abduction that had unsettled her. She had felt extremely nervous when I described the experience of my patient and had battled with herself for over a week before calling for an appointment.

"I've worried about this for several years now," she confided. "I seem to remember being taken on board a UFO against my will. In fact, just talking about it now makes me feel very anxious." Tears spilled down her cheeks as she reached for a tissue. "I'm really scared that I'm losing my mind. Sometimes I think I'm going crazy!"

"You seem fine to me," I told her. "Why do you think that having memories of a possible UFO encounter means that you're not sane?"

"It's my husband. He not only laughs at the whole idea of flying saucers, but thinks that anyone who claims they've been captured by extraterrestrials is a crackpot. He's so sure he's right . . . and if the topic ever comes up, his friends all jump right in and agree. If he ever found out why I'm here, he'd probably kick me out . . . divorce me or have me locked up!"

After more questioning, it did appear that she had seen UFOs on many occasions and had had some close encounters of the fourth kind (CEIVs), those in which there is an abduction by or contact with aliens. We only had time during that session for me to make a recorded tape of hypnotic suggestions to encourage restful sleep at night and to help her to be more relaxed in general and feel better about herself. Unfortunately, her fear got the better of her and she never returned. I have often wondered, particularly since then, how many other suffering people resist the very treatment that could give them the relief they so desperately need, because of their fears of finding out about contacts with the visitors and the consequences of that discovery.

◢

Almost one-half of U.S. citizens, according to a 1987 Gallup poll, believe in UFOs, and one out of eleven report having seen them. However, most new ideas and theories throughout history have met with resistance and ridicule. Even now, some Christian groups believe that UFOs are evidence of Satan at work and that those who accept them need prayers for their salvation.

We need to investigate these phenomena and help the people who have been traumatized by their encounters with aliens. I believe it is crucial that we have open minds, being neither gullible nor terminally skeptical, in order to rationally assess the evidence. I feel my work with hypnotized patients who seem to have remembered UFO abductions and contacts adds to the growing fund of data and knowledge of extraterrestrial visits to our planet.

✒

The first chapter of *Encounters* introduces you to the general subject of close encounters of the fourth kind and explains how hypnotic regressions work. It is followed by thirteen chapters, each a case history of an individual who appeared to have had experience with extraterrestrials. Names and identifying data have been changed in order to protect the privacy of my patients and subjects.

Perhaps you have wondered if you have been contacted or abducted. In Chapter Sixteen, I have described a technique for investigation that may help you find out, the pendulum. James Harder, Ph.D., and Leo Sprinkle, Ph.D., both known and respected UFO researchers, as well as others, use this method to help people discover whether they have had contacts with aliens. In the privacy of your own home, you can use a pendulum to tap into your subconscious memories. I have designed questions you can use and also have given you pointers on how to go beyond my questions. If you find that you are an abductee or contactee, you may want to pursue it further. In the Appendix, you will find lists of organizations, researchers and hypnotherapists specializing in UFO sightings and CEIVs. At the end of *Encounters* is a list of books I have compiled, which offers you an opportunity to continue to educate yourself in the area of ufology.

As you read *Encounters,* it would be helpful for you to keep a notepad nearby and record anything at all that you suspect as being evidence of a close encounter. Notice, for example, any signs of anxiety: fear, apprehension, heart acceleration, sweaty palms, dizziness, shortness of breath, etc. Mark the margin or highlight the material and record the page number so you can check back later when you start exploring your own possible contacts. You also may start remembering seeing lights in the sky, or recall a dream you had totally forgotten. This book could bring closer to the surface of your conscious mind experiences that have been deeply buried for years.

❦

Having read Whitley Strieber's *Communion* and Budd Hopkins's *The Intruders,* as well as other books on close encounters, I realized that probably thousands of people in our country have been abducted and/or contacted. My patients' and subjects' experiences were similar to, but at the same time quite different from, those reported in the above-mentioned books. Usually their experiences involved being taken against their will and examined thoroughly and, at times, painfully. With some, however, the encounters were meant to educate them, and, in a few cases, even help and heal them.

I wrote this book to expose you to another dimension of the contact/abduction phenomenon. *Encounters* may frighten you. I hope it will educate you. But my greatest reward would be if it helps you.

Acknowledgments

I wish to express my gratitude to:

The thirteen people who allowed me to present their case studies;

My patients and subjects, whose courage and experiences contributed to my understanding of the close encounter of the fourth kind phenomenon;

Ormond McGill, whose encouragement and friendship helped me keep on schedule with my writing;

Ted Chichak, for emotional support and friendship that go beyond his responsibilities as my literary agent;

Jim Fitzgerald and Mark Garofalo, my editors, for the interest they showed in this work;

Kate Hendon, for her patience, skill, friendship and interest while transcribing the tapes and collating the material.

This book is not meant to be a substitute for medical or psychological help. I always recommend that my patients see a qualified physician for their physical problems. If you have emotional or mental problems, you should seek the help of a professional therapist or counselor. In the Appendix, I have listed organizations and individuals who specialize in helping people who have had close encounters with extraterrestrials.

"Empty Your Mind.
Think of Nothing."

"I was home alone. Scared. As long as I can remember, I've always been frightened of being alone, especially at night. I still am. Then, I was either twelve or thirteen. My parents had taken Bill, my older brother to the junior-senior prom, so I turned on the TV to keep me company. Suddenly my eyes noticed a very bright light out the window right over the TV. It was dark out, about nine. The light was on the hill to the east. A very brilliant single light at the top of the hill. It seemed to be calling to me. I got very scared. I just sat still in the chair. I noticed that my body was immobilized. The TV turned to black-and-white snow. I couldn't take my eyes off of it. I don't know how much time elapsed. Then the TV started blinking and the color came back on. I looked up, but the light was gone . . . vanished. I felt funny. Strange. Heavy. I tried to move my arms and legs. I was so relieved to take my eyes off the TV and to be able to move . . . that I was back."

1

Sandi "forgot" about her experience for nine years, until a friend, Kathy, told her about a UFO she had witnessed in the desert night sky, as she and her husband were driving in the Southwest. Kathy later remembered having been abducted by extraterrestrials. As she was describing her reactions to it, Sandi began to feel anxious and tingly and commented that she wasn't feeling well. Kathy, having developed some psychic sensitivity since the incident, suggested that Sandi had been abducted.

Five years later, in my office under hypnosis, Sandi reexperienced a very frightening and physically painful two-hour encounter on board a spacecraft, a UFO, in which she had been examined and questioned. You'll be reading her account of this experience in Chapter Two. Officially, Sandi had an encounter of the fourth kind and could be classified as an "abductee."

Sandi is one of thousands of people who have been abducted or contacted by extraterrestrials. As a result of her close encounter, she experienced fears until she remembered the trauma under hypnosis fourteen years later. Many other abductees/contactees have developed phobias, anxiety, depression, amnesia, nightmares and other emotional and mental disturbances. Another, occasional, outcome of these encounters is various types of physical symptoms, which have been reported in the literature. A very common consequence of the abduction/contact phenomenon is that people begin doubting their own sanity. If they remember the experience, instead of being helped with compassion and understanding, they are often ridiculed and treated as though they were crazy, which, of course, further adds to the problem.

Interestingly, in at least one-half of the cases I've been involved in, the people were greatly helped by their encounters. Operations, usually involving lasers, and other treatments relieved symptoms, even correcting some conditions that were potentially fatal.

Despite the often traumatic effects, in almost every case it appears that the extraterrestrials were not motivated to hurt or frighten humans. Sometimes they expressed sorrow when their examinations or treatments elicited pain or fear.

As a hypnotist, it was fascinating for me to hear the verbatim (hypnotic) suggestions the visitors used to invoke relaxation and amnesia. Often they are the very words which any hypnotist uses regularly. In one case, the person was instructed to "empty your mind. Think of nothing." In most cases, just before the experience ended, the people were told, "You will remember nothing. It will be as if nothing has happened. You will forget everything." It seems too that the aliens have devices they employ to induce not only relaxation and cessation of fear, but unconsciousness. You will be reading accounts of individuals being rendered unconscious who still continued to experience what was happening from outside of their bodies, usually from a vantage point above and looking down, observing examinations, operations and treatments. It appears that we have another body, sometimes referred to as "astral," "etheric" or "spiritual," in which we retain awareness. This is consistent with the work of the last decade in the area of the near-death experiences (NDEs), in which people who have (temporarily) died actually left their physical bodies and retained full consciousness, minus the pain and/or fear they had felt prior to leaving them. In *Encounters,* you will see that the majority of my patients/subjects reported similar experiences.

Some of the following case studies may seem like unadulterated science fiction. The case of Dan, whom you'll read about in Chapter Twelve, is especially intriguing. Not only will you see him as a cosmic warrior, but one who totally possessed, by "replacing," a young boy. I found it helpful while working with him to remain particularly objective and nonjudgmental. The interesting thing about his work under hypnosis is that it had a profoundly positive effect on him, helping him to resolve deep inner conflicts (even though he was not a patient) and answering many questions that had troubled him for years. Despite the violence of the material, he felt much better about himself and much more self-confident.

In the next thirteen chapters, you'll be reading the personal accounts of people who have had close encounters of the fourth kind. Some of these individuals were patients who uncovered the hidden experiences in the course of their therapy. Often, the encounters caused the very symptoms that had changed their lives, driving them to seek help. Others were friends, or people whom I heard about through mutual friends, whose "dreams" or sightings of UFOs led me to invite them to my office. Our goals were to investigate their experiences in order to expose possible encounters and/or resolve any resultant symptoms or problems.

I used the technique of hypnotic age regression with each one of these people. Some had never been hypnotized before.

Hypnosis is now being used widely throughout the world as a way of helping people overcome problems and symptoms. There is no agreed-upon definition for hypnosis. However, I believe that every hypnotist would concur, at least, that the patient/subject is in an altered state of awareness, i.e., not in the usual conscious mode of thought. Hypnosis does not invoke sleep, nor unconsciousness. Even in the deepest state, there is awareness, which is focused and heightened. Therapists use hypnosis generally in two major ways: to induce a state of suggestibility in order to impress upon the subconscious mind thoughts and images of wellness and improvement, and as a tool for uncovering repressed experiences, ones that are no longer available to the conscious mind. Hypnosis is an extremely powerful way of helping the subconscious reveal its secrets. When in an altered state, subjects are very susceptible to suggestions. The general suggestions I use in age regression are to go back in time to the event being studied. Since all experiences are recorded in the subconscious mind exactly as they were originally perceived, they are available to be brought to the surface of the mind. However, it must be understood that hypnosis does not improve upon the original perceptions of the encounter, so what is being revealed is only how the person experienced it at the time.

In explaining to my patients how repressed traumas operate, I use the analogy of a thorn in the flesh. While it is embedded in the skin, it is painful, and the wound festers, as the body tries to expel the thorn. When it is finally removed, the healing process starts immediately. The thorn can be held in the palm of the hand and examined. It is not a pretty object, but it no longer causes pain and discomfort. When the frightening memory is brought out of hiding, it is there, usually not forgotten, unless the trance was at the very deepest level, somnambulism. The memory, like the thorn, is not pleasant, but no longer is it doing any damage, and the mind has been healed.

My patients and subjects (the ones coming only to explore a possible UFO encounter) usually went into one of three major levels of hypnotic trance: light, medium or deep. Often, after hypnosis was induced, the person would be in only a light to medium trance, but as the session continued, the level deepened, sometimes to the point of the person's actually reliving the experiences. At these times, the patients/subjects often cried, trembled, flailed about, cringed, etc. On occasion, the experience became too overwhelming, and they brought themselves completely out of the trance, eyes wide open, back to normal consciousness. Usually a few reassuring comments would ease them back into hypnosis so they could continue and benefit from the work we were doing.

Another therapeutic tool I used was finger signals. After the patients/subjects were hypnotized, I asked their subconscious minds to select and lift one finger to designate "yes" and another for "no." Once this mode of communication was established, I was able to ask questions of their inner minds of which their conscious minds were unaware. Although at times unreliable in terms of accuracy, this technique was generally very helpful.

I am a therapist, so my primary goal in doing regressions to close encounters is to help the patient overcome symptoms, problems and difficulties. Recently, I've taken on the additional role of a UFO investigator, in which collecting data (exposing the event) is the primary objective. Often in doing an investigation, I decided to ask questions that may actually have led the person in the suspected direction in order to facilitate our work. If a strict researcher had been peering over my shoulder, he would have frowned and shaken his head, because he would have been after proof of the validity of the contact, whereas my goal may have changed to quickly relieving anxiety that had surfaced.

When you read the cases and verbatim transcripts (which have been edited for clarity and to avoid repetition), you will see how the experiences unfolded for the patients/subjects. Some transcripts show evidence of confusion, contradictions of earlier statements, even flat denials of happenings patients/subjects later revealed. This is because people in trance are still very aware and conscious of what they are saying. If they are in a light to medium trance, they often are simultaneously judging, analyzing and, at times, censoring. Patients have later confessed that they have deliberately withheld material that came to their minds, or, even more confusing for me, have actually lied. Dan, whom you'll meet in Chapter Twelve, nicely summed up his experience under hypnosis the first time as follows:

"I thought there would be more of the sensation of blacking out or going under. And it's so light that it doesn't feel like anything's been done, until you start to let things come out. And you find you're saying things that you're not consciously thinking about. That was a strange experience. At first it was a little disconcerting. But after you relax and accept it, it's not bad. The conscious mind was scurrying around like mad, saying, 'This is not right. You're making this up. You're doing this, you're doing that.' The conscious mind was busy trying to put it down, and the subconscious mind was blabbing its fool head off. It's a very strange feeling, like your mouth is operating on its own, and your mind is saying, 'Shut up, you idiot!' "

In the majority of cases there were very strong resistances to remembering. This came from two main sources: hypnotic suggestions given to the abductees/contactees by the extraterrestrials (often the ones supervising the encounter) that, on waking, they would not remember anything, and from their own inner unwillingness to remember and especially relive an exceedingly traumatic event. Also, many people did not want to feel themselves or be seen by others to be different, to be "weird" and/or "crazy." As Gloria (Chapter Nine) put it before beginning her second regression to an abduction, "It was hard to accept in my mind that this really happened . . . no sense in trying to deny it anymore."

Hypnosis is a less than perfect tool. It is not a "truth serum." But it is helpful. In the hands of a skilled therapist and/or researcher, it can elicit a great deal of valuable repressed material.

When doing any kind of regression, I take a position of remaining very objective within my own mind as to an event's validity;

did it really happen? For example, each week at least three or four of my female patients find, under hypnosis, that they had been sexually abused as small children. They have no conscious memory of these events. We will never know, unless it is corroborated by other family members (which is extremely unusual), whether the material that emerged was an actual memory or a fantasy. What does impress me are the immediate and lasting cures that resulted from their hypnotic work. Besides eliminating debilitating symptoms, age regressions were followed by dramatic changes in many areas of these patients' lives. I often saw the same therapeutic effects after regressions to close encounters. For me, this is clinical validity, and I have no desire to prove that the experiences really happened, any more than I do with my patients who "discover" they've been sexually abused.

The next thirteen chapters are offered to you, therefore, not as proof that the encounters actually took place, nor as accurate portrayals. I am presenting them as case material, accounts of what these thirteen people experienced under hypnosis. You are invited to analyze the material and then to draw your own conclusions.

"They Put Something
in My Rectum."

"My friend Sandi thinks she may have seen a UFO when she was a child," Les said, as he put all his strength into the final stretch of my spine. I got off the treatment bench, and, while checking the alignment of my head and shoulders, he added, "She would be glad to talk to you about it. She just told me the other day that she thinks she may have had an encounter." Frowning, he commented, "Your head is just a fraction of an inch off. I think we've almost got it where we want it."

Leslie Szasalay, D.C., is one of the new breed of young doctors who are open to alternative methods of healing. At thirty-four he is developing a private practice in chiropractics in Saratoga and is the kind of person whom I like immediately. During my weekly treatments for low-back pain, we've become good friends and often share tidbits about our lives. After he had told me about an art show at our local junior college he and his friend Sandi had attended, he had asked me what I had done over the weekend.

"I spent both days working on my new book, *Encounters*. I just started it, and it's been very rewarding so far."

"What's your book about, Edee?"

"It's about people who have had, or at least appear to have had, close encounters of the fourth kind. Do you know which ones they are?"

"No. I saw the movie, *Close Encounters of the Third Kind.* What's the difference?"

"Let's start at the beginning. Close encounters of the first kind are those in which someone sees a saucer, a UFO, in the daytime and/or nocturnal lights. Close encounters of the second kind involve visual evidence of impressions made by a spacecraft, like burned areas or irradiated soil, grass or trees. Close encounters of the third kind, the ones Steven Spielberg's movie was about, are those in which the witness observes or directly confronts occupants of a UFO. And last, but certainly not least, are close encounters of the fourth kind, CEIV. They're the ones in which people claim to have been abducted or contacted by extraterrestrials. And that's what my book is about. Case studies of individuals who have had this type of experience. Many times they have phobias or other problems that are caused by these encounters, but they have no conscious memory of them, so we use hypnosis to help them recall what's happened. It's been fascinating work."

Not surprisingly, Les seemed very interested and open-minded about intelligent life on other planets and the possibility of our being visited by aliens. However, he is basically a pragmatist and takes a stance of being scientifically objective about such topics.

The following Saturday, Sandi, Les and I met in my office. Despite the relaxed atmosphere, since the building was empty and we were in very casual clothes, Sandi was obviously tense, yet excited about doing a regression.

Sandi is a very attractive twenty-seven-year-old bookkeeper. Trim and petite in her peach sweatsuit, her light-brown hair short and curled away from her pretty face, she smiled a little too often and giggled anxiously as she began her story. You read the beginning of her account in Chapter One, so I'll just summarize it at this point.

As a child, Sandi lived with her parents and older brother, Bill, in Eastern Colorado in a very rural area, where her family had their ranch. On a Saturday evening in the late spring of her twelfth year, she was alone, which was unusual. Her parents had taken Bill to his junior-senior prom. Sandi recalled being nervous, and so, for company and to distract herself, she made a bowl of popcorn, turned on the TV and sat down to watch one of her favorite sitcoms. The large picture window just above the TV looked out over pastures and nearby hills. In the daytime, it created a beautiful indoor-outdoor feeling, but this particular night the darkness was scary, and Sandi made an effort to avoid looking at the window. A few minutes into the TV show, she noticed an intense bright light that attracted her attention away from the set. Looking up and out, she saw what she thought were car headlights on top of the hill, which was about a mile away. No, it can't be a car, she thought, because it is a single light and much too bright. She then reasoned it must be a searchlight that their neighbor, a rancher, used to find lost sheep or cattle. She began to feel fear mounting, for somehow the light seemed to be "calling" her. Gradually she became immobilized. The TV shifted spontaneously to black-and-white snow. She found herself spellbound by it. As she remembered, "I seemed drawn into the TV." The next thing she was aware of was that the TV was blinking, the color had returned and the ten o'clock news was on. When she looked up, she saw that the light had vanished and noticed that she felt "funny" and tingly. A great sense of relief flooded over her when she realized she could move her arms and legs and take her eyes off the TV. A thought flitted in and out of her mind, I'm back!

"Sandi, at that age, did you know about UFOs?" I asked, slipping a tape in my recorder.

"I can't remember even hearing about them as a child. I did tell my parents what happened. Of course, they had no explanation. They thought it was a bad case of nerves. It was only five or six years ago when I first began to wonder about it."

"What happened then?"

"I had lunch with a friend, Kathy, and she told me about an experience she had had in which she had been abducted by aliens and taken aboard a UFO."

"How did she remember it, Sandi? Did she see a hypnotist?"

"No. She just remembered it. Or, at least, some of it. She's a psychic and has had all kinds of weird experiences that we talk about. While she was telling me her story, I began to feel funny again, and it reminded me of that night when I was a kid, with the TV and the bright light. I told her what I was feeling, and she tuned in to me and said she thought maybe I had had an encounter too."

I noticed that Sandi was getting quite uncomfortable; the more she talked about the possibility of her having been abducted, the more uncomfortable she became. "How do you feel about our doing the regression?"

"Scared . . . and excited. I guess it would be best to know for sure. But I've never been hypnotized before and I don't know if I can be," she said, twisting her hands together and looking into her lap.

"Sandi, let's not worry about that. There's nothing mysterious about being hypnotized. Have you ever cried when you saw something sad in the movies?"

"Sure," she said brightening up a little.

"Well, you were in a state of hypnosis. You had forgotten for a while that you were in a movie theater, watching a screen with lights projected onto it. You forgot that the people were only actors and that what was happening was not real. In other words, you had suspended disbelief, one of the things that sometimes happens in hypnosis."

"But I didn't feel hypnotized. I felt like I always do," Sandi said, her brows creasing.

"Almost every single person who has sat in that chair," I said, gesturing toward the reclining chair she was in, "is convinced he or she was not hypnotized. That's because there is such a misconception about hypnosis. It's a very natural state that we slip in and out of probably hundreds of times daily. Let's begin and you'll soon see what it's like."

She nodded in agreement. Les leaned forward in his chair and asked, "Would it be all right for me to stay in the room and watch?"

"With my therapy patients, I never allow it, but this is different. I don't want you slipping into hypnosis, Les, so make sure you stay alert, keep shifting your eyes around and resist any urge to close them."

He smiled broadly, nodded, tilted the chair back and crossed his arms behind his head, looking particularly alert.

After covering Sandi with my lavender-plaid mohair blanket and pushing the chair back to its full reclining position, I began the hypnotic induction. As soon as her eyes closed, her eyelids immediately flickered, a sign of trance. She quickly seemed to slip into a deeper state as her body relaxed, responding to my hypnotic suggestions. When I felt that she was ready to regress back to the possible close encounter, I asked her to go back into her memory banks to the night when she was alone and had seen the light.

I looked over at Les, who was leaning forward resting his elbows on his thighs. He looked a little concerned and gave me a quick smile. He waited, and soon Sandi began speaking in a slow, almost hesitant way.

✦

SANDI: I am sitting in the corner watching TV, and there is something on the hill. I looked up through the window. There is a light. I didn't know if it was on the road or in the pasture. It got brighter, like it was turning toward me. I looked at the light a long time. The longer I looked, the heavier I got. My arms were heavy. My legs were heavy. I felt like a balloon that was heavy. I felt like I was all blown up . . . that I was too heavy to move. I sat there and I looked at the light. I couldn't move . . . I was so heavy. And . . . the TV had gone off. The TV had gone toward snow and it was really loud. It was very loud! I tried to get up to turn it down and I couldn't get up. I was so heavy. Then I started looking at the TV, at the snow, trying to find something in the snow, trying to find a word or a face. [*Sighs*] I couldn't see anything in the snow that I could recognize. But I kept trying, and then . . . then I looked back up at the light. And I looked at it for a long time more. [*Long pause*] I feel like my body . . . is . . . is raising up. It's raising up higher and higher out into the night . . . [*Grimaces and sighs*] My other body is still in the chair, and I feel light. It's like I'm going up, up into the night, higher and higher and . . . higher . . . higher . . . way up into the sky and looking down, going higher . . . higher . . . [*Long pause*] Now I feel like I'm lying down on a slanted board, my feet down toward the ground. Just lying there, feeling so light, feeling so good. [*Pauses*]

DR. FIORE: And now what's happening?

SANDI: I'm in a large room with other beds, with other stations . . . and I'm on a slanted board. It's . . . it's big. There's . . . there's about six other stations. And it's oval. Yes, it's oval. [*Long pause*]

DR. FIORE: Let yourself remember.

SANDI: [*Sighs painfully*] I don't know . . . I can't . . . I can't see any . . .

DR. FIORE: Let yourself know everything you experienced. Tell me more about what it feels like to be on the bed.

SANDI: It feels like I can't get up. I feel like I'm so heavy that I can't get up. I don't think I can see clearly. It's cold. It's really cold, and I can't see. Everything's kind of fuzzy. And there's . . . there's some kind of light up above me, 'cause I'm lying on the slanted board with my head . . . back like it is now.

DR. FIORE: Tell me more about what's happening. It's crystal clear in your mind.

SANDI: I just wish it would end. I'm so cold, I just want a blanket. I just don't want to be there. [*Pauses*]

DR. FIORE: What else are you experiencing?

SANDI: I see a head, and it's got wings on it, the way . . . it looks. [*Sighs*] It's got big wings for eyes, that go . . . they go off the side. They look angry. I see that . . . face. Looking at me . . . I feel like he's . . . he's talking, talking to me. But he's not saying words, he's just talking to my mind. But I don't know what he's saying.

DR. FIORE: You will remember now exactly what he said to you.

SANDI: He wants me . . . to relax, not to be scared . . . [*Shivers*] But it's so cold, and I'm so scared. [*Long pause*] I keep . . . I get messages. It's like he's . . . like he's communicating, but I can't remember what it was. I can't understand what it was. I try to understand it. I try to just let it, let it come in, but . . . I just . . . I can't.

DR. FIORE: Where is he?

SANDI: He's right next to me. He's very close. He's standing over my face, over my body. I think I had a sheet on me, because it was so cold. It would touch me and I would shiver, it was so cold. And I wished that they would just take it off of me, because it was making me colder.

DR. FIORE: Tell me more about the being.

SANDI: I think they might be on both sides of me. I think they are. And there's three of them. Four of them.

DR. FIORE: What are they doing?

SANDI: They just seem to be standing. I think there's three on one side, and there's one on my right side. I think they're just standing there, looking down at me. I'm low to the ground. My head's probably . . . two feet off the ground . . . three feet off the ground. I keep feeling like I'm going to fall off the board, but I don't. I feel like I'm going to slide off, but I don't. I feel like all the blood is rushing to my feet, I wish they'd take me off of that board. [*Pauses and seems to look around*] They're moving around. There seems to be more of them. And they're moving around really fast, just scurrying around. Now they're kind of leaving me alone. I'm just lying there. I can see them, and they're going really fast. They look real cute.

DR. FIORE: What do they look like?

SANDI: I'm not sure now. The one with the weird eyes, the wings . . . they don't look like that . . . anymore.

DR. FIORE: Are you saying that one looks different from the rest?

SANDI: I thought it did, but I don't see it anymore. A little while ago he was there and he looked . . . he looked very angry and he had great big eyebrow things . . . cute . . . they stuck way out, with . . . deep eyes.

DR. FIORE: What color were they?

SANDI: Dark . . . black or brown, I think. They were way deep-set and the eyebrow was way out over it.

DR. FIORE: You're going to let yourself remember anything they have done to you.

SANDI: They're turning my head to look at the back of my neck. My neck doesn't go that way. But they're gentle. I feel flat, yeah . . . I'm not on the slanted board anymore. I'm on a level surface. And they're turning my head. [*Pauses*] They might have white robes, I'm not sure. It's like some of them . . . some of them that are looking at me have robes, but maybe the rest of them don't. What else did they do to me? They were gentle. They were cold. When they touched me, they were cold. I didn't like it, but they were gentle. I remember telling them, ''No! No, don't you do that to me! Don't you do that to me! [*Cries*] And they were telling me that it would be okay. They were trying to settle me down. And I didn't want them doing that to me. They were going to put something up my rectum, and I . . . [*Crying hard*] . . . didn't want them to do that to me.

DR. FIORE: Tell me all about it.

SANDI: I think it was a needle. And . . . they were pushing me . . . I was on my back, and they were pushing me onto my right side, and I was pushing back as hard as I could. I didn't want them to do that. They were pushing. They were so strong and so cold. At first when they talked to me, I trusted them. They were very gentle, and I trusted them. And then . . . and then they made me do something I didn't want to do.

DR. FIORE: What was that?

SANDI: They made me turn over. They made me turn over onto my side . . . and I didn't want to do that, because I was afraid of what they were going to do to me. And they put me on my side so they could spread my cheeks, so they could do something . . . I don't know . . . [*Whispers*] with a . . . probe or something. I don't know if it was sharp like a needle, but it was thin like a needle.

DR. FIORE: You are remembering everything as though it is happening now.

SANDI: I think they quit. Maybe they did something really fast . . . and then it was over and they let me go. I was so happy. I laid back down and I was never going to let them do that to me again. I'm so glad it was over.

DR. FIORE: You are going to let yourself remember everything exactly as it happened. Take it second by second.

SANDI: I'm lying there, and they're pushing on my hip. They're pushing, and I'm pushing back. And they push harder, and I push harder. And . . . and then they push really hard, and I flip . . . flip over on my side and they push my one knee up. And then . . . then they . . .

DR. FIORE: Continue speaking out.

SANDI: I'm so scared. I'm just so scared. [Crying] I guess maybe I gave up then. I was so scared. I knew they were so strong. I think I gave up . . . and I just, I laid there and . . . it was a terrible feeling. They put something in my rectum! It was terrible! Whatever they were doing, I didn't want it anymore. And then they pulled it out. And they left. They left me alone, and I was so happy it was over. I pushed back, and I had to lie on my back. I wanted to lie on my back so that they couldn't get to me again. I was still scared, but I wasn't as scared. It was over. I was still cold. I was still really, really cold. It seems like there was a light above me. So I just laid there and looked at the light and tried to think that it's not that bad. Tried to relax . . . tried to relax. [Sighs] And then . . . then I relaxed a little more. I looked around the room. It seemed like I was conscious. It's like I was . . . becoming more conscious at that point or something, like I was getting my faculties together. It seems like I had this feeling that I should look around and see what this is. I need to look around and . . . see what it is, see where I am. I have to remember all this. And I just remember a real urgent feeling to . . . to just . . . memorize every detail, but I can't. . . .

DR. FIORE: What is it you're noticing to remember later?

SANDI: The shape of the room. . . . The end that I was look-ing at is curved. Again, it was the long end of the oval, I think. It wasn't that huge of a room, but I was looking at the seam. It seemed like it was domed. And the seam, the seam between the top half and the bottom half. I thought, How unusual. I remember thinking, How weird. I don't know what it looked like. How did they do that? What does it do? Things were so weird. But it was . . . it was domed on the top and the bottom. There weren't square corners. You'd fall down if you walked over there, I thought. You would slip and fall because the bottom of the thing was curved. I remember looking at that one wall.

DR. FIORE: Tell me more about what you're noticing.

SANDI: I didn't recognize the material . . . I didn't know what it was made out of. It felt like we were in a cave, but it was smooth. You know how the back of the cave is rounded on the top and the bottom—it felt like that, but it wasn't natural like a cave. It was smooth. It felt like maybe . . . maybe it wasn't that tall. I felt that maybe if I stood up, it wouldn't be tall enough for me.

DR. FIORE: Was it tall enough for the other beings who were there?

SANDI: Hmmm. Yes, it was fine for them. They must not have been . . . they were so cute. They were littler than me.

DR. FIORE: And then what happens to you?

SANDI: I just feel like I'm sinking back down into my chair that I was sitting in. It feels like I'm there and then I'm not, I'm there and then I'm not . . . and then I'm there a little bit more . . . and then I'm not. And then, little by little, I'm there more and more . . . back in my chair . . . back in my living room. And then I just become more whole and more whole. And . . . I was afraid that I wasn't still all there. I was afraid that they had taken something . . . that they hadn't put me back together. [*Cries*] And then they talked to me . . . [*Sobbing*] They talked to me and told me not to be afraid, to be calm, and everything was okay and all that. They were very reassuring again. Just somehow I was sitting in my chair. I was back in my chair in my living room. Then . . . then they just seemed to be gone. I woke up . . . I looked into the TV some more, because it was still snowy. I looked into the TV, still looking for a message, then it blinked . . . blinked and came back on, a program was on. So I was looking down at the TV. The TV was in front of the window that the light came through. I was looking down at the TV, and when I looked back up to check and see if the light was still there, it was gone. And I got up . . . and I went . . . I looked at the window. I went to the front-door window and I looked all over and there was no light . . . it was gone. It was there on the hill, and then it wasn't there anymore. And then I . . . kind of shirked it off, and . . . sat back down and watched TV some more.

DR. FIORE: You're going to let yourself remember if there's anything else they did. Let yourself remember everything that happened. It's crystal clear in your memory, at the count of five. One . . . two . . . three . . . four . . . five.

SANDI: The stuff that felt like cotton was . . . was in a tub . . . was in a big, submarine-looking tub with a big hole in the top. And . . . [*Sighs*] They put me in there and it felt so soft. It was . . . like . . . jelly, but it was dry. It was so weird. I thought . . . this feels so nice, but what is it? And they put me in there and I kept sinking down. I don't know how deep it was, but it scared me, because I thought, If I sink in this stuff, it's thick enough to suffocate me. I don't want to, so I kept crawling back up. It was thick enough . . . it was thick enough . . . to like . . . grab onto, to get to the top, but it wasn't thick enough to keep me from sinking. It was in a big tank that looked like . . . looked like metal, I guess. It was like a big propane gas tank, like a big torpedo submarine. And it had an opening in the top, not big enough for me to lie out flat. I had to lie kinda with my feet drawn up, a little bit, because the hole wasn't big enough. I don't know how they got me. It seems like they were so gentle. I guess maybe they just lowered me in. They were so nice. The ones with robes were so nice. They seemed like women. They seemed female to me. They were so gentle and so empathetic and so nurselike. They were nice. That was in the corner of the room. The room was basically oval, but it had on one whole side little coves, or quite big coves. It was kinda like the shape of a shell, and in one of those coves was this tank. There was the one cove and there was a big scooped out place on one side. It was like the second cove, and it had a counter, pretty low to the ground. I can't remember them doing anything else.

DR. FIORE: Did they ask you any questions?

SANDI: It seemed like they were pressuring me, they were asking me why I was questioning them. "Why are you fighting us? Why are you questioning us?" And I kept thinking, Well . . . 'cause it was weird! [*Laughs*] And I told them, "Just leave me alone." [*Whispers*] And they . . . they kept making me feel really bad. They hurt my feelings. [*Cries*] They made me feel like I was wrong, like I was bad.

DR. FIORE: How did they do that?

SANDI: It's just that they kept on me and on me, "Why are you questioning anything we do? How dare you?" And that made me feel bad. There was more.

DR. FIORE: It's all coming back, it's very easy to remember.

SANDI: It was that one with the weird face. He wasn't nice. He's the only one that did bad things to me. He's the one that made me feel bad. He's telling me that I was bad, telling me that I was no good, that I didn't matter, that I was expendable, why should I care about my little self so much, and how dare I question him.

DR. FIORE: When he said that to you, how did you feel?

SANDI: I just felt really defenseless. I kind of thought maybe he was right. After a while, he did it to me. I just fought and fought. With whatever communication we were using, I just kept telling him. . . . I tried to fight back, "You know I'm just asking questions because I'm curious." I tried to defend myself, but he was strong. He just kept overpowering me and telling me that I was bad and . . . and finally . . . finally I thought maybe I'd better do what he said.

DR. FIORE: What did he want you to do?

SANDI: He wanted me to . . . he wanted me to empty my mind. I remember him telling me that. He said, "Don't think about anything." And I said, "How can I not think about anything? There's so much here that's going on, I have to think." And then, slowly, he told me to empty my mind of everything. "Don't think about anything."

DR. FIORE: When he said that, how did you feel?

SANDI: I said, "Okay," and he helped me. He talked to me. [*Sighs*] He just kept saying, "Empty your mind. Don't think about a thing. Let it all go away. Just empty it." And I remember . . . [*Sighs*] . . . I remember doing that. And I just . . . I just felt like I was in the blue skies . . . I felt like I was just air. I remember feeling . . . nothing. I guess I emptied my mind, because I thought that I was up in the blue sky . . . just floating . . . just nothing.

DR. FIORE: Now you're going to do something very interesting. You understand now that he hypnotized you, don't you?

SANDI: Yes.

DR. FIORE: You're going to remember what happened when you were under hypnosis. You're going to remember everything that happened. You emptied your mind and then what happened?

SANDI: I see a schoolroom and an American flag. [*Laughs*] Sheep, I don't know.

DR. FIORE: Trust your mind. Where are the sheep, and what are they doing?

SANDI: They're grazing in a pasture with a fence around them. I see a classroom, a little old-fashioned classroom with desks, and a chalkboard and an American flag.

DR. FIORE: Go back to that oval room. Your body was in that oval room, and there was a part of your mind that was observing and witnessing what was happening. You're in the oval room. You've emptied your mind. You're not thinking about what's happened with part of your mind. But the subconscious part of your mind is registering everything exactly as it happened, and now you're going to remember. When this being told you that you were going to empty your mind, did he also tell you that you would not remember anything?

SANDI: Yes.

DR. FIORE: Tell me what he said.

SANDI: It was a threat. He said, "You're not going to remember!" And I kept thinking, Yes, I am! I'm going to remember everything! And he said, "No, you will not!"

DR. FIORE: This is your chance to remember everything. Now you're going to remember everything that he thought you would not remember.

SANDI: He's asking me questions.

DR. FIORE: What questions does he ask you?

SANDI: [*Pauses*] I can't remember. [*Becomes upset*]

DR. FIORE: You can remember. You have every memory in your mind, and the only reason why you think you can't remember is because he tricked you into thinking you couldn't. And he was wrong. You can remember everything. You would like that, wouldn't you? Okay. Now you're going to prove that you are stronger than he is, because you are going to remember everything that happened that he thought you would never remember. What were the questions he asked you?

SANDI: He asked me about water, about the ponds. I didn't know the answers to his questions. It seems like all I had to do was think about things, I didn't have to say things. I remember something about water . . . picture of it, of a dammed pond, ponds that we had all over . . . fish . . . He kept asking me really . . . hard questions I did not know.

DR. FIORE: Like what? What was a really hard question that you did not know?

SANDI: I can't remember.

DR. FIORE: Now you can remember everything. You do want to remember, don't you?

SANDI: Yes.

DR. FIORE: We're going to undo his suggestion. Now he may have told you that you would never, ever remember what happened, but you see you have already remembered, haven't you? So he was wrong. So he doesn't have as much power as he thought he had, because you have already remembered a great deal about the encounter with these beings. Now you're going to remember at this point whether he asked you any personal questions; that would be much easier to remember. Did he ask you anything about your family, or about yourself, or about your life?

SANDI: He asked about my house and my family. He seemed to have been watching me . . . he seemed to know so much about me, and he wanted to know where my . . . I think he asked me where my . . . where my souls were. I think he meant my family.

DR. FIORE: When he used the word soul rather than family, what did you think?

SANDI: I was just trying to interpret what he was asking me. I thought it was kind of strange, but, in a way . . . I was real close to my family and they're like part of me, so maybe he was wondering where the rest of me was.

DR. FIORE: What did you say?

SANDI: I told him they're right here with me, they're inside of me, they're always close to me. And I was afraid he was going to take them away. [*Cries*] But he said he wasn't going to take them away, he just wanted to know where they were. [*Relieved*] He wanted to know more about them, he wanted to know a lot more about them. But I thought . . . he just wanted to know more about me. He was very nice. He was very kind. That it would be okay. He told me not to worry, it would be okay. [*Pauses*] He wanted to know . . . He wanted to know more . . . He wanted to know about the dog. We have a dog, and . . . he asked me if the dog was my soul too. I told him that we loved our dog, but he wasn't my soul. And . . . and then, then he wanted to know about love. He wanted to know about my family. And about love. I had to think about each one. I just thought. He told me, "Just open your mind and think about each one. Think about your mother, think about your father, think about your brother, and now think about yourself." So I did. [*Sighs*] He seemed to be real pleased about that. He was very happy. He said I was doing very well. He had the attitude like . . . now that we've done the part that's uncomfortable, you can do this and it won't hurt at all. He said it wouldn't hurt at all, that it would be fine and I was safe. It was fine. It was okay. It wouldn't hurt me anymore, and he was very nice then.

DR. FIORE: What part had they done that had hurt you?

SANDI: They . . . poked, poked, poked, poked . . . and . . . just poked everywhere . . . every little rib and bone and muscle. I didn't like that very much.

DR. FIORE: This conversation with him was later, is that correct?

SANDI: Yes. I think when I was lying on the flat table with the light up above, when everyone left. I don't think he was really there, he was just talking to me. His power was immense, but I don't remember anyone . . . being there with me. Although he was, you know, he was there, but he wasn't there. I think I was alone.

DR. FIORE: Let yourself know if there's anything else that he said to you.

SANDI: He wanted to know about feathers. [*Pauses*] I see feathers. I see birds. He's making me think about them. He puts his little ideas in my head and then he has me think about everything I know about them. The sheep and the pasture . . .

DR. FIORE: He put that idea in your head?

SANDI: Yes. He said just relax and let it happen. "Just see whatever you see in a classroom, and the feathers. . . ."

DR. FIORE: Now I'm going to ask you a few questions at this point. You will remember everything because you want to remember. When you were being poked everywhere, did they do any kind of vaginal examination?

SANDI: I don't think they did.

DR. FIORE: Now you're going to let yourself know if they put a needle in any part of your body, other than the rectum.

SANDI: No. They were carrying needles around, big ones, and I was scared for a while they were going to put one in me, but they didn't. [*Body tenses*]

DR. FIORE: Now, just let yourself relax. At the count of three you're going to remember whether they did put one of those big needles in you. If they did, know that you're safe, and it's all over, isn't it. And if they didn't, you're going to remember that too, at the count of three. One . . . two . . . three.

SANDI: They did.

DR. FIORE: Now let yourself know all about it.

SANDI: [*Crying in pain*] And they were pushing my head over, and they put it in my neck, in my back. And somewhere. [*Whispers*] I was so scared.

DR. FIORE: What did they do with the needles?

SANDI: I can't.

DR. FIORE: You're letting yourself remember. They pushed your head over and they put one in your neck and in your back. Tell me where they put them.

SANDI: [*Winces*] In my neck. In my neck, in my head. In my . . .

DR. FIORE: Did they put more than one needle in your neck or just one?

SANDI: Just one.

DR. FIORE: You said you saw them carrying around big needles. How many needles did you actually see?

SANDI: Ten.

DR. FIORE: And where else did they put the needles?

SANDI: In my arm, in my forearm. They ran it right under the skin.

DR. FIORE: Did it hurt when they put the needles in?

SANDI: Yes. It hurt going in. It didn't hurt once it went in. It just felt like something was in there. It felt like I was deadened. I could feel something hard in there, but it didn't hurt. It just hurt when it went in.

DR. FIORE: Where else did they put them?

SANDI: Between my toes, between my big toe and the next toe. That one was awful! [*Cries in pain*]

DR. FIORE: Did they explain to you why they were doing this, or what they were doing?

SANDI: No.

DR. FIORE: How did you react to the needles?

SANDI: I was scared, but I couldn't react. It was like I was drugged. I wanted to just jump off the table, but I couldn't. I was so heavy. And . . . I'm not sure I cared. I did . . . on the one hand, I did care. I wanted to leave. On the other hand . . . I was so heavy and so sleepy that I didn't care what they did. But when I saw them, especially the one between my toes, I thought, Oh . . . my God!

DR. FIORE: What did they do? Did they put the needle in and leave it sticking in you?

SANDI: They seemed to stick it in and then wiggle it around. They were wiggling it around like they were . . . I don't know. They would wiggle it. And on my arm, they just kept sliding it and kept sliding it in. And . . . I don't know. I don't think they injected anything. It seems like they were just probing in there, to see . . . to see something, to find out something.

DR. FIORE: Were any needles put in your abdomen or your navel?

SANDI: I think so.

DR. FIORE: Tell me about that.

SANDI: [*Pauses*] It's not so clear.

DR. FIORE: You are going to remember at the count of three. It's so easy. Look how much you've already remembered. One . . . two . . . three.

SANDI: Yes, they did, through my navel.

DR. FIORE: How did that feel?

SANDI: It felt like sticking your finger in a balloon. It felt like putting a pin in a balloon. It stretches and it stretches and it stretches and it finally punctures. It was like that.

DR. FIORE: And when it punctured, how did it feel?

SANDI: It was fine.

DR. FIORE: And what did they do once they punctured it?

SANDI: They wiggled it [the needles] around. I couldn't tell what they were doing. I think some of them were . . . like tubes. And I thought that maybe they were taking something. Yes . . . some of them were like tubes, especially the one in my arm.

DR. FIORE: What were they taking?

SANDI: I don't know.

DR. FIORE: Did you see it?

SANDI: I didn't look. I was too scared. Then I did look. They [the needles] were metal or stainless steel or something. I couldn't see what was in them. I couldn't see what they were taking. But in my arm, that one . . . that one was like a tube. It couldn't have been blood, because it would have run out.

DR. FIORE: The male being who was questioning you and put you under hypnosis, did he look like the female type who was very kind and gentle? Did they all seem to be the same species?

SANDI: Yes.

DR. FIORE: Did they tell you where they came from?

SANDI: No.

DR. FIORE: Did you ask them?

SANDI: No.

DR. FIORE: When you left your living room, you said you left one body in your chair and floated in another body. I want to know if that's really true. I want you to go back to when you are leaving your living room. See if there's anybody in the living room with you. You're looking at the light. I want you to move to the very moment when you start to leave the chair and tell me everything that you experience.

SANDI: No one's in the room. I don't feel a presence, but someone is talking to me in my brain.

DR. FIORE: What is the person saying?

SANDI: They told me that I would be going up. [*Pauses*] ''We're going to . . .'' no, ''You're going to feel like you're going up. You're going to go up. And don't be scared. Everything's okay.'' And I started to go up.

DR. FIORE: Tell me what part of you started to go up.

SANDI: Everything . . . it felt like everything was going up.

DR. FIORE: I want you to look back at the chair or the couch you were sitting in. As you were going up, what did you see there?

SANDI: I didn't look back. It felt like I was just leaving maybe a skin on the chair, just like a snake does . . . just a skin.

DR. FIORE: Did it feel like the physical body was going up?

SANDI: Yes.

DR. FIORE: Now what?

SANDI: I just went up and up and up. I didn't think it would ever end. I just felt lighter and lighter. . . .

DR. FIORE: How do you get from going up to being in the oval room.

SANDI: I don't know. It's just like I was there.

DR. FIORE: Okay. Now you're going to let yourself remember if you saw a craft of any sort.

SANDI: I don't know.

DR. FIORE: Now, I want you to remember the very last thing that was said to you by those beings.

SANDI: I think they said, "Goodbye."

DR. FIORE: Did they thank you?

SANDI: In a weird sort of way, I think so. But it wasn't the way we do it. It wasn't so much thank you as it was . . . they knew that I knew. It's like they didn't have to say it. They knew that they . . . had benefited and they knew that I had benefited.

DR. FIORE: Let yourself know how you benefited from that experience.

SANDI: It's like . . . they gave me an experience to make me a more whole person. To experience that, they said, would be good . . . or they implied it would be good for me.

DR. FIORE: Did you ever have any experiences with them or other aliens before that experience?

SANDI: I don't think so.

DR. FIORE: Have you had any experiences with them since then?

SANDI: Maybe . . . I'm not sure. It seems like they've been here again. It seems like they've talked to me and I've talked back. It's a . . . like a warm feeling.

DR. FIORE: A warm feeling?

SANDI: It's like deep inside. Very positive.

DR. FIORE: Are you saying that you may have been telepathically communicated with?

SANDI: I think so, yes.

DR. FIORE: And it's something that you welcomed?

SANDI: Yes.

✒

As I brought Sandi out of hypnosis, I looked over at Les, who had been listening attentively for almost two hours. He looked relieved that it was over and delighted at the same time.

Sandi seemed a bit disoriented at first, which is not at all unusual, especially after being under hypnosis for such a long time. I got her a glass of water, and Les watched her rather apprehensively as she drank it.

"How do you feel now, Sandi?" I wanted to have her start talking and orienting herself to her surroundings. It is very easy for people to slip back into a trance as they mull over what they just experienced.

"Fine. Just a little sleepy." Les moved his chair closer to her, and they smiled at each other.

"You've been under hypnosis for almost two hours, Sandi."

"It seems like just a few minutes. I'm surprised. What time is it?" Les leaned over and showed her his watch. "I can't believe it!"

"That's time distortion, a very common feature of hypnosis. By the way, do you feel you've been hypnotized?"

"No. I didn't go under, but I don't understand how it could have been so long. I didn't feel any different." She looked up and off to the left. "I was pretty scared during some of that. I guess I must have been hypnotized though, because it was so real. And I never knew that all that happened before."

The three of us talked about her regression, and when it seemed that she was back to her normal waking consciousness, I suggested we end our session. Sandi agreed to do some drawings that are included later in the book.

As she and Les were just about to leave, she turned back. "Thanks a lot for clearing up the mystery. I have a lot to think about now."

". . . They're Coming Down Here, Wanting to Mix with Our Race . . ."

⬤ I agreed to see Mark as a special favor to his grandmother, Betty, a former patient. I work with adults (over the age of twenty-one), and Mark was only eighteen. Since I particularly liked his grandmother and his grandfather, also an ex-patient, I made an exception by taking Mark on for treatment.

Mark was the only person in the waiting room and got up eagerly as I came over to introduce myself. He greeted me pleasantly, and as he walked to my office, I noticed he had a very severe limp, yet there was something graceful about the way he moved his body. Mark was a clean-cut-looking young man, about five feet five inches tall. His body looked somewhat out of proportion, as though the top had grown to manhood, yet the bottom had not caught up.

Once in my consultation room, he got quickly to the point. "I've got arthritis. A couple of years ago it was real bad, now it's in remission." He continued, "I've got it in both hips, my lower back and ankles."

"When did it start, Mark?"

"When I was eleven. I was an athlete . . . in the soccer league. I got kicked in the ankle, but I ran on it. It got worse and I finally had to quit the game. It turned into arthritis, and three months later I was in the Stanford Children's Hospital."

Mark told me more about his life, his goal of going to college in the fall, his frustrations with his disease. As he put it, "It's such a big thing in my life. The doctors just treat the symptoms. I feel it's almost impossible to cure."

After he discussed his grandmother's plans to take him to a special clinic in Mexico, I asked him if he had had any recurrent dreams. He recounted several, but one in particular piqued my curiosity. It sounded like a possible abduction. I asked him to tell me everything he could remember about it.

"It's almost scary, like it wasn't a dream. There's nothing I can do. I'm paralyzed. I see a person for a split second. It's not even a person. He's like the dude on the cover of that book. The one with the picture of the UFO guy."

"*Communion?*"

"Yeah. But not exactly like that one. He has that long face, but in the dream it doesn't have much detail to it. The eyes are round and an emerald green. The body is all one color. After he takes hold of me, it's like I'm shrinking and I'm scared. That's all I can remember."

"How often have you had the dream?"

"Many times over the years."

I suggested to Mark that he might be remembering actual close encounters of the fourth kind and asked him if he was interested in UFOs.

He leaned forward with a lot of excitement showing on his face. "I'm very interested in them. I think about them a lot . . . about their technology . . . the places they hide in the ocean. And how they study us. While I was in Children's Hospital, I was hoping they would come down and take me away. I've taken astronomy classes and I look at the stars a lot. I look for a ship."

"Have you read about abductions? Have you read *Communion?*"

"No. I picked it up in the bookstore and read a few pages."

"Did you have any reactions to the pictures or the cover or what you read?"

After he answered negatively, I decided to continue exploring his dreams. "Have you had any dreams about UFOs?"

"A couple. I'm getting into a ship once and taking off . . . and then the dream is over. They don't make me get on, though. In some other dreams, I'm on the ground and the UFOs fly by me. In some, I'm scared like it's a nightmare and in some I'm not."

We seemed to have gotten off on a tangent. One that interested me greatly, but Mark was seeking my help for his arthritis, and I didn't see any possibility of a connection. I decided to initiate hypnosis at that point in order to do some work on the major issue in his life.

Mark quickly slipped into a moderate trance, and I immediately began to work on his symptoms. After about fifteen minutes, he mentioned seeing a picture of a UFO. Following my intuition, I decided to regress him to the cause of his recurrent dream.

✦

MARK: I see my house I used to live in. Here in the Bay Area. And . . . I'm seven. I think this is right after I got diabetes, maybe before. And they're taking me up. They're levitating me up to the ship.

DR. FIORE: Tell me about that in detail.

MARK: I don't have a blanket on me, so I just go up, and part of the roof just . . . I don't know, it's, like it's transparent, and I go through it into . . . and then there's a compartment in the bottom of the spaceship that I go up into. And there's two aliens, one on one side of me and one on the other. I'm a little frightened here. This feels like even the second or third time I've been abducted. And they put me on a little table that has wheels on it. And they roll me down the hall . . . and they're lifting my eyelid back.

DR. FIORE: What does that feel like?

MARK: It doesn't hurt. They're not lifting it, they're just pushing it back. I guess they're just looking at me. In the room they put me in, there's another little boy.

DR. FIORE: What's happening to him?

MARK: It looks like he's sleeping.

DR. FIORE: Are they doing anything to him?

MARK: No. He's just lying there. He's on a table.

DR. FIORE: What emotions are you feeling at this point?

MARK: A little frightened.

DR. FIORE: Where are the aliens in relationship to you?

MARK: They left.

DR. FIORE: Are you in the room alone with this boy?

MARK: Yes. I know the boy is there, but it's like I don't really care if he's there, I'm just worried about myself. I'm lying down, trying to fall asleep.

DR. FIORE: Why are you trying to fall asleep?

MARK: Because I think it's a dream and I want it to go away.

DR. FIORE: And now it's a little later.

MARK: We're both awake, and we both have our own alien with us. And we're holding hands with it, and we're using it as a crutch and we're walking. I think they're watching the way we walk. And we go back, we go across the room a few times. I'm not really paying attention to the boy. It's like I don't feel like I should.

DR. FIORE: Why do you suppose they're looking at the way you walk? Did they say anything to you?

MARK: They don't say nothing. I kinda just know what to do. I kinda read the body language.

DR. FIORE: Is there anything unusual about the way you walk?

MARK: Not the way I walk. They're like looking at my knees, ankles and hips. It only happened a couple of times. They put me back up on the table. I'm lying down now.

DR. FIORE: Now what's happening?

MARK: I kind of have a feeling that they're coming down here, wanting to mix with our race, you know?

DR. FIORE: What gives you that idea?

MARK: Because they're getting like a real small, real thin wire, and at the end of this wire is a tube, and they've been squirting medicine in it, and they stick the wire down my penis and squirt it into me. And I'm out of it though. I'm not awake. I feel like I've got anesthesia.

DR. FIORE: Where do you feel you are?

MARK: I feel like I'm on the table. I know what's happening to me, but there's nothing I can do about it.

DR. FIORE: Do you see what's happening?

MARK: Yes.

DR. FIORE: And where are you in relationship to your body?

MARK: I'm inside my body lying down, and also above it a little bit, above and to the right side.

DR. FIORE: Do they explain to you why they put the wire in your penis?

MARK: They keep telling me, this is just going to help us in the long run.

DR. FIORE: When they say "us," whom do they mean?

MARK: I guess they mean their race.

DR. FIORE: What causes you to lose consciousness?

MARK: They just put their hand on my forehead. Just gently they touched it, and I kinda just went out.

DR. FIORE: That's when you left your body and went unconscious?

MARK: Yes.

DR. FIORE: And then it was after that they inserted the tube?

MARK: Yes.

DR. FIORE: Speak out anything that comes into your mind.

MARK: Kind of like when a doctor presses on your stomach, feels for an ulcer or something like that. I see myself from the top, right now. The aliens are feeling around, like my testicles. I guess they're feeling for the wire or something. It's almost like a fishing wire, fishing line. And they pull it out, real fast.

DR. FIORE: What thoughts are in your mind as you're looking down?

MARK: I don't want no problems with that area when I get older.

DR. FIORE: Are you saying that you don't want them to hurt you permanently?

MARK: I don't want them to hurt me, whatever they're doing. I don't want there to be scars or damage to it later on or something.

DR. FIORE: Now what happens?

MARK: Some of the medicine or fluid or whatever it is leaked out, and they clean it up. It's kind of a pale blue color. Then they're checking my chest area. They're just touching. They take my neck and they move it from side to side. And they cut off a little piece of my hair. [Pauses]

DR. FIORE: Just report everything that comes into your mind.

MARK: One of the aliens takes both hands and grabs the sides of my face, gently, and his thumbs or fingers are on my temples, and I wake up.

DR. FIORE: Do you feel that what he did wakes you up?

MARK: Yes.

DR. FIORE: Tell me exactly what he did.

MARK: He uses both hands. He takes his forefingers, puts them behind my head, puts the palms on the cheekbone with the thumb on the temple and kinda just presses, and I wake up.

DR. FIORE: And then what happens?

MARK: He helps me off the table, and he walks me to this little chair. There's a round bowl that comes over my head, like you go inside a beauty shop and it dries your hair. And it covers me. I feel this warm feeling over me. Kind of really relaxing. I fall asleep. It's just so relaxing. And then a guy comes over and picks me up . . . lays me like on the floor, and . . . boom. I'm gone.

DR. FIORE: What do you mean by that?

MARK: He put me back in bed. If I remember correctly, I woke up with a slight headache.

DR. FIORE: Go to any time when they did a healing on you, if they did, of any condition that you have. If they've healed you for a number of things, go to the one that has had the strongest impact on you, at the count of three. One . . . two . . . three.

MARK: They have a big clamp around the left side of my side, my gut. It's sending pulses, shock waves into my pancreas, for my diabetes. I don't know what it's for, but it tickles sometimes, and every time it sends one of these waves through, my body twitches just a little bit.

DR. FIORE: How do you know they're sending it to your pancreas?

MARK: Because that's where it's at, that's where they have this clamp. And I have diabetes, and I have a feeling that's what it's for.

DR. FIORE: How do you feel about them doing this?

MARK: I don't mind.

DR. FIORE: Do you have any other feelings or thoughts?

MARK: I just wonder when they're gonna get done with me.

DR. FIORE: What do you mean?

MARK: 'Cause I felt like I've been there a long time, with them working on me. Nothing they did was painful. I'm just real, real impatient, just to be lying there, having this thing hooked to the side of me.

DR. FIORE: Are you alone in the room?

MARK: Yes.

DR. FIORE: Do they explain what they're doing?

MARK: No. I kinda feel that they're just putting, this energy in me, this thing that's hooked to me.

DR. FIORE: How many extraterrestrials are there with you?

MARK: Just one.

DR. FIORE: Tell me about this being.

MARK: His form's kinda flat. It's not round like ours. And he has pretty broad shoulders and a thin neck. His arms are much longer than humans' arms are. His fingers are much longer and more bony-looking, the knuckles are.

DR. FIORE: How many fingers does he have?

MARK: Four.

DR. FIORE: Does he have a thumb in addition?

MARK: Yes.

DR. FIORE: So does he have five altogether?

MARK: No, four. Three fingers and a thumb. It's a big thumb.

DR. FIORE: What does his face look like?

MARK: He has real sharp cheeks, they stick out there. He has a real small mouth. It doesn't open. And his nose is just a little mound. And his eyes look like a cat's almost. They're concave. And his head's almost like egg-shaped.

DR. FIORE: What is his hair like?

MARK: I don't see hair. There's a few little hairs, but not many of them.

DR. FIORE: Does he have eyebrows?

MARK: No.

DR. FIORE: Ears?

MARK: Doesn't really look like an ear, though. They're pretty small. It's like a little piece of skin, sticking up a little bit, with a hole. The hole's bigger than the piece of skin.

DR. FIORE: What color are the eyes?

MARK: Almost black, but also green a little bit, a dark green.

DR. FIORE: And how big are the eyes?

MARK: They're pretty big . . . big eyes.

DR. FIORE: At this point, what is he doing to you?

MARK: He's messing with his machinery, his equipment.

DR. FIORE: You say he's been working on you a long time. What have they been doing all this time? Think back. Remember.

MARK: He's been hooking me up to his machines.

DR. FIORE: What part of your body?

MARK: He was taking blood out.

DR. FIORE: Where did he take the blood out?

MARK: He took it out of my arm.

DR. FIORE: And then what?

MARK: He put this thing over my chest, like a big thing of rubber, well, it was pretty heavy. Like lead almost, like what they use in X-ray machines. They put it over me, over my chest. And on the machine, it showed my lungs and my heart. And he'd move this thing up and down, and it would show my internal organs, and the bones, you know.

DR. FIORE: Could you see it too?

MARK: Yes. I looked over at it. The machine was right by me.

DR. FIORE: And then?

MARK: He also has another machine that takes pictures of what this screen had showed on it. It'd keep track of everything that it showed, and as this paper stuff came out, he would mark little *x*'s and *o*'s and he would draw little things on certain areas of the paper, like for my heart or my bones or something. He put this thing on my head, like a bandana, and it made me sweat, and he's scraping the sweat off. He's going to keep it, to study it or something. This thing he put on my head, it's real hot. My forehead broke out in a sweat.

DR. FIORE: Did he explain why he was doing any of this to you?

MARK: No. He don't talk to me. I feel that he's going to study it all, examine it, for future reference.

DR. FIORE: Now he's just scraped off the sweat, now what?

MARK: That's all.

DR. FIORE: When does he put the clamp on you?

MARK: That's not till later.

DR. FIORE: What does he do in between?

MARK: He went out for a minute.

DR. FIORE: During this time, did you think of escaping or protesting?

MARK: No. It's kinda like being in a doctor's office.

DR. FIORE: Did you have the feeling that it was familiar, that you had done this before?

MARK: Yes.

DR. FIORE: Can you actually remember having done it before, or is it just a feeling of familiarity?

MARK: Yes. Familiar. 'Cuz that alien that was working on me is real friendly. He seemed like a pleasant person, like he's seen and talked to me before.

DR. FIORE: Move to the moment when he comes back in the room.

MARK: He has the clamp with him now. And another person's coming in with him. He put the clamp on me, and then the other alien hooked it up to the machines. Then he left the room.

DR. FIORE: Did they both leave?

MARK: No.

DR. FIORE: Who left the room?

MARK: The one that hooked the wires and plugs and stuff that the clamp was to.

DR. FIORE: The one that came in, did he look similar to or very different from the other aliens?

MARK: He looked a lot alike.

DR. FIORE: What were they wearing?

MARK: Nothing.

DR. FIORE: Could you see their skin all over their body?

MARK: Yes, something like a chameleon, they can change their colors. It has to do with the lighting. They can change their color. They can't go from like a black to a white, but they can go from a lighter to a darker color from what their skin color is.

DR. FIORE: They're not wearing any clothing at all?

MARK: No.

DR. FIORE: Can you see their genitals, for example?

MARK: No, I don't look at them. I just see them from the belly up.

DR. FIORE: Do they have a navel?

MARK: Yes.

DR. FIORE: Is it different from ours in any way?

MARK: It looks basically the same.

DR. FIORE: Was anything said to you about your diabetic condition? Any questions asked or anything said about it?

MARK: Nope. But they knew what was wrong with me. They knew I had diabetes.

DR. FIORE: Did their treatment help your diabetes?

MARK: Nope.

DR. FIORE: Did it make it worse?

MARK: Nope. It didn't do nothing to it.

DR. FIORE: What do you think they were doing? Why do you think that clamp was there?

MARK: I think the shock waves were . . . there's something unique inside this shock wave that would hopefully stimulate the dead part of the pancreas to make that start working once again. It didn't work.

DR. FIORE: Do you feel they have helped your arthritis in any way?

MARK: I don't think they're helping with it. They're just looking at it and studying it, as I go on. They're not doing nothing for it.

DR. FIORE: As you have reached maturity, do you feel they have taken any of your sperm?

MARK: Yes.

DR. FIORE: You're going to remember that at the count of five. One . . . two . . . three . . . four . . . five.

MARK: Yes. They have a fishing wire-type of thing. On the end of it is like a miniature thing you stick up a baby's nose to get the mucus out. It's like that, but it's real small. And that was painful. And I guess they used that as a suction. And on the end of it, was like a little camera so they knew where they were going. They must know anatomy pretty well, and they went to the part where the sperm was being made, and sucked some of it out.

DR. FIORE: And that hurt you?

MARK: Going in hurt.

DR. FIORE: But did it hurt so much that you had to leave your body?

MARK: I was out. They put me out. I'm asleep during this. I see myself from the top now.

DR. FIORE: How do you know now that it hurts?

MARK: Just by watching myself, I can tell that it hurt. And I just remember something now. I don't have kidney stones, but when I go to the bathroom, sometimes it hurts bad, and that can be from them doing that.

DR. FIORE: How many times have they extracted the sperm from you?

MARK: Twice, I think.

DR. FIORE: When was the last time?

MARK: Age fifteen comes to my mind.

DR. FIORE: Is there anything else you want to remember before we stop?

MARK: That's it.

✦

After Mark was out of hypnosis, he shook his head. "I can't believe all that happened. But it was so clear, and I could feel those scared feelings, just like it was happening right then."

"We'll never know for sure, Mark, but what you experienced is very similar to what other people have remembered about that kind of encounter."

"So do you think my dream was real then? I mean like not a dream, but really happened to me?"

"It's very possible, Mark. There is nothing in your regression that I haven't heard before, or at least heard something very close to it."

✦

Mark left my office satisfied that he had done his best and excited about his experience with the aliens. I was very interested in the visitors' efforts to help his diabetes and perhaps his arthritis as well. Yet even their advanced technology could not give him the relief he so desperately wanted and needed. The fact that he had remembered experiences and procedures that were painful and frightening meant that he had healed himself of the negative effects from those buried traumas. Not only had Mark helped himself, he had contributed to our growing knowledge of the most exciting and remarkable happening of our age, the interaction of extraterrestrials and humans.

"I Wouldn't Let Them Make Me Forget."

Barbara eased her huge body into my Danish black leather reclining chair and burst into racking sobs. "I've been real sick. It's all this weight. Three hundred and forty-seven pounds! And now I have panic attacks all the time."

I handed her a box of tissues and waited for the crying to subside. From the biographical data sheet she had returned to me before our appointment, I knew that she was in her early fifties, married, the mother of grown children, and worked full time in a position with considerable responsibility. I saw before me a suffering human being; obese, terrified and probably feeling completely hopeless.

"The moment I arrived in your parking lot, I started to have a panic attack, but I feel better already," Barbara said, blowing her nose noisily. "You're my last hope." Barbara's face reflected the desperation she was feeling. "I've tried counselors and doctors. They just tell me to take off the weight and relax."

She gave me a "laundry list" of her many physical problems, including "heart attacks," hemorrhaging, a hysterectomy, allergies, headaches, seven surgeries to repair a bad break in her leg and torn muscles in her knee, and borderline diabetes. As she settled back more into the chair, she described other, psychological problems; a lifelong claustrophobia that had worsened during the past twenty years, and, more recently, the panic attacks. Her stormy marriage of over thirty years was an ongoing source of unhappiness and stress. "I'm sure it's all tied in with my 'iceberg' . . . a lot of anger and hatred that I hold in. I put on a smile and go on with life." She spent some time telling me about her marriage and then appeared to have run out of steam. She looked at me as though the ball were now in my court.

"What's your top priority, Barbara? We have about an hour left today, and we can get started with the treatment now."

"The panic attacks are the worst problem. The others have been around for ages, but these started about three years ago, back in 1983," she said, reaching forward for another tissue. Wiping her face and neck, she gazed up to her left, obviously remembering something. "I was driving home at night, about 10:40. All of a sudden, I saw a flash of light . . . in an instant, twenty minutes had passed. I felt real confused." She leaned forward in her chair and almost whispered as she confided, "I started feeling anxious from that point on. Later, I was in the hospital, when all of a sudden I woke at 3:00 A.M. and something said, 'UFO.' I looked out and saw a strange streak in the sky. I wasn't sure what it was. I started reading articles on UFOs, and they made me really nervous, but I was fascinated at the same time."

"Why were you in the hospital, Barbara?"

"One of those heart attacks I was trying to have," she said, chuckling. "They started about a year ago. My heart would speed up, chest pains were really bad, I'd get faint and just about pass out."

"What does your doctor say about them?"

"He says they're due to stress—pressure. I find if I have a real rough day at the office, they occur."

I wanted to use hypnosis with her before she left, since she lived near Sacramento, about two hours away, and would not be able to come on a regular once-a-week basis. Often panic attacks can be relieved relatively easily, if we are able to "hit the nail on the head" without a whole lot of resistance. But before starting the treatment, I needed a few more clues. I asked her to tell me more about the panic attacks.

"After the first one, I noticed I had sore spots on my body. It was scraped, but I couldn't remember bumping into anything. If I relaxed, my mind would be bombarded with thoughts so fast I couldn't grab onto them."

"Was there any theme?" I asked.

Barbara looked down with a sheepish smile on her face. "Please don't think I'm crazy . . ." She glanced up at me for reassurance.

I smiled at her. "Barbara, you're not crazy and you know it. I'm very used to hearing unusual things. I doubt whether anything can shock me anymore."

"Well, occasionally thoughts of UFOs come storming into my mind and, believe it or not, a day or so later someone will say they have seen one." She let out a big sigh of relief and relaxed back into the chair. "I'm psychic. I've been sensitive that way ever since I was a kid. It's a liability! I get severe headaches before natural disasters, especially earthquakes. I have to call the doctor, and he gives me a shot."

"How frequent are the panic attacks, Barbara, and where and when do they occur?"

"There's one section of the road, just past a bridge, and unfortunately, I have to go that way to get home from school at night. I'm taking some night courses. I have them [panic attacks] there. I haven't had a good night's sleep in three years! I wake up in the middle of the night, terrified." Crying, she twisted a wad of tissues around her fingers and looked up at me beseechingly. "They're crippling me!"

I had planned to make a tape of relaxing suggestions that would help her to sleep and from there proceed into a regression to the cause of the panic. I judged that the remaining fifty minutes would give us enough time.

"Barbara, usually people's body temperatures drop a bit when they're relaxing," I said as I covered her with the mohair blanket and eased her chair into a reclining position.

I settled back in my Danish rosewood chair, slid a thirty-minute tape into the small Sony on the end table, picked up the mike and began speaking to her in a soft, modulated voice, asking her to close her eyes, sink down into the chair and concentrate on her breathing. I studied her face and saw the muscles giving way to my continuing suggestions to relax and drift deeper.

Suddenly, she started squirming in the chair, throwing the blanket off and breathing rapidly. I realized she was panicking and immediately decided to do the regression. Quickly slipping the relaxation tape out of the recorder, I grabbed a ninety-minute blank tape, pushed Record/Play, swung the boom around close to her face and placed the mike in it, to record the session.

●

DR. FIORE: Tell me whatever comes to mind, without censoring the material for any reason. What are you aware of now?

BARBARA: I'm driving along about fifty-five miles per hour. Something in my mind says UFO, and I look around at the sky through my windows, but I don't see anything except a very large bright moon. But the feeling is very strong. There's a flash of light. [*Pauses*] A UFO stops over my car and brings my car to a halt. [*Getting upset*] I am taken out of the car.

DR. FIORE: How is that done?

BARBARA: By a light. The light seems to pull me from . . . pulls me out of my car. [*Becoming agitated*] I don't want to go. I'm taken aboard a . . . a . . . ramp. [*Crying*] I'm scared. I can't see anything. I'm scared. [*Pauses*] I'm on a table. I can't move. They keep telling me, "Don't be afraid. We won't hurt you." "I want to leave," I say. They say, "Not yet, not yet. You'll be all right. You won't remember." [*Calmer*] There are people there, but I can't see them. But I know they're there. They have equipment they run back and forth over me. It doesn't hurt. It's just I don't like being in close quarters. I don't like it and . . . [*Much more relaxed*] Then I go down the ramp to my car and I start driving home.

DR. FIORE: Go back to the moment you entered the UFO. You will remember everything that happened accurately at the count of three. One . . . two . . . three.

BARBARA: They are walking with me.

DR. FIORE: Who are "they"?

BARBARA: There's two. I think they're men. I can't tell. They're in gray. I see a gray hood, kinda like . . .

DR. FIORE: Is it like a jumpsuit?

BARBARA: Kinda like that, only it's closer fitting than that.

DR. FIORE: Are they talking to you as you walk?

BARBARA: They're not saying anything, but I hear what they're saying in my mind. "Don't be afraid. We won't hurt you." [*Shivers*] I'm cold. I'm inside now. When they undressed me, I said I didn't like it. "I don't know you guys." They just kind of chuckled and said, "Well, you won't remember anyway, so it doesn't matter." Then I told them I was cold, so they gave me a robe. There was this kind of cabinet under the table, and they got it there. Then they helped me onto the table.

DR. FIORE: Are you lying on the table?

BARBARA: Yes. On my back.

DR. FIORE: Remember exactly how they examined you.

BARBARA: They took a skin scraping.

DR. FIORE: From where?

BARBARA: My arm. My leg. They looked at my bad leg.

DR. FIORE: What did they say about that?

BARBARA: They said, "You had an accident." And I said, "Yes." They said, "You had your female organs removed," and I said, "Yes." And they wanted to know how I felt about it. [*Becoming upset*] Uh! I don't like the vibration. The rocking disturbs me. I have an inner ear problem, and the motion bothers me. They told me it doesn't take long. [*Jerking her hands away*] My fingernails. They clipped my fingernails and a piece of my hair. [*Pauses*] They took a blood sample.

DR. FIORE: From what part of your body?

BARBARA: From my finger. [*Extends right index finger. Long pause*]

DR. FIORE: Did they examine you vaginally?

BARBARA: No. They mainly used the machine . . . a big black machine . . . they ran it over my body. It didn't touch me, but it was close. And they were kind. They didn't want me to be upset.

DR. FIORE: Did they tell you why they chose you?

BARBARA: Because I was there.

DR. FIORE: Tell me everything that's happening.

BARBARA: They say something about my skin. They keep talking . . . something about my skin.

DR. FIORE: Just relax. I'll count to three, then you'll remember. One . . . two . . . three.

BARBARA: How white I am. My skin where it hasn't been exposed to the sun is very white. They keep calling it fragile. They keep telling me it's different.

DR. FIORE: Do they comment on your weight?

BARBARA: No, nothing about the weight. They're more interested in the white skin.

DR. FIORE: Do they say anything else to you?

BARBARA: They put blocks . . . they don't want people to know they're doing this, so they put blocks on the memory.

DR. FIORE: Did they say why they were doing this? Why they didn't want us to know?

BARBARA: They said they were exploring and finding out about other people, and because we're such an emotional people . . . uh . . . I'm fighting the block . . . emotional people, they don't want us to know they're there . . . but they want to find out what we're like. We're similar, but we're different. They tell me they're from Sirius. Uh! Uh! [Squirming] The vibration's getting stronger. [Pauses] The propulsion . . . that's what the vibration is. They take off out of sight of any other cars and then when it's clear, they bring you back to your car.

DR. FIORE: Is there anything else you need to remember?

BARBARA: They told me not to be afraid. That they do not hurt people.

DR. FIORE: Did they say anything about being in further contact with you?

BARBARA: They said I might feel their presence in the area because I have some psychic ability. I might feel their presence when they're there and that I should not be afraid and not let it bother me. They're very kind. They keep telling me, "Don't be afraid. You don't need to be afraid of us."

DR. FIORE: How many people did you see in the ship?

BARBARA: I saw three . . . and I keep seeing a panel of some kind. There's not a lot of light. I can't really tell . . .

DR. FIORE: What shape is the room you're in?

BARBARA: Oval . . . round. Round.

DR. FIORE: Tell me more about it.

BARBARA: There's doors and kinda like . . . I see a big metal wall that comes out into the room. Kinda like covering something. When I come up the ramp, it's kinda like you're in a steel corridor, then you come into the room where the table is. It's kinda like a medical room. It's not the control room of the ship. There's one person who's in charge. He seems to be bigger than the rest of them. He's taller and he keeps projecting kindness. He keeps telling me not to be afraid. He doesn't talk, but I keep hearing him in my mind telling me not to be afraid. They won't hurt me and I feel kindness from him. And he puts his hands on my eyes.

DR. FIORE: He touches your face?

BARBARA: Yes. He touches my forehead. He covers my eyes and my forehead with his hand. He says I won't remember.

DR. FIORE: Did you say anything?

BARBARA: I said I wanted to remember. I didn't want to forget. I'm very interested in things like this.

DR. FIORE: Did you deliberately try to undermine his suggestion to you?

BARBARA: Yes. I kept saying, "I want to remember."

DR. FIORE: You said it to yourself?

BARBARA: Yes. "I want to remember."

DR. FIORE: And now that you've remembered, how do you feel?

BARBARA: I feel better.

DR. FIORE: Do you feel there's anything to be afraid of?

BARBARA: No.

DR. FIORE: Now the panic you've been feeling . . . do you realize it's how you felt when you were going up the ramp?

BARBARA: Yes.

DR. FIORE: You've been having flashbacks. Do you understand that it's because you gave yourself the suggestion to remember? When I hypnotized you today, the memory came right up because you had already told yourself you wanted to remember. All these panic attacks have been your remembering . . . you were remembering the panic you felt as you approached the ship and were forced up the ramp. You didn't feel that way after the tall one in charge calmed you down. Let's go back over that again. You will remember what you experienced. You're going up the ramp again.

BARBARA: Oh! Jesus! [*Crying and agitated*] Oh God! What are they going to do to me? [*Crying harder*] I'm scared. What are they going to do to me? [*Shouting*] God! No! No! [*Flailing her arms about as though to break free*] I'm trying to run back to the car. . . . [*Becomes calmer*]

DR. FIORE: What's happening now?

BARBARA: He's saying, "Don't be scared. We won't hurt you. It's all right. It's okay. Don't be scared. It's okay. It's okay. It's all right."

DR. FIORE: Do you feel calmer?

BARBARA: I'm not scared anymore. I know he won't hurt me. I'm looking at the table.

DR. FIORE: I want you to remember the time you felt the best with him. You've already remembered the worst; now remember the best.

BARBARA: Just before he put his hands on my head, kindness, just nothing but kindness flowed from him. He said he didn't like to upset people, but it was his job to check people out to see what they were like. And I understood that. I keep feeling kindness . . . kindness . . . kindness.

❡

I brought Barbara out of hypnosis with suggestions of well-being and told her she would remember everything.

She opened her eyes and smiled broadly.

"How do you feel?"

"Much better."

"Is there anything to be afraid of now?"

"No," she said softly. "I wouldn't let them make me forget." A big grin lighted up her face.

"That's why you had the panic attacks, Barbara. You were actually reliving the anxiety you had felt during the abduction each time you passed that spot. When you relaxed the guard in your mind, for example when relaxing or sleeping, your subconscious mind tried to heal you of the trauma by bringing it to the surface of your mind. But it was too painful, so you pushed it back down. Have you ever had a boil?"

She leaned forward in her chair, looking puzzled. "Yes, a few times."

"When that happens, what your body is doing is bringing poisons to the surface so they can be released. Your mind has been doing the same thing."

She nodded, understanding.

"When you passed the place of the abduction, or any place very similar to it, the repression holding the memory down was weakened, and it started to come up. You were actually reliving what you had once experienced."

"Why doesn't it fade with time?" Barbara asked, shaking her head incredulously. "It's been just as bad lately as the first time."

"That's an excellent question. The subconscious mind has a memory bank of everything we have ever experienced, exactly as we perceived it. Every thought, emotion, sound of music, word, taste and sight. Everything is faithfully recorded somehow in your mind. Your subconscious mind's memory is perfect, infallible. The charges on traumatic memories are like thorns in our flesh. They fester . . . they cause all kinds of problems and symptoms, until the energy associated with them is dispelled. How this happens is not known, as yet, but that it does is very evident. Now I've given you a psychology lesson," I said, laughing.

"Are the panic attacks gone?" Barbara asked.

"The proof of the pudding is in the eating," I replied. "We won't know what we've accomplished here in the office until we see how you are in your daily life. When can you come back?"

We set up another appointment as soon as possible. As she stood up to leave, we both spontaneously moved toward each other for a hug.

With the door open, she paused, smiled and said, "Thanks. I feel so much better. Best of all, I now have hope."

✦

When I saw Barbara ten days later in the waiting room, she smiled and eagerly got up to come into my office. Before she had even settled herself into the chair, she spread out her arms and said, "I'm so much better! I only woke up one night with a panic attack. And I'm not as tired, despite an allergy flare-up and the headache that goes with it."

"How did you feel when you left here?" I asked, picking up my yellow notepad and preparing to take my usual verbatim notes.

"Fine. I didn't feel any dread when I left Sacramento for home. I did a test. I deliberately went past the bridge and the place on the road I told you about. That section still bothers me. I feel some apprehension, but I know why. I have more insight. The first time, I just pulled over and parked . . . and waited it out. No panic, just apprehension."

I commended her for her progress, as well as her willingness to face her fears. Usually when a repressed event is exhumed, it brings in its wake more material that surfaces little by little when the mind is relaxed. Sometimes patients report whole scenes flashing before their eyes on the drive home after a session, or later as they're just about to drop off to sleep, or even when doing the dishes or other routine chores.

"Barbara, has anything more come into your mind about the event we dealt with last time?"

She leaned forward in her chair, bursting to tell me all that had happened. "I remember that two technicians pulled me from the car. They willed me to walk between them. When I got closer to the ship, I started to panic. The same panic I've been feeling. I yelled, "No!" They grabbed my arms, and the third man, the one in charge . . . he was in black, calmed me down. I walked up the ramp into the ship. The two technicians followed behind me. I felt a struggle between fear and curiosity. At the doorway, I stopped. I don't know or remember how I got undressed and on the table." She paused, and her eyes became distant. "The two technicians did undress me, now I remember, and gave me a robe because I complained I was too cold. I became aware of a slight vaginal and anal discomfort. But I don't remember much. There was a rectangular light panel. I hopped out of my body, astrally projected. I've done that since I was a kid, and I stood next to the door looking at my body on the table. The man in black said, "Damn psychics! Get back here!" He was disgruntled and ordered me back. So I went back. The machine is clearest in my mind. The three men looked the same as us. One technician kept talking about my skin and how white and fragile it is. They commented on my blood chemistry, but wouldn't tell me anything more about it." She sat back and took a deep breath.

"I'm impressed with how much you're coming up with. How did your body feel after our session?" I asked.

"My eyes were sore for two days. Not the same day, but the next two. The night of our session, I slept without any panic attack waking me. It was the first time in years!"

"How have you been sleeping since then?"

"Just fine. Oh! Something interesting! They told me it was only twenty minutes, but it must have been more. Since then, I find I'm suddenly distrusting clocks. I'm double-checking them."

"Barbara, how's your energy level been since last time?"

"In the past year, I've been totally exhausted. Since our visit, I'm not exhausted. Of course, I'm sleeping better, but I'm still tired. And I have not been at all depressed since our meeting." She smiled brightly, adding, "And I'm not eating as much."

I felt we needed to review the UFO contact again, since she was not completely free of anxiety. Also I had a hunch there was still more for her to remember. If we had time, I planned to regress her to the source of her claustrophobia, so I induced hypnosis.

✑

DR. FIORE: Move back in time to the event responsible for the soreness in your eyes. At the count of ten you will remember. [*Counts to ten*]

BARBARA: The machine . . . the lights on the machine were directly over my face, and that's why I split. I left my body. The one tech said, "Are you about through?" And the other one said, "Yes." And they moved the machine back to my feet, and then the leader covered my eyes with his hand.

DR. FIORE: Let yourself remember what happened that caused you the irritation in your vagina and rectum.

BARBARA: When I was out of my body during the exam, they propped up my legs and did a vaginal and rectal exam.

DR. FIORE: Okay. Go back to one minute before you left your body and see what caused you to leave it.

BARBARA: The light and the machine over my face. I don't like that . . . anything close to my face. They moved the machine over my face, so I jumped out and stood by the door.

DR. FIORE: How did they do the vaginal and rectal exams?

BARBARA: It was something black attached to the machine . . . a round object.

DR. FIORE: Do you know if it hurt or not?

BARBARA: No, I don't. I was just watching.

◢

This session, unlike the first, which was a double session, was only fifty minutes long, and there was no time left to work on Barbara's claustrophobia, which had predated her abduction. We had worked up to the last minute, so I brought her out of hypnosis. After ascertaining that she was fine, I reminded her not to drive for ten or fifteen minutes, and asked her to set up her next appointment with my secretary. We gave each other a hug and exchanged best wishes for the Christmas holidays.

*

On 15 January 1987, I saw Barbara for the third time.

"No panic attacks! Not one single one!" She announced happily. "And would you believe? I've lost twenty-seven pounds since I first saw you."

I checked my notes and said, "That was only seven weeks ago."

"Yes, and remember, I've been through first Thanksgiving and then Christmas and all the celebrating of the holidays!"

"Did you put yourself on a diet?"

"No diet. My appetite's decreased . . . and I don't feel at all deprived. It really hit me Thanksgiving evening after dinner. I hadn't overeaten. In fact, I left food on my plate without even realizing it. And I only had one helping!"

I was really puzzled, because I have worked with a great many obese patients for years and have always found some plausible subconscious reason for the overweight, which is often a defense against being sexually attractive. I could see no logical explanation for the change she had noticed.

She interrupted my thoughts by saying, "I feel some UFOs are back in the area. I asked, 'Are you there?' I got back a strong feeling that they were."

Barbara and I continued to work on a once-a-month basis for two more sessions. Although our investigation of her UFO experience was over, she still had many things to clear up in her life. Each time I saw her, she reported progress. She was no longer fatigued, the panic attacks were a thing of the past and her relationship with her husband was improving.

In May of 1987, she wrote saying she felt so well that she no longer believed that she needed therapy. In her own words, she was ". . . feeling well. I am happy, and I am losing weight. One of the things that prompted this decision [to discontinue therapy] is my passing a very crucial test recently. In the past when I have been upset or had a problem, I have always headed straight for the refrigerator. This time, I was extremely upset and heartbroken, but instead of heading for the refrigerator, I looked at the problem, accepted it and decided that I was not going to let it bother me. In other words, I have learned for forgive myself for my own stupidity and to forgive others too. As a result, everything is working out great."

I called Barbara just before writing her chapter, to get her permission to use her material, and was delighted to hear that she has continued to make tremendous progress in every area of her life.

5

"They Can Come and Take Me Any Time They Want!"

Tom had been my patient for over one year when the topic of CEIVs came up. He is a very warm, intelligent person, a specialist in computer programming, who had sought my help for chronic depression and severe anxiety attacks that had immobilized him from time to time. His basic problem was a real lack of self-esteem and self-confidence. We were making some headway on these crippling issues, but there was still more work to be done before he would be able to actualize his potential and achieve the personal happiness and success that he so richly deserved.

Tom walked over and hung up his navy blazer on the rosewood coat tree in the corner of my office and then settled himself in the chair. He slipped out of his loafers, put his feet up on the black leather ottoman, pushed the chair back into a semireclining position and crossed his arms behind his head.

"What's your new book about, Edee?"

As I described the topic of *Encounters,* he listened attentively. Within seconds, he uncrossed his arms, fidgeted a bit and then folded them across his chest, holding onto himself tightly.

"What are you feeling, Tom, as I'm talking about this?"

"Real strong anxiety. I feel they're out there somewhere and will pick me up . . . again." He frowned as though a little surprised. "Then what will I do? Maybe what I feel is a fear of an impending contact and having to go through that again." He laughed nervously. "It sounds like I've been abducted, doesn't it?"

"It certainly wouldn't surprise me."

"I'm feeling a real strong spooky, spine-tingling, hair-standing-on-end feeling! However, it's totally outside of my belief system that this could happen to me."

"Have you read any books on the subject?"

"Yes. I read Whitley Strieber's book, *Communion.* When he talked about the abject terror he felt, it certainly struck a note with me. It sounded somehow very familiar. Since having read the book, I've had that same spooky feeling more often. I had it before. I can remember times even when I was a kid that I felt like that. I think that it usually happens at night, when I'm alone. One of the recent times was sometime last summer. I was going out to get something to eat. And then, on an impulse, I decided to drive up the road toward Mt. Hamilton Observatory. There are places you can stand and look at the city lights. That particular night I was really feeling good about things. It was a beautiful, balmy night, and I decided I would treat myself to the experience. I did enjoy it. But I was standing to the side of the road, and there were several very gnarled-looking trees. It was real dark, and that feeling came over me: What if they come and pick me up right here? [*Laughs nervously*] That real, absolutely terrified, real spooked, verging-on-terror sensation. I controlled it for a while, but I went back a little sooner than I otherwise would have. I stopped at more than one place. And the feeling kind of ebbed and flowed and came back a couple of times."

"Has it happened often, Tom?"

"Yes. Three or four times a year."

"Tom, it sounds like you may have had a contact and what's happening is that whenever you're in a similar situation or in any way you're reminded of it, you are actually reliving what you once felt. The very best thing we can do now would be a regression."

"Fine, but first there's a possible piece of evidence. There's this funny lump I've got in my nose. And I'm not sure what it is. It's on the inside of my right nostril, on the septum in the center. It feels hemispherical in shape and sort of hard, bony. It appeared overnight. I went to bed one night not having had it and the next morning, got up with it. It was back in late '76 or early '77. I had had surgery on my ear and was still seeing the ENT doctor periodically, so I made a point the next time I saw him to have him take a look. He examined it and then didn't make any comments about it at all. I went away with a question mark in my mind and for some reason decided not to push it."

"Do you remember whether there was any blood on the sheets or anything to indicate a nosebleed or anything of that sort when you woke up that morning?"

"Not to my recollection."

I noticed that our time was slipping away, even though we had a double session. I wanted to do a regression, so I hypnotized Tom and asked his subconscious mind to take him to the event responsible for the "spooky, spine-tingling feeling." I counted to ten and asked him to report whatever came into his mind.

*

TOM: I'm in a forested area at night, a dark night. And I'm meeting some unearthly looking beings. Rounded heads and generally humanoid, but definitely not human. They have smaller, shorter bodies than an adult human and they're very lightweight. I have the feeling . . . that's an image that I made up, that's not what they really look like. I didn't want to look at them close up, to see what they looked like.

DR. FIORE: Let yourself remember everything that you experienced, just as though it's happening now.

TOM: When it happened, I didn't want to experience it, so the memories I have of it are not complete. I was taken against my will. Had I been given my choice, my choice would have been absolutely not. I'm not ready for this kind of a feeling.

DR. FIORE: Where were you when you were taken against your will?

TOM: I may have left the house, intending to just go out into the yard or something, and then I was taken from there. I wish I had never gone out. If I had just stayed inside, maybe I would have been safe . . . but then, maybe I wouldn't have been safe. And the thought went through my mind that I'm never going to feel safe again, wherever I am . . . that being inside isn't safe either. The only way I can feel safe is if I don't allow myself to believe that this ever happened. It's a very frightening feeling to feel like I'm never going to be safe again. I can't quite face that. There's an inner conflict between belief and disbelief. This is something that happens to somebody else, it doesn't happen to me.

DR. FIORE: Let yourself remember what happened, exactly as you experienced it, at the count of three. One . . . two . . . three.

TOM: I'm inside some sort of a roomlike area, on a table, undressed, nude, and I don't like this at all. I'm totally out of control. One of the things I really hate about it is the feeling of being out of control, completely in their power, the feeling of being probed. I don't have a recollection of any severe pain, but definitely discomfort and fear. Apprehension. They could do anything they wanted to with me, and I have no choice in the matter. At times being handled kind of roughly, being touched and pressed in different parts of my body with hard, cold objects. Very unpleasant, very disagreeable. My genitals were being handled and examined. That's a real feeling of being violated . . . my person being violated. [*Pauses*] I hate it! [*Squirms*] I hate it! [*Long pause*]

DR. FIORE: Continue to report whatever comes into your mind.

TOM: I kicked and screamed and tried to resist, at least initially. They overcame my resistance. Any attempts they made to communicate with me were really limited to trying to calm me down and keep me under control.

DR. FIORE: You're allowing yourself to remember more of this in order to heal yourself of this trauma.

TOM: There's definitely resistance within me now to not remember. There's a part of me that does not want to remember that. Part of me that didn't want to believe it in the first place. I think that feeling of being completely out of control is perhaps the most difficult to deal with. The feeling that if I really believe this, then I have to believe that I'm just not in control of my life. They can come and take me any time they want.

DR. FIORE: Let yourself remember something easier to face.

TOM: I think the first event was when I was very young.

DR. FIORE: Let yourself remember that event now. Go back to the very first event, at the count of five. One . . . two . . . three . . . four . . . five. Just report everything that comes into your mind.

TOM: It was early in the evening. When it began to happen, the sky wasn't completely dark. There was something in the sky. And there's a being in the woods . . . and then it's later. I'm cold and shivery, and that was when they first took my clothes off. That coldness didn't last the whole time, but it was very uncomfortable and unpleasant at the time . . . and connected with that feeling of being out of control.

DR. FIORE: You're allowing yourself to remember exactly what happened to you.

TOM: A much stronger feeling of this tingling sensation. I'm getting a number of confusing images of different times, kind of mixed together, perhaps out of sequence. Of having been carried through the air, above the trees . . . and I don't know how this is happening. I'm not being supported by them. They're not carrying me physically. I find myself flying through the air all of a sudden. It's exhilirating and frightening all at the same time. It's so strange! And unbelievable. I mean, this must be a dream. And yet I don't think it is. I think it's really happening, but part of my mind doesn't want to accept this as anything happening to me. But . . . it is. I'm looking down, seeing the trees below. And the fear of falling becomes quite strong. And yet, somehow, there's a part of me that knows I'm not going to fall, [but] there's another part of me that's terrified that I am. And if I could just let go and enjoy this, it would be great! If I didn't have all these fears attached to it.

DR. FIORE: Now what's happening?

TOM: I'm still sailing through the air above the trees, in the most inexplicable way. I have no idea what's going on. How in the world are they doing this? [Pauses]

DR. FIORE: Continue to report everything that you're aware of.

TOM: I'm still experiencing that same sensation. I'm trying to let go and enjoy it . . . and I'm beginning to do that.

DR. FIORE: Are you continuing to fly?

TOM: Yes. I'm being carried up to the ship . . . the ship is hovering up above. And it's a dizzying sensation of motion. The trees become a blur below me. I feel like I'm suspended there in midair, being carried along.

DR. FIORE: What do you see?

TOM: I'm looking down at the moment, but the ship is up above. It's a disc with a hemispherical bulge above it. The explanation that comes to me now is that I was in what might be called a tractor beam, a beam that was pulling me up to the ship.

DR. FIORE: Now it's just a little bit later. What's happening?

TOM: I was brought inside the ship. I'm not quite sure how.

DR. FIORE: It's very clear in your mind.

TOM: I'm in a room or a chamber that is somewhat dimly lit, a reddish orange, quite dim. No harsh lighting. I'm in the presence of . . . at least three or four different beings. Because the light is so dim, I experience them as shadowy figures. I don't want to look directly at them. There's a part of me that is very interested, but I think the stronger feeling is uneasiness. Uneasiness and apprehension. [*Pauses*] Something's draped over my body. Some or all of my clothes have been removed, and some sort of a blanket is being draped over my body. It came down to about my knees, and my feet are bare. They folded it back and exposed my genitals and I'm . . . I didn't like that. And it made me uneasy. It intensified my feeling of uneasiness.

DR. FIORE: What's happening?

TOM: They touched me with their hands. Maybe they had gloves on, a fairly coarse, woven cloth. But they also touched me with instruments. And they were cold, hard, probably metallic. They were prodding and probing and poking. Something was inserted in my penis, and that was distinctly unpleasant, but not painful.

DR. FIORE: You're going to let yourself remember that at the count of three. One . . . two . . . three.

TOM: A real strong feeling, intense feeling, of having my person violated, but surprised that it's not painful. I force myself to try to relax, but I couldn't completely relax. Oh, I think it went really deep. Oh! [*Cries out in pain*] Ah! . . . [*More pain*] It's very unpleasant to even think about. [*Moans*] I want this to be over with! [*Sighs*] It makes me angry too. I don't like being treated that way. They're trying to tell me that it's for a very good reason. I don't really care.

DR. FIORE: Let yourself remember exactly what they conveyed to you.

TOM: They're telling me to hold still. And I don't want to hold still, and yet if I do try to struggle, it's going to result in my being hurt or injured. So I better hold still. [*His body tenses*] And it's the hardest thing in the world to try and hold still and submit to this.

DR. FIORE: Did they give you a reason for what they're doing?

TOM: I don't remember. I think I'm so young that I probably wouldn't have understood. There's a thin, flexible tube. Somehow it's almost like it moves on its own. It went back in through the urethral canal and down into my scrotum . . . it's probing down into my scrotum. [*Squirms*] It's distinctly unpleasant and disgusting to experience that. It was both unpleasant and a relief when it was withdrawn. It kind of stung slightly when they took it out, and yet it was a big relief at the same time. They're telling me that it's not going to have any lasting negative effect. I don't want to think about it anymore. I have the distinct feeling of wanting to block that memory from my mind. So, so unpleasant!

DR. FIORE: Did they suggest that you block it from your mind?

TOM: They were aware of my desire to block it from my mind, and they assisted me in doing that. Without really saying it to me, they were going to help me do that, in order to try to make me more comfortable. [*Sighs*] I was subjected to a rectal probe as well.

DR. FIORE: Let yourself remember that.

TOM: I found that also to be unpleasant, but not nearly so unpleasant as the other. Somehow it didn't seem quite so threatening. In fact, that went quite deep too. There were times when I felt a sensation up inside my abdomen that . . . that was not as alarming as the other thing though, but somewhat alarming.

DR. FIORE: And now?

TOM: Something's being inserted down my throat, and I'm gagging. And again, feeling a probe inside my chest from that. It's those sensations of something probing inside my body that I definitely find very alarming. I panicked momentarily because of feeling suffocated while it was going on. I wasn't sure I was going to be able to breathe normally.

DR. FIORE: Let yourself know if you ever saw the beings. If so, remember what they looked like.

TOM: They're inside that room. Kind of dark, shadowy figures, with some kind of clothing that is like a cloak with a hood. A glitter of light from the eyes, probably reflected light. But they're shorter than . . . Hmmm . . . I think I'm confused with another experience where I was older. They're between three and four feet tall. I didn't look at them very closely, but I do remember a relatively flat face. [*Pauses*]

DR. FIORE: Continue to report everything that you're aware of.

TOM: What at first I thought was another type of creature is an instrument or a tool that was connected into the wall of the ship.

A tube with something on the end of it. Two to three inches in diameter. My first reaction to it was that it was some sort of a serpent, but then I realized later it wasn't alive. And now I get the feeling it might have been . . . some kind of a vacuum apparatus. I'm put into a sitting position in some sort of a chair. Maybe the table that I was on folded into a chair, like a recliner chair. [*Pauses*]

DR. FIORE: And?

TOM: I'm resting on something that was to some degree form-fitting but it was too big for me. It was like sitting in something that was not completely hard . . . kind of like the feeling of a padded dash in an automobile. And then, for some reason, having my legs strapped down. [*Pauses*]

DR. FIORE: What is your reaction to this?

TOM: I'm looking forward to it being over with. A feeling that maybe the worst is over with, that the worst is past. And so, I guess there's some relief from that.

DR. FIORE: And now what's happened?

TOM: I'm being dropped back down out of the ship on like a cable or something, in a chair. There's some more of them waiting on the ground below to take me back.

DR. FIORE: And now?

TOM: Now I'm feeling really tired, both physically and emotionally. And I want to go back to sleep. And I somehow know that they're going to take me back home.

DR. FIORE: Now what's happening?

TOM: I am back in my bed and . . . I'm drifting off to sleep with a feeling that if I remember this, it's going to be like a dream.

❦

Before I brought Tom out of hypnosis, I gave his inner mind suggestions to prepare him to remember easily and accurately under hypnosis the next time we met, everything that he needed to remember about close encounters with extraterrestrials. I reinforced the suggestions that this preparation would go on at a very deep level of his subconscious mind and would in no way disturb him. I emphasized that he would feel particularly calm and have a wonderful sense of well-being. Then I counted him out of hypnosis.

❦

Two days later, I saw Tom again because he had called my office saying he needed to see me immediately. He got right to the point as soon as he sat down.

"I felt strong anxiety on Monday when I left your building. Since then, my energy level's been down, all day yesterday and today as well."

"It sounds like we stirred up something last time that's not resolved, Tom."

He nodded, looking quite distraught. I immediately initiated hypnosis and regressed him to the event that was responsible for the anxiety.

❦

TOM: It's the UFO issue. I have two conflicting reactions to those experiences. One part absolutely refuses to accept it and resists any further contacts or experiences. The other part of my mind is intrigued and would like to understand and be able to communicate and be at peace with it and look for whatever value might be in those experiences.

DR. FIORE: Let yourself remember what is causing the anxiety.

TOM: The very initial reaction when it first happens is disbelief combined with a strong feeling of being threatened. A sinister threat to my well-being. Something to avoid at all costs, if possible. But it was not possible. In that initial experience of being carried away from the house, I struggled to the best of my ability, but it was useless.

DR. FIORE: Let yourself remember another experience that has had a strong negative impact on you.

TOM: I'm in the car with my parents. I'm still young. I'm sitting in the dark in the backseat with my brother and sister. I saw the ship again. I didn't have a clear conscious memory of what had happened before, but I was filled with a sense of dread. You see, a part of me did remember and knew I was not able to avoid it. There was a wish that my parents would protect me. The fact that they couldn't increased my sense of helplessness and panic and an extreme feeling of defenselessness.

DR. FIORE: What happened?

TOM: I was taken along with my brother and sister. My parents were temporarily out of commission, unconscious, while this was going on.

DR. FIORE: Then what happened?

TOM: We were taken into the ship and there was a physical exam again. That's the hardest part for me, because it's extremely uncomfortable to think about those intrusions into my body.

DR. FIORE: What happened with your brother and sister?

TOM: I'm not aware of them being in the room, but being taken to the ship with me and our being returned together.

DR. FIORE: What happened to you during the examination?

TOM: I'm on that table again, being probed. [*Body tenses*] Into my penis again and a rectal probe . . . a tracheal probe or esophagus or both. [*Gags*] That feeling of something probing inside my body is . . . intensely unpleasant. Especially the genital probe. One or more of those probes, almost like a live thing, a thin, tiny finger moving around and probing. [*Squirms*] Oh! it was just . . . makes me want to squirm and writhe and get away from it. The feeling and having to hold perfectly still is almost too much to bear. At some point on the way back, I compared notes with my brother and sister. She found it much less disagreeable than I did. She was able to exchange information. I was intrigued and envious, and I wondered what was wrong with me. Why couldn't I react like that too?

DR. FIORE: Then what happened?

TOM: I thought if I ever had to face that again, I would try to talk to them first to get them to explain to me why it was necessary. And if it was absolutely necessary, why couldn't they render me unconscious? It still makes my skin crawl, thinking I had to submit to that.

❧

Tom looked somewhat upset after he came out of hypnosis. We talked for a while, and then I noticed him finally relaxing. After about five minutes, he seemed back to normal and ready to leave.

❧

Two weeks later, Tom reported feeling much more relaxed about his CEIVs. Also he had been handling stressful situations very well. We started hypnosis early on in the session, and I asked him to go back in time and space to another CEIV that was still having a negative impact on him.

❧

TOM: There's some sort of a ship, sitting on the ground, and an extraterrestrial standing outside it. And I'm just a very short distance away, just looking on.

DR. FIORE: Tell me all about it in detail.

TOM: It's a disc with sort of a bubble shape above it, in the center.

DR. FIORE: Let yourself know what time of day or night this is.

TOM: It's dark, so it's nighttime.

DR. FIORE: What do you feel and think as you're watching it?

TOM: [*Pauses*] I don't seem to be feeling any real strong emotions, other than interest and curiosity. I was watching this from a hiding place sort of far away. Maybe hiding in some bushes or something.

DR. FIORE: Let yourself remember it in detail.

TOM: I'm with someone else, a friend, who told me about it. I went to see it out of curiosity.

DR. FIORE: How old are you approximately?

TOM: About twelve or thirteen.

DR. FIORE: Tell me everything that you're aware of.

TOM: I'm up closer, maybe even touching it. I don't know . . . [*Pauses*] Maybe I'm confusing two experiences or something. Something's not quite right. This seems to be in the daytime. I'm standing and watching it fly away into the sky . . . in daytime.

DR. FIORE: It's going to be very clear in your mind. You're going to remember it exactly as it happened, at the count of three. One . . . two . . . three. First thoughts.

TOM: I had a flash of being inside the ship. [*Pauses*] That seems to be in the daytime also. Perhaps I came back the next day and . . . went up closer. I was with a friend when I first saw it at night . . . and then I came back the next day alone.

DR. FIORE: It's all coming into your mind. Just report everything that you're aware of.

TOM: I seem to be getting another image, or a slightly different image, again a nighttime image. Of a dark night with a full moon, and hearing a dog sort of howling in the distance.

DR. FIORE: Then what happened?

TOM: I'm walking through a wooded area. But it's a pleasant area to be in, at least in the daytime. And I'm having a mixture of feelings. Some pleasure and enjoyment, because I like that place, and I'm also feeling kind of spooky and anxious at the same time.

DR. FIORE: And?

TOM: I noticed a bright white light that at first I thought was the moon and then realized it wasn't. It's a very, very bright light, like a searchlight or something, except that it's portable. It's like a flashlight, but it's much brighter and bigger than a flashlight. [*Long pause*]

DR. FIORE: What happens? Let yourself remember.

TOM: I'm back and the experience is over with, but somehow it doesn't seem quite real to me. I'm going over it in my mind and I'm trying to figure out what it means. It's almost like I'm trying to decide, Okay, this really happened and this part of it didn't really happen. This was just my imagination.

DR. FIORE: What are you remembering?

TOM: Remembering seeing this strange ship and these strange beings and . . . and remembering watching the ship fly into the sky, into the distance.

DR. FIORE: You're going to go back to the time when you're watching the ship. At the count of five. One . . . two . . . three . . . four . . . five. What comes to mind?

TOM: I seem to have been up close to the ship and possibly even having communicated somehow with the beings.

DR. FIORE: Let yourself remember that clearly. Go down deeper into your mind now and retrieve these memories. Let it happen, at the count of five. One . . . two . . . three . . . four . . . five. What are you aware of at this very moment?

TOM: I'm close to the ship and noticing how big it is. It seems very, very big, and I feel quite small in comparison. [*Pauses*] I seem to have met at least one being that's taller than I am. [*Long pause*]

DR. FIORE: What happened?

TOM: I'm climbing up a sort of a ladder into a hatch underneath and just looking inside and then climbing right back down again. And I'm standing there looking at it disappear into the sky and feeling frustration. The frustration is coming from the fact that my curiosity was left unsatisfied, that I have a lot of questions about where it came from, where it's going, what is it, who are these people? What does all this mean? Combined with a frustrated feeling that I can't talk about it without being subjected to ridicule, that I'll be accused of making up stories or being crazy, or, you know, being off my rocker.

DR. FIORE: Let yourself know where these thoughts came from.

TOM: Once before, I tried to tell someone. [*Pauses*] I was really, really laughed at, hooted at, by several friends, and I felt so embarrassed and humiliated that I made up my mind that I was never again going to try to convince anyone who hadn't also seen it. And I was accused of being crazy to a point where I started to wonder myself. At times I questioned my own sanity, in regard to the experience.

DR. FIORE: Move to the experience you did have, the one you were ridiculed for telling about. Just report whatever you're aware of. Trust your mind.

TOM: [*Pauses*] I don't seem to be getting any visual images, but I'm noticing a sensation in my hands. A sensation like maybe my fingers were pulled and stretched out over a ball of some sort. My fingers and my thumbs feel like they are pulled into a very painful position.

DR. FIORE: You're remembering it exactly as it happened to you. What comes to mind?

TOM: [*His body tenses*] Something is being pressed down on top of my hands. My hands were squeezed between two . . . it seemed like they were both sort of hemispherical surfaces like, part of an instrument. There was enough pressure for it to be distinctly uncomfortable. I was experiencing some fear that it was going to injure my hands. It certainly hurt. [*Pauses*]

DR. FIORE: Let yourself remember what's being done, just as though you're there right now.

TOM: My ankles are in some sort of a clamplike shackle or vise. My ankles aren't being hurt the way my hands are, except that it's just very disagreeable and unpleasant to be constrained that way. [*Pauses*] Something is being put over my face. And other parts of my body as well, my chest, my genitals. . . . [*Pauses*] There's something around my waist. [*Long pause*]

DR. FIORE: And?

TOM: I have a feeling of wanting it to be over with.

DR. FIORE: What's being done?

TOM: They don't intend to hurt me. But the feeling is they don't really understand that even though it may not permanently injure me, that it is extremely uncomfortable and somewhat painful, and emotionally . . . very disturbing. They don't seem to really understand that. Either they don't understand it, or they don't completely care. Or a combination of both. A feeling of being out of control, of not being able to control what's happening to me, which I find very, very threatening. And fearful. A feeling of being completely at their mercy. They have made some attempts to reassure me, but I don't completely trust them. That's a very frightening thing, because they could do anything they wanted to me. [*Squirms*] A catheter was inserted into my penis and maybe a sample of urine was taken. [*Arches his back*]

DR. FIORE: How did that affect you?

TOM: A feeling of being in someone else's control and having very uncomfortable, disagreeable things done to me and not being able to do anything about it. And having my privacy invaded . . . being violated. I'm able to keep my feelings under control in this particular situation. But I don't like it. It's really disagreeable! I'm not completely panic-stricken, but sort of resigned. I have a very strong wish that I did not have to go through this.

DR. FIORE: Who is doing this to you? Look around and describe who they are and what they look like.

TOM: There's at least three or four. When they were pulling on my hands, there were two on my right and one on my left, and another one moving around or something.

DR. FIORE: What do they look like?

TOM: [*Pauses*] Humanoid appearance. Kind of a cloudy white color. [*Pauses*]

DR. FIORE: Tell me more about them.

TOM: They're about my own height.

DR. FIORE: How tall are you?

TOM: Around four feet.

DR. FIORE: What shape are their heads?

TOM: I'm looking at their heads from the side. They remind me of these dummies that are used in automobile crash experiments. Their ears are not the same as a human ear, maybe more like a crescent-shaped opening. Their features are flatter and less prominent than the human face.

DR. FIORE: What about the eyes?

TOM: I found it disagreeable, somewhat frightening, to look at them directly. They don't have eyelids in the same way we do. The eye seems to be covered by a translucent membrane similar to what I've seen on birds.

DR. FIORE: What's happening to you?

TOM: I'm lying in a semireclined position. I was released from whatever it was that was holding my arms and my ankles and brought up to a sitting position. Something is lowered down against the top of my head. And it feels like it's a very hard surface, probably metallic. The part of it that's against my head is kind of like a ring, a circular shape. It was pushed against my skull with a fair amount of pressure. I found it somewhat uncomfortable, not unbearable. Less uncomfortable than what I've just been going through, so that maybe I'm experiencing a slight sense of relief from being released from what they had just been doing to me.

DR. FIORE: And now what's happening?

TOM: [squirms] My abdomen is being pierced by a needle of some sort, and . . . [He flinches] that caught me by surprise. When it first happened, I felt a very quick, fearful reaction, but that passed very quickly because it wasn't nearly as painful as I would have expected it to be.

DR. FIORE: What are you aware of now?

TOM: Now I'm back outside.

DR. FIORE: Let yourself remember how you got there.

TOM: I was carried back outside by several of these same beings.

DR. FIORE: Let's find out if you were given any kind of suggestion not to remember.

TOM: Several times during the experience something in my mind kept saying, this can't be really happening to me. It's a dream.

DR. FIORE: Let yourself remember whether the extraterrestrials gave you any suggestions that this was a dream or that you would not remember.

TOM: They were somehow aware of my thinking that and reinforced it. [*Pauses*] They suggested that it would be easier to think of it that way and to just forget about it. Somehow I was disturbed about that. I felt that's taking the easy way out, and that it would be better if I could really understand it and be able to talk about it with people. [*Pauses*] But if I didn't completely believe it myself, how could I expect anyone else to believe it? And maybe that it would be easier just to forget about it.

DR. FIORE: Let yourself remember what you did after they took you out of the craft.

TOM: I walked back home. It was some distance. It was at night.

DR. FIORE: How do you feel?

TOM: Still disturbed. My parents are going to wonder where I've been, and I'm not sure what to tell them.

DR. FIORE: And now you're home and what happens?

TOM: I'm being confronted by my mother, wanting to know where I've been, what I've been doing. I tried to say that I went for a walk. I am totally unable to give her an explanation that she's satisfied with. She's very suspicious that maybe I've been doing something that I shouldn't have been doing. And I feel like if I tell her what really happened, she'll accuse me of making up a story and that that won't help. I really don't know what to say. She asks me why I went out, and I said I don't know. She's not satisfied with that. I ended up being punished. I felt it was very unfair.

✔

I asked Tom's inner mind to bring him back to the present, gave him positive suggestions and then counted him out of hypnosis.

He seemed a little groggy for a few minutes, but calm and oriented to his surroundings.

"No wonder I didn't want to talk to anyone about those meetings. Look what happened."

"It's obvious, Tom, that you've been traumatized by those close encounters. First you were taken against your will and then subjected to painful procedures that were not for your benefit. You were terrified and couldn't confide in the people who were important to you. I feel that a lot of your anxieties, your feelings of vulnerability and helplessness, and even your need to hide in your apartment when you're under stress are all due to these experiences. You should start feeling lots less anxious and more energetic. But we need to explore any more CEIVs that you've had. And as we do, you'll heal old wounds."

"It certainly makes sense. I would like to be over my fear of them. When you think of it, it's really an extraordinary experience to be in the presence of beings from other worlds."

"Exactly! I personally think it's the most exciting discovery of the twentieth century."

"They Said
I Had Cancer!"

Linda had been my patient for three months when we first discovered she was a contactee. She had sought my help for a number of problems, especially a deep sadness that had swept over her from time to time during the past sixteen years. She is a talented artist and also very sensitive psychically, especially as a healer. During our first session, she told me that her whole family is psychic, that they often worked together as a team doing healings.

Linda, a trim attractive brunette, looks ten years younger than her forty-five years. She is a pleasant person, someone whom one likes instantly because she exudes a goodness and a kindness.

During her months of therapy, Linda developed into an excellent hypnotic subject. During one session, going along with a hunch, I decided to explore the possibility of her having had a close encounter with extraterrestrials.

DR. FIORE: I'm going to ask your inner mind to take you to any UFO experiences you may have had that you have completely blocked from your conscious memory. If you have had more than one, you're going to go to one that is very important, at the count of ten. [*Counts to ten*]

LINDA: It's green inside. There's this light flashing over here somewhere. Somebody's sitting over here. I want to peek around the corner. I'm curious to see what's going on. [*Pauses*] They put me in this room . . . it's really bright and small. [*Pauses*] Ouch! . . . Why are they doing this? Why are they looking at my body? What did I do? [*Crying*] Leave me alone! I can't move! I have to just lie here. [*Getting frantic*] They're opening me up. How can they do that?

DR. FIORE: What part of you are they opening up?

LINDA: They're opening me here, my stomach.

DR. FIORE: How are they opening you up?

LINDA: I don't know, I don't understand what they're doing. There's no blood. They just open me up. It looks real dark inside. They're suctioning something up . . . kind of cleaning me, inside. Getting this dark stuff out of me.

DR. FIORE: Where are you seeing this from?

LINDA: Up above . . . I'm looking down at myself.

DR. FIORE: What do you see when you look down?

LINDA: I see these heads . . . and they're working on my body. And they've opened me up . . . and they're cleaning this black junk out of my stomach region. They said I had cancer! They were trying to help me.

DR. FIORE: How did you feel when they told you that?

LINDA: Confused. I'm all right, there's nothing wrong with me. I don't understand how they could see inside me. [*Pauses*] They put something on me. It's like glass, little round pieces of glass. They aren't like crystals. They're round and smooth and they had little lights on them. And they placed them all over my body. And then somehow they ran something over the top of it, kind of like a sensor of some kind.

DR. FIORE: Did it touch you?

LINDA: No. It stayed about . . . about so far away. [*Six inches from her body*] Until they came to here [*Points to abdomen*] and something was wrong here.

DR. FIORE: How do you know that?

LINDA: I can feel pain there. I just want to be home. My little girl's crying. [*Cries*] They took her too. What did they do to her? They tell me that they are helping us. I don't understand why they're doing this. Why don't they just leave us alone? [*Long pause*]

DR. FIORE: What do they look like?

LINDA: Kind of very, very small . . . very small heads . . . kind of really pointed. And they look . . . not human flesh. It's like greenish, sort of knobby looking. They've got big eyes. I wish they'd hurry and finish up. I want to go home.

DR. FIORE: What are they doing now?

LINDA: Somehow they're pressing my flesh back, and it's going back together. [*Sighs*] I feel I can breathe easier. There's this bright light.

DR. FIORE: Where is the bright light coming from?

LINDA: Some kind of source over here, to my right. It's like I'm enclosed in a . . . like a capsule kind of thing, and it's moving through a corridor almost like a chute . . . down a chute. [*Pauses*] And then it goes into this . . . some kind of vehicle. And there's other ones too, with people in them. They're putting us in them.

DR. FIORE: Tell me more about that.

LINDA: It's almost like a conveyor belt or something, with rollers bringing these capsules with people onto it. And they're closing the door. [*Pauses*] And I just lie there for a while.

DR. FIORE: Now what's happening?

LINDA: I'm just lying there. It's dark. I hear some people groaning, mumbling.

DR. FIORE: How do you feel, and what are you thinking?

LINDA: I just want to go home.

DR. FIORE: What are you doing now?

LINDA: I'm moving. It feels like it's fast. [*Pauses*] We land. They open up the capsules and they help us get out. It's quite a view.

DR. FIORE: Tell me more about that.

LINDA: I feel like we're walking. . . . It's more like a desert area, there's not much around. They put us in smaller vehicles. They're full of light. There's lots of lights going. There's about four of us in each one. There's a driver. They take off. We're going over some trees. Aha . . . I'm home. I'm back in my bed.

DR. FIORE: How do you feel?

LINDA: Tired.

DR. FIORE: How does your body feel?

LINDA: I feel tingling. My hands are tingling. My head hurts still. [*Touches forehead*] I just roll over and cuddle my husband. I'm so glad to be there.

DR. FIORE: What was that on your forehead that you touched?

LINDA: They gave me a third eye. It still hurts. It's all tight.

DR. FIORE: How do you know that's what they gave you?

LINDA: They pulled it apart. That's what they said they were going to do.

DR. FIORE: Now go back to another encounter with them, at the count of five. One . . . two . . . three . . . four . . . five.

LINDA: God, the light's so bright! What's going on? Ahh . . . I can't see. Everything's too bright. [*Pauses*] I don't even know where I am.

DR. FIORE: Tell me everything you're aware of.

LINDA: Just this bright, bright light. It hurts my eyes. I wish I could see what's happening. Someone's pushing me back, making me move. [*Pauses*] I'm going in an elevator . . . kind of a glass elevator. [*Sighs*] I feel like I'm way up high and I can see all over. The earth looks real small. . . . I'm way, way up.

DR. FIORE: Where are you?

LINDA: I'm in some kind of a bright room. There's other people with me. I don't know who they are. I never met them before.

We're being asked to go in this door . . . down this darker corridor. It's a long corridor.

DR. FIORE: Tell me about the other people.

LINDA: We have these white things on. I guess it's kind of like a hospital-type gown. We're just doing what we're told to do, to walk down this corridor into this room at the end.

DR. FIORE: Is there anybody you recognize?

LINDA: [*Turning her head as though looking around*] My brother Ralph's there. [*Pauses*] And Mark.

DR. FIORE: Who's Mark?

LINDA: My other brother. And my sister Sherry. Looks like a family reunion here.

DR. FIORE: Are there other people besides your two brothers and your sister?

LINDA: Ralph and Mark, Sherry, Betty, my brother-in-law, Bill, my niece Barbara, my sister Sally, there's Margie, my other sister. My mom . . . my dad . . . What are they doing with all of us? I don't understand? [*Long pause*]

DR. FIORE: What are you doing?

LINDA: We're sitting down on kind of a bench. My family . . . we're all holding hands. It's like the room's spinning.

DR. FIORE: Besides your family, are there any other people there?

LINDA: I think my Aunt Eloise is there too, and there's some people I don't know. It's getting more crowded all the time.

DR. FIORE: How many people would you say there are alto-gether?

LINDA: Oh, gosh, it's like fifty to sixty people. Now we're going down some steps of some kind. [*Pauses*] Looks like a work center. They're having us do something . . . like working.

DR. FIORE: Tell me about it.

LINDA: There's this big machine, it looks like a pump . . . pumping something out.

DR. FIORE: What are you doing?

LINDA: I'm turning a wheel. I just keep turning this wheel and turning this wheel.

DR. FIORE: Who is telling you to do this?

LINDA: This . . . I don't see him. I don't know who it is.

DR. FIORE: Move to the first time you do see him.

LINDA: Sort of a bald head, great big eyes, long nose, pointed chin. Like something out of a comic book or something . . . something someone's made up.

DR. FIORE: How tall is he?

LINDA: Very tall. Very, very tall. I feel really tiny compared to him . . . very tall and thin.

DR. FIORE: What is he wearing?

LINDA: It looks like a big collar that comes up, and this long . . . long robe. They're wearing similar outfits, but all different colors, very pale colors. They shimmer a little bit. The clothing shimmers. And their hands are long, long . . . thin fingers that come out to about here. [*About five inches longer than her hand*]

DR. FIORE: What are they doing?

LINDA: They're instructing us.

DR. FIORE: Tell me about that.

LINDA: They're telling us we have to learn these things, it's for our survival. The world will come to an end if we don't learn these things. We've got to help our people. They're going to teach us. [*Pauses*] My whole body's . . . vibrating. Especially my hands. Telling me to point my fingers certain ways. Teaching me to be sensitive. It's all this . . . power coming through my hands. It's like electricity. Strong. [*Pauses*] Oh God! . . . I'm being told I can learn to heal, myself. It's okay to use this power. They've known about it for thousands and thousands of years. I can learn to scan, like they do. But first I've got to be healthy. I've got to take care of myself. [*Long pause*]

DR. FIORE: What are you experiencing?

LINDA: I'm being taught . . . how to feel the energy coming through my hands. And to feel what happens when I move the energy around and scan my body. I can feel it inside my body. As I pass my hands over [my body], the energy moves inside. This is fascinating. [*Long pause*]

DR. FIORE: They said first you have to be healthy, you have to take care of yourself. Did they give you any advice?

LINDA: I have to watch what I eat. To notice that if something I eat doesn't agree with me, then it's not good for me. And to stop eating it. Chew more carefully. Get more exercise. Meditate every day.

DR. FIORE: Did they tell you how to do that?

LINDA: They gave us lessons.

DR. FIORE: Tell me about that.

LINDA: We went into some place that looks like a . . . chapel. It's cool there, peaceful and quiet. There's like a crystal, sitting out in the middle of the room. It's really bright and shining. All different colors come out and form a circle around the crystal. We're being told to put our hands up and feel the energy of the crystal. And just go in our minds. Just relax.

DR. FIORE: Did they give you any other advice?

LINDA: Be patient. [*Long pause*] My head hurts.

DR. FIORE: Go back to what is causing your head to hurt.

LINDA: Something's drilling my head. I don't want these head- aches anymore. [*Cries*] They're telling me I have to let go, not to be afraid. It's the fear that's giving me the headache. Some kind of metal tubing . . . going through my head, right up my ear. [*Pauses*] And there's some kind of fluid being put into the tube.

DR. FIORE: Who's doing this?

LINDA: One of those . . . tall people.

DR. FIORE: Are they saying anything to you as they're doing this?

LINDA: Trust him, I'll feel better.

DR. FIORE: How does it feel as they're doing this?

LINDA: Pressure, like a drill. I just want to pull it out.

DR. FIORE: Where is it?

LINDA: It's right here. [*Points to her right ear*] They took it out. [*Sighs in relief*]

DR. FIORE: Did they say anything more about it?

LINDA: Be patient, it'll get better.

DR. FIORE: Did they tell you what was wrong?

LINDA: No.

DR. FIORE: Now let yourself know if anything else was done or said during that encounter.

LINDA: That I wouldn't remember.

DR. FIORE: How did you feel when they told you that?

LINDA: That's not fair. I want to know what's going on. There's too much information, they say, for me to understand at once. I just have to learn it slowly. Just be patient. I'm not ready yet. About five more years.

DR. FIORE: Did they say anything about having contacted you before or that they would contact you in the future?

LINDA: Many times.

DR. FIORE: Tell me verbatim what they said to you.

LINDA: "We'll be back next month to teach you some more."

DR. FIORE: How did you feel when you heard that?

LINDA: Okay. I'm getting used to it now.

DR. FIORE: What do you mean by that?

LINDA: They come so often.

DR. FIORE: How often do they come?

LINDA: Once a week, for a while. I always feel so tired after they've been . . . and sad.

DR. FIORE: Why are you sad?

LINDA: I don't know. I'm confused. [*Long pause*] I'm back home now, back in my room.

Linda seemed a bit disoriented when she came out of hypnosis. After a few seconds, she smiled and leaned forward in her chair, which was now in an upright position. "I've had dreams of UFOs. And when I read *Communion,* I felt it had happened to me. I'm so glad we went into that."

"I was just playing a hunch, Linda. Actually, it seems that psychic people do have contacts with extraterrestrials much more often than people who aren't so sensitive. Also I've found that people tend to develop psychically after close encounters. So I'm not sure which came first, the chicken or the egg."

"As I told you, my whole family's psychic. And there we all were! I can't wait to tell them."

About a month later, Linda came into my office obviously excited about something. "My sister Sherry called to tell me about a dream she had had the night before. And that in itself is unusual, because she rarely remembers her dreams. She dreamed she was taken into a spaceship and they treated her yeast infection with a blue gel. The next morning, the yeast infection was gone. She'd only had it for a few months, and it was pretty bad, but right after the dream it cleared up. She called me in the morning while I was still in bed, so I didn't relate it to myself until that evening, when I realized my yeast infection was completely gone. That's a miracle, because nothing the doctors prescribed did anything except get rid of the itching, never the discharge. It's been gone for a few weeks now. *And* my mother, who had a yeast infection for forty-three years, is cured too, since Sherry's and mine cleared up."

"Well, Linda, it seems like something happened to all three of you. Would you like to check it out?"

Linda agreed that would be important to work on, and so, after she was hypnotized, I regressed her to the encounter in which her yeast infection was treated.

✦

LINDA: I went to bed early that night. They come . . . there's two of them, they come into my bedroom. There's a tall one. He's got on a long robe. The one with the long fingers, he doesn't have any hair. He has a big cranial section of his head and a large, large forehead. He smiles and says, "Well, are you ready?" I say, "Okay." There's a small one there too. He looks more human. Almost dwarfish. They take me out the front door. There's some kind of a vehicle. It looks about the size of a car and has lots of lights, and it almost looks like a glass with a kind of bubble roof over the top. The three of us get in. They put me in the back part, and we go real fast. And pretty soon we're landing inside a large, large, large spaceship. It's huge! I can't believe the size. It's just huge. I can see the stars.

DR. FIORE: Where do you see the stars?

LINDA: Outside of this large spacecraft, I see lots of stars. There's like a cloud of brilliant lights, coming from the top of it, way up here. [*Pauses*] We're still going toward it. I see my brother Mark there. He's greeting me. I get out. He gives me a hug. He tells me that his subconscious will never let him remember this, but he enjoys it when he goes. He tells me that he won't give me a bad time and tease me, but he really does understand . . . because he's going through it too. There's four of us now, the real tall one, the real small one and another one larger than I. We're on a platform or something, and we turn right. Very spacious. Very, very spacious. And I hear a very gentle hum. It's very relaxing. We go into this big theater of some kind, with seats for people to watch a movie screen. They're showing us something, and what they're showing us is a picture of the earth from the way they see it. They see the earth on the screen and clouds surrounding the earth. They're pointing out a particular area on the earth to go to. I can't quite tell where it is. It seems to be some place in Europe. Northern part of Europe. I see where it is. I've dreamed of it before, but I don't know where it is. It's on a hillside, and it's like a big cave with doors that open up. It's a sanctuary, they say, to go there and find peace, comfort and learning. Once we go there, we won't be the same. We will be changed. Our energies will be vibrating at a higher level. I guess we're there with the crystal again. Everybody's holding hands, and we're singing a song. *"Om Shamda, Olom, Vaya, Ovee. Om Shamba Vaya."* I feel tremendous joy. [*Whispers*] It makes me cry, it's so powerful. [*Cries a little*] It's like everybody is being lifted up. It's almost like we're . . . floating. Still holding hands, and we're all . . . being lifted. And the vibrations are getting stronger and stronger and more powerful. I get a little scared. I don't know how much I can take, it's so overwhelming. [*Pauses.*] I'm back in bed.

DR. FIORE: I'd like you to go to the time when you were being healed of the yeast infection, at the count of five. One . . . two . . . three . . . four . . . five.

LINDA: I'm on the table, my feet are up. And they use an instrument of some kind. It looks like a big cotton ball on a stick. You know how when they take a throat culture? It's kind of like that, and they're swabbing me inside.

DR. FIORE: Where?

LINDA: They're going way up into my uterus too. And they're cleaning it out somehow, swabbing it out. They have this jellylike substance that looks like aquamarine blue, and it's clear, it's transparent. How are they doing this? It looks like they're putting it on something that's a squarish, rectangular sort of shape. And they squish it out of the rectangular shape, up inside me. I told them it feels cold. They say that's to help freeze the bacteria. And then they take that out.

DR. FIORE: What do they take out?

LINDA: They take out the applicator which they used to put the jelly in. [*Pauses*] And . . . my legs are still up. It reminds me of the circus, the people that twirl, kind of. And . . . I'm twirling with my feet up. But my feet are together, and they are attached somehow to something. It's not uncomfortable or anything, it's just like the people who, in the circus, twirl up in the air, kind of, and then they bring me back down. And it almost looks like a pad or something they're putting on me, between my legs. And then they put me on another couch. They cover me up for a little while, and I take a rest.

DR. FIORE: Did they explain what they were going to do?

LINDA: They said, "Don't worry, it won't hurt." It's for my own good. But they understand I have been trying to get rid of it by myself. They say now's the time I've got to get completely well, so they're going to help me some more. They say something about an infection of the liver. I don't know how that can have any relation to that.

DR. FIORE: What did they say?

LINDA: Infection of the liver. I damaged it as a child. When I fell from someplace. Damage to my liver, which over the years they have been slowly refurbishing, just as if building, like building it up. The salve penetrates the whole body and generates new cells that will fight infection and in turn will give off new life in my body. They tell me I'll understand more as we go along.

DR. FIORE: Tell me anything else that they say regarding the body.

LINDA: They say there are these portals, where you can gather energy and bring it up through the body, to cleanse and renew each cell. I see. They are showing me a cell and how the energy comes, uses something and is generated out.

DR. FIORE: Where does the energy come from?

LINDA: It comes from the universe. A magnetic system which is generated from the sonar field. I don't understand that. This is the main source of energy for all the universe, for all the one called Eli.

DR. FIORE: Let yourself remember what happens after your treatment for the yeast infection.

LINDA: I go and watch while the other people are being worked on. I just stand and watch them. There's seven, counting me. No, eight, because there's somebody on the table.

DR. FIORE: And then?

LINDA: There's a bright light over here and to my left, about two to three feet across. I'm feeling it shining its warmth on my face. I'm sitting on some kind of a chair and somebody's talking to me on my right. He has my hand and is calming me down. I got scared of something. It's upset me.

DR. FIORE: Move to just a few seconds before you were upset.

LINDA: [*Grimaces*] I feel threatened.

DR. FIORE: Let yourself remember.

LINDA: I don't want to. I don't want to!

DR. FIORE: What is it you don't want to do?

LINDA: I don't want to go through it again.

DR. FIORE: Let yourself remember.

LINDA: It's by the black hole. I fell into it. It feels like a cyclone or something. I'm falling and I'm scared. [*Her voice quavers*] I feel empty. [*Her body jerks*] I'm back in the chair and somebody's comforting me.

DR. FIORE: Are they explaining something to you?

LINDA: It was an accident.

DR. FIORE: What else do they say?

LINDA: I was in an area of the ship that I wasn't supposed to be in. For my safety, I have to stay with the others. They were able to rescue me, this time, but no guarantee about the future. They do not reprimand me.

DR. FIORE: Move back to that incident.

LINDA: I'm climbing up the stairs and I got lost. I thought I would investigate. There's a door at the end. I slipped and fell into the big black hole. I was falling around and around, and some being comes and grabs me. He brings me back up and holds me. He takes me back into another room. And talks to me. And I can see the color of his aura. I was crying.

DR. FIORE: Move back to the time when you were watching the others.

LINDA: I see someone on the table, with an instrument over his midriff. Metal goes around him. It's narrow and connected, attached to an L-shaped arm. Attached to something in the wall. That metal thing has parts that touch the person's body. I ask, "What is wrong with him?" And they tell me he has a stomach ulcer, so they are generating energy which is directed at the ulcer. Someone else on the table is tall and thin. Somebody is working on his head, doing something to his head. It's a smaller, circular thing that moves from point to point, and from temple to temple. Just above his eye. They're pulsing it to shrink the tumor, and I can almost see the tumor shrinking as they're working on it. He gets off, and a small child is put on the table. A little girl about five or six. They're scanning her whole body, giving her a physical, checking her out. She has worms, they say. They're going to eliminate them. No, they're going to inject something into her stomach area. It looks like a big syringe in the stomach. [*She points to her abdomen*] They put salve in and carry her off the table, and now they're laying her down and covering her up. They're lifting a big man onto the table. He's about forty. Dark hair, big burly-looking man. They're doing something with his left arm. He has a problem with his shoulder, they said. His shoulder dislocates and gets swollen, like bursitis. He's now inflamed, inside his shoulder. They're raising his left arm, to see the mobility. They're doing something with the left arm, they keep raising it into the air for some reason. The doctor does the same thing. They use an instrument with pulsing light. Then he gets off. My sister Sherry is on the table. I can't see what they're doing to her.

DR. FIORE: Let yourself remember everything at the count of three. One . . . two . . . three.

LINDA: They have her legs spread open, and they're doing something to her they did to me, putting salve in. Now they put her legs together, and they're twirling her around and around. Her head is down, and her feet are up there. [*She points into the air*] It kind of scared her. They take her down to the corner and cover her up with a cover. There's a young teenage boy, fifteen to sixteen years old, who lies on the table. He has very large feet. He used to have a hip problem on his right side. His hip is deteriorating, so they are trying to generate energy to promote new cell growth. A large machine with crystallized light. Eight inches around, attached to something on the floor. Like in an L shape. It sends out this green and yellow and blue and pink and white light, into this young man's hip area. They have somebody holding his shoulder because he's squirming. They ask him to squeeze his legs. They use their hands. And somebody's pressing on his side. Somebody else is pressing on the other side. He gets off the table, and he's walking fine. He's still limping, but it seems like an improvement. He's lying down, and they put a blanket over him. They say it's time to go back home. We've had enough for tonight.

DR. FIORE: And then what happens?

LINDA: All of us are walking down a corridor. They have us walk through the door. There are twenty-five other people. We sit and wait for a while for other people. Then they put us into a smaller craft that holds about fifty people. And they close the door, and we whiz off. We land somewhere, way out in the desert. We get out of that [craft] and go into smaller ones that only hold a few people. They strap us in something, and a protective arm comes across. We whiz over the top of trees. The very first thing I see is a lake, over to the right.

DR. FIORE: What time is it?

LINDA: About 2:30 in the night, actually early morning. It's 3:00 before they get me home. Somebody is walking with me. A tall being gives me a hug, and I climb back in bed.

DR. FIORE: Let yourself remember another important encounter, at the count of three. One . . . two . . . three.

LINDA: The room with a crystal. Standing there. Feeling the energy coming. I know I have to heal myself somehow. They're going to teach me what to do.

DR. FIORE: Speak out everything that you are aware of.

LINDA: I'm a little scared. There's a lump in my breast. I'm real worried about it. They tell me they can help me. They said direct the energy from my left hand to where the lump is. Take the right, put it over the top. Take a deep breath. Let energy flow through it. Visualize it getting smaller. I can feel the energy going through. [*Sighs*]

DR. FIORE: What happened to you then?

LINDA: It was like the energy suddenly stopped. We're going into some kind of a room.

DR. FIORE: Just report everything that comes into your mind.

LINDA: Some kind of a round table, a long table, like in a doctor's office. They're having me get up on it. They have some kind of an instrument over here. It looks like a metal tube with a light on the end, almost like a rounded crystal or something on the end of it. They're putting it over, right where the lump is on my breast. It sends some kind of energy through. They remove it. Get me off the table. There are other people there with me. I don't know who they are, but we're all together, and it's somebody else's turn to get up on the table. Several people taking turns, having different things done. There's just one really tall being with us in the room. He's got on a very dark, almost black robe. I see his long fingers. His hands look very bony. His hands are very long. They come out to about here. Especially the knuckle area is very bony.

DR. FIORE: What color is his skin?

LINDA: It's whitish, almost iridescent in a way. He's doing something with his hands.

DR. FIORE: What is he doing?

LINDA: His hands are at the top of somebody else and it's like they're cutting right over the top of the forehead a little bit. He's not touching them. I think it looks like Sherry. My sister Sherry. And he's working with her forehead somehow. He's coming around the sides of her ears. He's sending some energy somehow, to the back of her neck. He seems to be reaching over and going along the side of her body, all the way down to her feet. Working with somebody else there too. There's another being at her feet now. And they're both working on her at the same time. She's smiling. She says it tingles. Actually, she's laughing. [*Laughs*] My mother's there too. She says she wishes that we could live closer together rather than have to come together in our dreams. The room seems brighter all of a sudden. There's all this beautiful light coming out of everybody. And we just kind of glow. Now they've taken us back to the crystal again. I want to go and touch it, but they say don't touch it. It's turning purples and blues on the left side and pinks on the right. You just soak it up. It's very powerful. [*Pauses*] I'm back in bed again.

DR. FIORE: Go back into the ship. Let's see if they say anything about your appointment with me today.

LINDA: They say don't tell her.

DR. FIORE: What do you say?

LINDA: Why not? I feel it's important for people to understand. They say that people aren't ready. They'll just laugh. They have to be given time.

DR. FIORE: Let yourself know if anything else was said to you.

LINDA: You should understand that we mean no harm. We are here to change the world . . . to keep it from disaster. Which is imminent, if people keep living the way they do. We are here to help the people into a new age of living. There will be changes so powerful that only the strong will survive. We are here to give knowledge and understanding to the world of light and the world of children of God. We are here to change the world for a better development in the universe . . . to be closer . . . to surviving planets . . . in the nearby universe. We are here to give to all, new life, new force, a new being, an exciting, wonderful world of knowledge. Peace be with you forever and always.

DR. FIORE: How do you feel about that?

LINDA: Curious.

DR. FIORE: Did you feel that that message was coming through you?

LINDA: Definitely. I felt that if I had let go a little more, my voice would have changed. And that I would have been completely channeling it. A part of me still doesn't let go enough.

DR. FIORE: Just let yourself relax. I'm going to ask you to go back in time and space to another important contact. Just report whatever comes into your mind.

LINDA: Blinking red light over here. They're kind of beings. They're working at an instrument panel over here. It's inside a spaceship.

DR. FIORE: What do they look like?

LINDA: Very strange. [Laughs] They're kinda green and glowy and have real tiny eyes. They're real small beings. They have little tiny eyes, no nose at all, just kind of holes where we have noses, and kind of a round little hole where the mouth is, if it's a mouth; I'm not sure. One I see in front of me is working on some kind of an instrument panel. It has these lights, and it has cords coming out of some area, like an electrical type of wire that surrounds them. It looks like a . . . like a telephone type of thing. It has some wires. Like a switchboard. They won't let me go in the room. I can't go in, but it kind of curves around a little bit. And they take me down this hall. I'm walking with somebody very tall. It's like an old friend. I feel comfortable with him. He's got a hand on me, on my back. We're talking.

DR. FIORE: What are you talking about?

LINDA: We're talking about what I learned that day. I can't remember what we're saying.

DR. FIORE: At the count of three, you're going to remember. One . . . two . . . three.

LINDA: He asks, "Do you know that if you take the energy from your hands and lay it on your third eye, you can send it all the way down . . . through your body to a point of impact, where it will regenerate and come back out again . . . through your ear?" And then I can hear them. Hmm . . . We continue walking. Then we go into the room where Sherry and my mom are, and some other people too, where the table is. There are five other people and two other large, tall beings. And then the table and some of their instruments, all medical instruments, but they're very different from ours. There's a machine over here to the right. It looks like when they take people's blood in a centrifuge type of machine, and they're taking samples of our urine, and they're putting it in this machine for testing.

DR. FIORE: Where are you?

LINDA: I'm over on the other side of the table, and I'm just watching the work right now. It's like they're preparing. This is before they work on any humans. I ask them, why don't they take people who are healthier to do their work? And they say, they're not the right ones. They're trying to prove a point.

DR. FIORE: What is that?

LINDA: Trying to change the mental concepts of people. Then I'm back on the table. Someone's at my feet, another tall being's at my head. The one by my head has his hand, not touching me, but kind of directing the fingers toward my head. I feel changes . . . occurring inside my brain and in my head. At one point it hurts.

DR. FIORE: Did you say anything?

LINDA: I just told them I felt it go directly in me. It felt like an electrical beam going through my head. They teach me to use the instrument on the lump in my breast.

DR. FIORE: What instrument is that?

LINDA: It's a long silver thing with a rounded crystal on the end. And it glows out light. It pulsates, I guess. Somebody is working down at my feet. They're sending energy. It comes up through both feet and just keeps coming in waves. And I feel it at the top of my head, coming all the way through. They say, "You're okay now. You're ready to get off." And so I get off the table. And Sherry says, "I want to go next." So she hops up. And they work on her.

DR. FIORE: What do you see?

LINDA: I see them working right around her pubic bone. They're doing something there. It's almost like their fingers are going right through her body and they're cleaning something out of her ovary area over on the right side. It's like a white mass of something that they're pulling out. They bring it out of her and put it in the bag, like a plastic-type bag, and close it up. And somebody dumps it into a pail.

DR. FIORE: Does she say anything?

LINDA: She jokingly asks them if they can enlarge breasts too. [*Laughs*]

DR. FIORE: Where are you?

LINDA: I'm over on her left side, holding her hand.

DR. FIORE: Then what happens?

LINDA: They turn off the lights in the room, and we are directed out of the room, turn right, go down this corridor, and then we get onto—it's like a small spacecraft. And we sit down. It only holds about five people, and one—it's not a tall being, it's somebody small—one of the green ones. Somebody's coming, saying, "Wait. Wait, you forgot something." Giving something to somebody, a bag of something. It's sort of like rocks, but they're not rocks. They're glowing. All different colors, mostly golds and blues and browns. I don't see who they're giving them to. Then we take off. And then I'm back in bed.

DR. FIORE: Move back to the very first contact with extraterrestrials.

LINDA: I'm in Seattle. I'm looking out the window. In the sky, there's a light. I stand there watching. And it disappears. And then I don't see it anymore. Beings come into the room. They talk to me like they've known me for a long time. They say that I'm in a different body this time, but we'll continue working together. This will be an exciting time. Wonderful things will be happening. They tell me to not be afraid. I'm sitting on a tall being's lap. I'm four years old. They're telling me something. I don't know what he's telling me.

DR. FIORE: You will remember at the count of three. One . . . two . . . three.

LINDA: His arm is around me like a big father. I feel he cares about me a lot. He's telling me a story about another place. And another time. It's a city of lights, and things we do not have here on this earth. I see a lot of blue, brilliant lights. He is saying this is where you came from and you can go back when you're through here. This is your home, but for right now, you have to be here, on this earth, but they'll come visit me, and I can talk to them whenever I need them. But I can go home when I'm through.

DR. FIORE: What is his name?

LINDA: Revance. He's leaving now. And tucks me back into my bed and says goodbye. My little brother's crying. My mommy comes in and I tell her an angel came to visit me.

◢

When Linda came out of hypnosis, she had tears in her eyes. "They are so very, very loving. And the energy's so powerful, it made me cry."

"Linda, I'm concerned about the lump in your breast. Are you aware of one?"

"Yes. I just found it last night. I'll have it checked out."

"Fine. It's really important to have good medical care. Let me know what you find. I'll be very interested also in what happens with your yeast infection."

"It would be too good to be true, if it's cured."

"Do you think Sherry would be willing to come for a regression to the same encounter? I think it would be particularly interesting to see what she remembers under hypnosis."

Linda made arrangements with her sister, and Sherry did come several weeks later. You'll read her account in the next chapter.

Linda had to drop out of therapy temporarily, so I called her just as I was writing up her case. Her yeast infection has returned, and she has it recurrently. Sometimes it's a lot better and at times, worse. So it appears that the extraterrestrial "doctors" don't have a permanent cure for it, either. She had the feeling, though, that she is being treated for it by them. Both her sister Sherry and her mother remain free of their yeast infections.

"I've Let Those People Touch Me!"

🖜 "I don't know whether I can be hypnotized, because I have a very strong will and I don't think I can let someone else take over control." Sherry, Linda's sister, looked decidedly anxious about being hypnotized. Yet I felt she was just as concerned about not being able to do a good job. She had accepted my invitation to come for a regression, therefore she had a lot at stake. First, she wanted to solve the puzzle: How had her yeast infection been cured? And was her dream of extraterrestrials really a close encounter? Second, she wanted to perform well for her sister's sake. And third, she knew my time was valuable and I had given up a Saturday morning for our work. She was under a lot of pressure, especially since she didn't think she could be hypnotized, which is a very common fear.

"That's no problem, Sherry, because you are never under my control and there's no issue regarding will. In fact, the stronger you are, the better, because you can use your will to cooperate. It's really self-hypnosis anyway. I'll give you suggestions, and if you decide to go along with them, and I'm sure you will, you'll hypnotize yourself. One of the bonuses from our work today will be that you'll have a tool you can use all your life."

Sherry looked much more relaxed and a little curious. Smiling, she asked, "You mean, I'll learn how to hypnotize myself?"

"Yes. By simply giving yourself the very suggestions I'll be using with you, you can put yourself into a trance. In fact, let's have a practice run before we begin the regression and you'll see for yourself what it's like to be hypnotized. I'll teach you how to bring yourself out too."

After she had removed her contact lenses, stretched out almost flat with her feet up on the ottoman and was covered with the blanket, I asked her to close her eyes and concentrate on her breathing. "Just breathe easily and naturally without changing the pattern of your breath. Now imagine a miniature sun, just like the sun in our solar system, deep in your solar plexus. This sun is radiating through you, through every atom and cell of your body, filling you with light. It's shining out beyond you, an arm's length in every direction, creating an aura of brilliant, sparkling, dazzling white light of protection around you." Next I had her imagine herself at the top of a magnificent staircase, and as I counted down from twenty-one to zero, she was to take a descending step with each number, going deeper and deeper within. Once at the bottom of the staircase, I assumed she was in a good state of hypnosis, so I gave her suggestions to remember the three phases we had been through; concentrating on her breathing, surrounding herself with white light and walking down the stairs. I emphasized to her that at this point she could give herself positive suggestions to achieve any goal, and she could strengthen them by imagining the desired result as though it had already been achieved. I pointed out that her subconscious mind couldn't tell the difference between what was imagined and what was actual, that once it accepted the desired goal as a reality, it created a "blueprint" and immediately started to manifest it.

"Now when you are ready to come out of hypnosis, give yourself mental suggestions for well-being, for example, 'I'll be awake and alert and feeling fine in every way.' Mentally count to three and open up your eyes at three. Go ahead and do it now."

Sherry beamed with delight. She had learned self-hypnosis. Quickly, a slight frown of doubt crossed her face. "But are you sure I was hypnotized? I felt like I didn't go under."

"I can be pretty sure you were, and certainly with practice you'd allow yourself to go deeper. It will be very helpful as a way to relieve stress, and it only takes a few minutes. But there's one very important caution: *Do not use self-hypnosis to regress yourself!* It's sort of like opening Pandora's box. In fact, you can make things worse, because undoubtedly you wouldn't permit yourself to reexperience the anxiety involved in the event that's causing the condition you wish to alleviate. You'd only succeed in bringing the repressed memory closer to the surface, and it could cause you more problems. Otherwise, self-hypnosis will serve you well through the years."

Sherry was nodding in agreement. "No. I wouldn't do that, but I could work on a few areas. My weight and procrastination."

"Great! Once at the bottom of the staircase, give yourself positive suggestions and imagine yourself at your ideal weight and see all the tasks you've been putting off as already accomplished." I checked the clock and saw that it was time for us to get started with the investigation of Sherry's "dream."

Having just been in a trance a few minutes before helped her to into an even deeper one very quickly. Within two minutes, she was ready to regress. I gave her inner mind suggestions to go back in time and space to the cause of the dream, emphasizing that she would remember easily and accurately. I counted slowly to ten.

*

SHERRY: I was lying on a table or some flat surface that seemed like it was stainless steel. I don't remember any faces, but there was a doctor, or someone I perceived as a doctor, and there was some kind of machine that, I was told by mental telepathy, could analyze if there was anything wrong in my body and could also kill bacteria in my body that wasn't good. So I allowed them to do whatever . . . and the next thing I knew, I was being examined vaginally, and it seems like my feet were in some kind of stirrups or in something very similar to what you'd find in a doctor's office. And some kind of cream was being put inside of me. At times I felt feelings of fear, but somebody who seemed to be familiar or whom I trusted would tell me not to worry, that everything was okay. And actually, I think I felt kind of grateful. I was kind of thankful that I was being helped. And then I was put on something that made my head feel like I was spinning. I felt like my whole body was spinning, and that was pretty scary. And I was told not to worry, that it was okay, that I'd be okay, and then I blacked out. When I came to, someone asked me if I remembered anything. I said no. The next thing I knew, I was snapped back into my body.

DR. FIORE: Where was your body?

SHERRY: In my sleeping bag. I was camping.

DR. FIORE: Move to the very first moment when this experience started. Just trust your mind and report whatever comes into your mind. You're in your sleeping bag and what happens?

SHERRY: It seems like I see a flash of light. I feel this pulsating . . . pulling, kind of sensation. I don't see anything. It's dark except for violet and gold light. [*Long pause*] I keep on getting these feelings that I shouldn't be saying anything. I feel like there's some kind of block that I . . . I don't know if it's my own fear that I'm not going to remember anything or . . .

DR. FIORE: You're doing just fine. Just speak out whatever comes into your mind.

SHERRY: I feel real tense, real stiff. It seems like there's some kind of . . . form that seems to be mostly light. I feel kind of frightened. Every time I feel like I'm getting close to something, I start to tense up.

DR. FIORE: That could be because you're remembering how you once felt, which was tense. So just speak out.

SHERRY: I feel like I'm lying somewhere and I'm seeing silhouettes above me. It's kind of a silhouette of something that . . . there's no hair or anything, just a form with a head. But it's making me shake like I'm cold. I don't see anything definite, just the feeling of being looked down at, by maybe five or six figures.

DR. FIORE: Do you remember ETs of different heights? Or were they just one general height?

SHERRY: It seems like all the forms were about the same height.

DR. FIORE: How tall is that?

SHERRY: It's hard to say, because I was lying down. Much taller than I am, maybe . . . eight feet or so. And it didn't seem like there was any clothing. . . . There was nothing to clothe, there was nothing to hide. It was just a form. I did see just a brief picture of a . . . a form with very large, dark eyes . . . just very briefly.

DR. FIORE: You're going to remember that form very well and you're going to tell me the details.

SHERRY: Hm . . . Now I'm seeing something different. Seems almost like a . . . leathery, almost amphibian-type skin. It's kind of . . . greenish-yellowish and wrinkly . . . large eyes, but they were . . . ooohhh! [*Grimaces*] I really don't want to remember. It's pretty scary.

DR. FIORE: You're going to allow yourself to remember, because the more you get rid of your fear, the more you will feel good about yourself. It's just because they're different. They did not harm you, so let yourself remember.

SHERRY: The one thing that I do see is that the eyes are very caring and loving. And . . . I really sense that they are . . .

they really don't want to scare and they really worry about that. The caring is really evident in the eyes. [*Pauses*] The face I saw is gone. It was more amphibianlike than anything else.

DR. FIORE: Let yourself know if they all look like that.

SHERRY: I sense that they don't, but I don't really see anything.

DR. FIORE: Tell me about their bodies.

SHERRY: They seem to be very trim-looking. It's not like there's any fat. . . . They seem to be the same, I don't see any big differences.

DR. FIORE: Now let's get back to what's happening. You believed you were lying on something.

SHERRY: I'm lying flat.

DR. FIORE: What is your body feeling?

SHERRY: I feel cold.

DR. FIORE: What are your emotions?

SHERRY: I feel afraid, even though I feel like I don't need to be.

DR. FIORE: Is anything being relayed to you in any way?

SHERRY: I feel like they're . . . it's like light . . . some kind of light that's making me calm. It's calming.

DR. FIORE: What color is the light?

SHERRY: It's purple and gold.

DR. FIORE: Where does the light seem to be coming from?

SHERRY: It seems to be emanating from whoever is around me. There seems to be kind of a merging of forms or something. It's like seeing an aura around somebody. It's not like actually seeing an actual form, and so the colors merge. But it's mostly like gold.

DR. FIORE: Now you're going to move ahead to the time that something does happen to you.

SHERRY: It's not like I'm actually seeing anything, but I feel like I'm being operated on.

DR. FIORE: Tell me about that in detail.

SHERRY: It seems like they're taking something out of my breast, but I don't know if I'm making this up.

DR. FIORE: Don't be concerned about that. Where do you feel you are in relationship to your body?

SHERRY: I can't feel what's happening. I can't feel . . . there's no feeling of touch.

DR. FIORE: When you say that, do you mean no body sensation or no emotion?

SHERRY: No body sensation.

DR. FIORE: Where do you feel you are in relationship to your body?

SHERRY: It's like being within and also watching.

DR. FIORE: From what vantage point?

SHERRY: From above my head. [*Long pause*] It's like I'm looking at somebody's brain or an X ray of someone's brain.

DR. FIORE: Tell me more about that.

SHERRY: It's not an X ray, because I can see . . . It's like there are colors. Light.

DR. FIORE: Tell me about it in detail.

SHERRY: I think something was being taken out.

DR. FIORE: Was that somebody else's brain, or was it yours?

SHERRY: It was somebody else's.

DR. FIORE: Was it anybody whom you knew?

SHERRY: No.

DR. FIORE: I'd like you to remember how many other people were in the room being examined, treated, and/or operated on.

SHERRY: There were many.

DR. FIORE: Tell me about that, you're allowing yourself to remember so very much now.

SHERRY: There's a child being pushed by me. It looks like I could see light around him. I could see his aura, the golden aura around him. I definitely sense that I'm not alone.

DR. FIORE: You're going to do more than just sense, you're going to know, you're going to allow yourself to remember now, at the count of three. One . . . two . . . three. You are remembering just as though it's happening now.

SHERRY: There seems to be one central figure that is like the head. I guess he would be almost like a head surgeon. He's wearing some clothing with a high collar. I . . . just saw him from the back. He has a large brain . . . a large head. [*Pauses*] I'm not too concerned about what's going on around me, because it's happened before and it's not like it's new, so . . . I don't really see anything definite. I suppose I could leave my body and look around, if I wanted to. [*Pauses*] It's pretty interesting. You can have the opportunity to see what the inside of a body looks like. It's like I can see somebody with their whole abdomen opened up. I can see their lungs. I can see the heart beating. [*Pauses*] There's somebody that had . . . it's almost like their legs are wrapped. It's not a cast. It's kind of like a bright, iridescent blue. [*Pauses*] It's pretty busy. There's a lot of activity. I don't want to get in the way.

DR. FIORE: How many people would you say are being operated on?

SHERRY: A hundred come to my mind, but I don't know. It's a round space and it's pretty full. [*Pauses*] I see something spinning. It's almost like a roulette wheel, but there are different parts of it going in different directions. It's almost like looking down from the top. I don't know what it is.

DR. FIORE: Do you see anyone whom you know?

SHERRY: Not yet. I feel like I'm moving outside of a certain space and then back in. I'm not staying in the same place. It's almost like I can come and go.

DR. FIORE: What do you mean by that?

SHERRY: My etheric body can come and go.

DR. FIORE: Where is your physical body?

SHERRY: My physical body is on the table.

DR. FIORE: What's happening to it?

SHERRY: They're still working . . . it seems like they're working on my abdominal area.

DR. FIORE: What are they doing to it?

SHERRY: I'm not sure.

DR. FIORE: Take a look.

SHERRY: [*Pauses*] My mind says they're looking for cancer, but I don't know that.

DR. FIORE: Let yourself know if they conveyed that to you.

SHERRY: They're just looking. There's nothing there. They're just looking to see if there's any obstruction. It seems like they're trying to move things around so my colon is straightened out. [*Pauses*] They fill the space with light. It's not like it's being done with . . . tools, really. [*Pauses*] I can see there's a machine over somebody, and I can see all the bones in their body through the top. It's like an X ray, but it's . . . it's like a fluorescent green, and they're lying on a table. It's a man. They're mostly checking. It seems like they're trying to help people who have problems. There's so many people to help. I get the feeling that as our bodies are healthier, it enables us to better help others. It seems like it's because we won't be worrying about ourselves and we'll be more clear and allow the light to flow . . . flow better, easier. [*Pauses*] It seems like it's all about . . . energy . . . and sharing light and helping others. [*Pauses and looks up*] You can look up and it's like a light show. It's pretty interesting.

DR. FIORE: Let's move to what's been done to you in the way of treatments. You said that you thought they were taking something out of your breast. And then what were you aware of?

SHERRY: I felt like my system was being flushed out, somehow.

DR. FIORE: Is anything being conveyed to you mentally or through speech?

SHERRY: Mostly not to fear, that there's nothing to fear, that they're trying to help.

DR. FIORE: Did they say why they're trying to help you?

SHERRY: I just get feelings of love. But I don't know that there's any connection other than that.

DR. FIORE: Let yourself remember if something was done about your yeast infection.

SHERRY: [*Pauses*] It was like a cream. It was put inside of me . . . real deep inside of me. It was not done with an instrument. It was done, I guess, with a hand and it was a little cold and really messy. It felt . . . gushy. It wasn't really cold, but I could tell that it was like a cream.

DR. FIORE: How did you feel about this being done?

SHERRY: I felt uncomfortable, but I knew what it was being done for. They told me why.

DR. FIORE: What did they say?

SHERRY: They said it would take care of the yeast. [*Long pause*] When I feel like I'm going to remember something, I start to tense up and I . . . feel like I can't. Either I'm not supposed to, or I'm afraid to, I don't know which one.

DR. FIORE: At the count of three, you're going to allow yourself to remember, even if you feel that tension. One . . . two . . . three.

SHERRY: The feeling I get is that I'm out of my body and I'm looking at it as if I were the doctor. And I'm looking at what they're doing.

DR. FIORE: And what do you see?

SHERRY: I'm looking at it like I'm standing in front of my body with my legs spread. And it's almost like I could go inside and see what it looks like . . . inside. [*Pauses*] It seems like I ask them to examine me because I was so worried about this fungus infection. So I don't get the feeling that anything would be done without my consent or asking. I'm being given a different perspective of what is going on with my body. It's almost like I can see the lining inside my vaginal area. Like it's . . . almost like being blown up on a screen . . . magnified. [*Pauses*] But there's nothing really wrong. Hmm . . . It's almost like there's this . . . I can't explain it. It's something that moves along with it. It's kind of like an iridescent green. There's a light on the end of it so you can see. [*Pauses*] It's like I need to know my body and what makes it work so I can understand more. And I get the feeling that the reason for it is so I can help other people. But I don't know if I was told that or it's just a feeling.

DR. FIORE: Let yourself remember if you're told that.

SHERRY: [*Long pause*]

DR. FIORE: Trust your mind and just report whatever comes into it.

SHERRY: It's like I'm being drawn toward a light that's like the light of a candle. And pretty soon, it's . . . not just in front of me, it's like it's within me. [*Pauses*] It's almost like some kind of a ceremony. Something's happening that is very emotional. There's some kind of special group that I'm a part of, and it makes me want to cry. [*Cries*] It's a . . . it's like being . . . all for one for the higher good of all of life. [*Long pause*]

DR. FIORE: Now go to the time when you're spinning.

SHERRY: It was really scary. I didn't understand what they were doing. Now I think there was something connected to me, to my head, and it was making my mind spin. It's just giving me that feeling, like pulsating. I felt like I was going to black out. I knew that was what was going to happen. And when they asked me if I remembered, I said no, even though I did remember.

DR. FIORE: You said no, but you did remember?

SHERRY: I did remember some things, but I said no because I wanted to go back. [*Pauses*] But I don't remember any faces. They didn't want me to. It seems like they only want me to remember them as light. Because that's what we have in common.

DR. FIORE: Why do you think they put that thing on your head?

SHERRY: Because it would erase the memory. It seems like I would not ever allow that to happen again if I knew everything . . . if I remembered everything. I might not allow myself to be open.

DR. FIORE: What do you mean by that?

SHERRY: In a sense, it's like letting yourself be used for a higher purpose. Not like a guinea pig, but because they're helping at the same time it's helping them also to have a deeper understanding.

DR. FIORE: A deeper understanding of . . . ?

SHERRY: Of humans. Of the human body. It's like we're helping each other. Whatever we give comes back in return in other ways. Like the gift of being healed is giving and receiving.

DR. FIORE: Do you feel there have been other experiences before and after? And if so, how many?

SHERRY: [*Long pause*] Hmm . . . Too many to count.

DR. FIORE: Do you feel that they have worked on your body or healed your body either before or since?

SHERRY: I feel that, but I don't have any recollection. Sometimes I'll wake up in the middle of the night and a certain place on my body might hurt and I'll get a distinct feeling that I've just been operated on, and then by the morning it's gone.

DR. FIORE: Have you ever seen any marks on your body that you couldn't explain?

SHERRY: Yes.

DR. FIORE: Tell me about them.

SHERRY: Once I saw a very fine red line, but it was gone in a matter of hours. It was on my abdominal area, on the right side.

DR. FIORE: Do you feel that the ETs have extracted eggs or fetuses?

SHERRY: Eggs.

DR. FIORE: Tell me about that.

SHERRY: It's being used for study. And . . . and I have a concern about pregnancy for some reason.

DR. FIORE: What do you mean by that?

SHERRY: I just felt that there was life inside me before. And . . . I actually consciously feared that some kind of intercourse was taking place. [*Long pause*]

DR. FIORE: Continue to speak out.

SHERRY: But I don't know. . . . I just don't know if there's . . . I don't know. [*Seems very upset*]

DR. FIORE: Would you like to remember if that has happened?

SHERRY: No.

DR. FIORE: But you feel that eggs have been extracted?

SHERRY: Yes.

DR. FIORE: How do you feel about that?

SHERRY: I feel that I don't want it to be used to create a life, but that for study it would be okay.

DR. FIORE: Was any explanation given to you?

SHERRY: It seems like the purpose was for education. But that . . . concerns me.

DR. FIORE: What do you mean by that?

SHERRY: It concerns me because life is . . . is so fragile, and I don't want to . . . allow myself to be a part of something that's not . . .

DR. FIORE: Let's move to the end of that experience, the one that you had in July. You're going to go to your last moments with them. Just report whatever comes into your mind, whatever you're aware of.

SHERRY: It seems like I'm moving. I'm moving toward an all-consuming kind of light, but it's not real. There seems to be a sense of excitement. [*Pauses*] I guess they're leaving. I see . . .

heads, through some kind of window area. There's kind of a bright pinkish light, and yellowish. . . . It probably looks like how you would envision a flying saucer.

DR. FIORE: Take a good look at it.

SHERRY: It seems to have kind of a dome like. . . . It's funny, this is a smaller . . . only a few people fit in this. Actually, this might be what they bring people back in. It has a lower area that comes around like an upside-down little saucer or something. But there's not very many, it isn't the big one. This is smaller. There's only about five beings in there.

DR. FIORE: I want you to take a good look at them and tell me more.

SHERRY: I could draw the outline for you.

DR. FIORE: Remember what happened. How did you get out of the craft?

SHERRY: It seems like they're dropping down, kind of like a tube. Hmm . . . It's almost like it's spinning. It's a weird feeling. I can almost feel it, like I'm in it right now, spiraling.

DR. FIORE: Let yourself know how you got from the craft to where you started.

SHERRY: [*Pause*] Let's see, it's hard to explain. It's almost like changing matter, like all the atoms were changed. It's almost like there was a physical body there, but the molecules were changed so they could be re-formed in another place and actually be in two places at once.

✦

Sherry came out of hypnosis easily. "Their eyes were different from what I remembered from my dream. I immediately backed

off when I got a glimpse of them. I would hate to think of someone touching me who looked like that." With dawning realiza-
tion, she covered her eyes with her hands. "Oh my God! I've let
those people touch me!"

" 'We Need You
as a Contact.' "

🖋 "The Pillsbury Doughboy came first. He put his arm around me and I felt better. He didn't talk to me, but did communicate mind to mind. There were three others like him in a row. One was taller than E.T." Ted stood up and showed me how tall they were, putting his hand at about his waist. He walked over to the chair next to my desk and picked up a portfolio of his drawings and began spreading them out on my burgundy-colored carpet. "I brought some of my pictures back. I thought you'd like to see them again."

Ted, mid-forties, tall and attractive, with dark brown hair and startlingly blue eyes, is a former patient. He was here to discover if he had had a close encounter of the fourth kind and had just finished describing a recurrent childhood dream.

I was reasonably sure our visit would be more than productive. When he was in therapy with me, he had shown me many professionally done pen-and-ink sketches, the majority of which were of UFOs. The twenty-odd beautiful drawings of spacecraft now on my floor represented more than ten years' work.

132

"How long have you been interested in UFOs, Ted?"

"All my life. As a child I used to spend a great deal of time watching sci-fi movies like *War of the Worlds,* and the early Hollywood B-movies of Martians coming to Earth. Then there was one movie that really had an impact on me. I think it came out around 1956, called *Forbidden Planet.* There was a flying saucer in it that was totally fascinating to me. I think that's when I started drawing spaceships, and it carried on in my artwork all these years. When I was ten years old, all of a sudden, I had to know more about stars and astronomy. It got to the point of almost an obsession, where I had to go down and get books constantly. Finally I got a telescope, and then I learned to identify star clusters by sight and by rote memory. The next thing I knew, I formed an astronomy club here in the Valley [Santa Clara Valley] and was active in it for years."

"When do you feel you may have had your first close encounter with extraterrestrials?"

"Probably when I was about two to three and a half years old. I woke up from a nightmare and looked up and there was a person next to my bed. I was terrified! I closed my eyes and went back to sleep. That was a particularly hard time in my life. When I was eighteen months old, I showed the first signs of an angioma, a vascular malformation. Remember we talked about that? I was born with an enlargement of blood vessels in my brain. Later, when I was older, I'd have spells when I'd be out of control, crying, nervous, overly emotional, at times I'd even have some paralysis. My parents took me for my first tests. The doctors said there was nothing that could be done, except medications, barbiturates. They didn't have the treatments forty years ago that they have now, of course. In fact, they told my parents I might be dead in six months, certainly I wouldn't live to adulthood. By then my vision had become very poor, I saw double. I had problems walking, to the point of having to crawl again. I stopped talking and had to be fed. The right side of my body had stopped growing. When I was a little older, about three, I kept telling my folks the doctors had cut the top of my head off. When I was about three and one-half, my parents took me to San Francisco for an exploratory operation. The surgeons were amazed. The growth had shrunk. Nobody could ever figure it out. By then I was walking, talking, feeding myself and could see just fine. I did continue to have some problems with it, though, mainly being supersensitive. My last major spell was in fourth grade, and then they finally stopped."

"Ted, let's start with the nightmare and the night visitors."

"Fine. I hope I can do it."

Ted had developed into an exceptionally fine hypnotic subject during our earlier hypnotherapeutic work, so he was in a trance deep enough for a regression within seconds. I asked him to go back to his very first close encounter. Before I finished counting to ten, he interrupted me.

✔

TED: There's a person here with me. His head is quite large. It's almost like the shape of a peanut. It's larger and rounder at the top. Then it narrows down a little bit and broadens at the bottom. The bottom is a little bit longer than the top. It's very strange looking. I've never seen anything quite like this before. He's got two eyes. They slant upward at about forty-five degrees. The eyes are long and narrow.

DR. FIORE: What color are the eyes?

TED: It seems like they're brown. When he opens his eyes, they get quite large. I don't see any ears. The head's very smooth. There doesn't seem to be any hair. The head's very white. It's almost like the texture of . . . like a honeydew melon, but smoother. In fact, it's white, but there's a slight greenish color to it. It's very, very pale green. [*Pauses*] It's very strange, because it seems like there's a number of them, all here at once.

DR. FIORE: Where are you as this is happening?

TED: I'm in a room in some kind of a craft. And the room is round and there's lights and dials along the wall. On one side there's all kinds of dials and lights in little screens. These dials are built into the wall of the room, but there's a table that comes out like they would use to write information.

DR. FIORE: How old are you?

TED: Three years old.

DR. FIORE: And what are you doing right now?

TED: I'm in this room, and it seems like I'm standing and these people are all around me. Some of them are . . . let's see, they're a little bit taller than I am. They're all different sizes and all different shapes. The ones that are a little bit taller than I am, their heads are very strange . . . kind of like a grasshopper. But the taller ones' heads are a little bit different. They're more like insects.

DR. FIORE: As you're looking at them, how do you feel?

TED: I don't seem to be extremely afraid of them. I find them kind of fascinating. They're not at all aggressive.

DR. FIORE: What are they doing?

TED: Well, they're looking at me. They're fascinated with me. I don't know if we're communicating anything. I can feel some emotions, some tears, almost like I want to just burst out and cry.

DR. FIORE: Tell me more about where you are.

TED: The room is small, but it's not supersmall, but it's not superlarge. I have a feeling it's maybe about twelve feet across. Maybe from the floor to the ceiling it's also about twelve feet.

It's very clean, very smooth, and it's domed. There's almost no furniture in it except for the panels of lights and this table that contours around the room. I believe the door is behind me, and all the people are standing in a semicircle around me.

DR. FIORE: How many are there?

TED: There are two short people, a little bit taller than I am. Then there are two people that are like adults.

DR. FIORE: Now what happens?

TED: There's no verbal communication. I can't tell whether they're saying anything to me. It's like a meeting. Aha . . . what I'm hearing is, "We're here to help you." I ask them, "What do you mean by helping?" And they say, "We are here to help you." Hmm . . . I don't know. "Why are you here?" "To help you." "How?" "With life." "Am I of this planet?" "No." "Why am I here on this planet now?" "Contact." "What do you mean by contact?" "Later, you'll be a contact between them and us." "What do you mean by them?" "Earth people." "Are you going to come back later?" No response. "Where am I?" "In space." "What is this room that I'm in?" "Control room." "What planet are you from?" "No planet. Space station." "Where is your space station?" "Near here." "Are we still close to the earth?" "No." "Do you have a message for me?" "Yes, we will be back later." "What do you mean by later?" "When you are older." "Can you tell me when?" "Older."

DR. FIORE: Now what happens?

TED: It feels like I'm being beamed back down to the earth.

DR. FIORE: Go back through this again to see if there's an examination.

TED: I see myself lying on a table. I'm out of my body, looking at myself.

DR. FIORE: Where are you in relationship to your body?

TED: I'm off to one side, next to them, and I'm watching them. They have a metal probe that's about the diameter of a pencil and about the length of a pencil. It has a blunt end. At the blunt end there is a little . . . almost like a needle that comes out. And they take this probe and they touch different parts of my body. But the needle doesn't go into the body. They just press it up against the skin in different parts. This probe registers information on the dials that are on the wall. As they touch different parts of my body with the probe, the gauges move.

DR. FIORE: Is the probe independent of the gauges or attached to the gauges?

TED: It's attached. There's a wire or something attached to one of the instruments on the wall. As they touch me with the probe, the information is being registered on the gauges, and then it's being fed into like a computer for storage.

DR. FIORE: Then what happens?

TED: They look into my eyes, look in my mouth, look at my hair. They look at my head. They're doing something to my head. [*Pauses*] "Is there something wrong with my head?" "Yes, enlarged tissues. If they continue to grow, you will not be able to survive." "Why are you doing this to me?" "To help you. We need you as a contact."

DR. FIORE: What are they doing to you?

TED: It seems like they take the probe and they touch different parts of my skull. I don't know whether they're putting energy into the skull or whether they're just registering information. [*Long pause*]

DR. FIORE: Continue to speak out.

TED: I'm still lying flat on the table. They bring over an apparatus that's on wheels. There's these little probes and this apparatus that fits around the head. The probes are like little miniature fountain pens attached to the apparatus. These fountain pens can be directed in any direction. There are four of them, two on each side. And at the ends, there's like a glass cover. There are needles that extend out from the glass cover. When they turn the apparatus on, a beam of light comes out. It's very straight and it's very thin. It's needlelike. It's very much like laser light. And it comes out and it strikes my head, but it doesn't hurt.

DR. FIORE: Are you still in your body when this is happening?

TED: I'm . . . I'm out of my body. For a few seconds. The beam of light hits the sides of my head, from the back end of the head, all the way up to the front, on both sides. Then they turn off the machine and remove it. Now they awaken me and have me stand up. [*Pauses*] They gather around me.

DR. FIORE: Your inner mind is going to let you know more about what happened. Let yourself know any details that you omitted.

TED: What I see now is that I'm in this chair and the top of my head is being removed. And they're looking at my brain.

DR. FIORE: What do you mean?

TED: They took an instrument and they cut open the top of the head, all the way around. And they were able to remove that part of the skull and look at the brain.

DR. FIORE: Let yourself remember everything exactly as it happens.

TED: In the beginning, I'm sitting in a chair and there's instruments all around me. They've taken like a laser device and they've cut around the skull. They've removed the top of the head, the skull, and they're looking at the brain. They do that first. Then they put me down on a table. They pick up probes that are hooked up to dials and gauges on the wall and they touch different parts of the brain very gently. The gauges register information. They're finding out something. I don't know what information they want to know. The brain fascinates them, and they're very curious about it. They watch the dials and the gauges, and they record the information. [*Long pause*]

DR. FIORE: What is happening?

TED: They're taking an instrument, it's like a laser, and they're able . . . after they've removed the skull, to heal something. They probe around the brain, they touch all over and they find the enlargement. And with the laser light, they're able to shrink it.

DR. FIORE: Tell me about that in detail.

TED: I watched them, and it's like the light beams out of a little instrument. And it's like fire with a very small beam of light, very thin. It's almost like silk. It's the thickness of a spiderweb, and it beams out and hits that part of the brain. And it just . . . causes it to shrink and change color. Change to bright red, and then it . . . turns to ash. To a grayish ash. And there's another instrument they take, like a suction instrument. And they move it around the surface and remove that ash, and it sucks it up and takes it away. Then they finish. They put the skull back on and fit it, and then with another laser light . . . Oh, the apparatus. They put the apparatus around my head again and they turn it on. And this time instead of cutting, it mends. It mends the skull 'back together. The atoms go back together, and there's no scar tissue. And when it's finished, there's no indication that the skull has been cut open.

DR. FIORE: Now what happens?

TED: I'm taken into a recovery room. There's an attendant there.

DR. FIORE: Are there any other patients?

TED: No. I don't see anybody else. I stay there for quite a while.

DR. FIORE: Where are you in relationship to your body at this time?

TED: I think I come back in. I feel my spirit coming back into the skull and reclaiming the eye sockets. And I feel my spirit body coming back in and just . . . molding to the skull, to the physical body, almost like pouring milk into a container. I feel myself just gently coming back in and feeling, feeling the skull come up against my spirit body. Feeling myself come back in contact.

DR. FIORE: Now move to the moment when you were returned to your home.

TED: I'm on this platform. In the center of a platform is a bell-like jar. I think it's a jar. Anyway, I see these apparatuses coming down from the sides, and they're like laser instruments. They point these at me, and there are four of them, and they beam energy down. And my body changes into a different kind of matter, into light particles. And I travel back to the place where I began, and at that point I materialize.

DR. FIORE: When you materialize, where are you?

TED: I'm inside of the house. I'm back in bed now. And . . . I wake up. And this person is standing in front of me. And I don't remember what happens, but he frightens me.

DR. FIORE: Which person is this?

TED: He's from the spacecraft. He came down with me to escort me back.

DR. FIORE: When you say you woke up, do you mean you just regained consciousness?

TED: Yes. It was like I was in a very deep sleep, and then I woke up, and I saw this person standing by my bed. He scared me very much. I didn't know what to expect. Then I closed my eyes and the person disappeared.

DR. FIORE: Then?

TED: I went back to sleep.

DR. FIORE: Let yourself remember another encounter.

TED: I see an arm extended out. At the end of the arm there's a television camera, in the center. It's a rectangular lens that fits into the arm and points at me. And there's a sensor in the center of the unit. A robot's moving his arm up and down my body.

DR. FIORE: Where are you?

TED: I'm sitting in a chair in a room in a craft. It's run by a group of mechanical beings. Metal robots. [*Pauses*] They're checking my body. The room is filled with different kinds of instruments and dials and lights. I'm in a chair that's similar to a dentist's chair, with contoured arms on each side. There's another robot behind me. I'm being studied, but I don't know why.

DR. FIORE: How old are you?

TED: Ten years old.

DR. FIORE: Are they talking to you?

TED: I'm being examined. I'm in a spacecraft somewhere. The people that are examining me are mechanical. They have artificial intelligence. They don't seem to be very frightening. They're pretty much like the ones in some of the movies I've seen.

DR. FIORE: How do you know that they're mechanical?

TED: Their arms are different than mine. They're jointed and they're shaped differently. They're made of metal. It's like a whole series of long, rectangular boxes, hooked together, that move. The body is fairly tall, fairly wide, and it comes to kind of a dome at the top, like their head. But it seems like they're almost all metal.

DR. FIORE: And you're not frightened by this?

TED: No. I don't seem to be frightened at all.

DR. FIORE: Now move back and see if there was a time during this encounter when you were frightened.

TED: It was in the very beginning, when I was asleep. This was during the night when I was taken.

DR. FIORE: Let yourself remember all about it.

TED: I fell asleep. And I was taken aboard. A beam of light came down. I'm not sure, because it feels like I'm a lot older here. It seems more recent.

DR. FIORE: Let yourself remember.

TED: Late thirties. It happened in the apartment where I live. It's like a beam of light came down through the apartment, surrounded me and changed me into a different molecular structure, and then it took me back into the small spaceship. And from there I was taken out.

DR. FIORE: Taken out?

TED: Taken out into space, away from Earth. And we came to this colony. Where all these different spaceships were.

DR. FIORE: What happened?

TED: I was taken on board a larger spaceship or space station. [*Pauses*] I'm in the chair. I'm being examined by the robots.

DR. FIORE: Tell me more about this.

TED: There's a robot standing in back of me. The other one in front of me has his arm up, scanning my body. It seems like the end of the arm is like a television screen camera with a sensor. And this sensor is going up and down my body and making readings. But I don't see it being registered anywhere. It's being taken into him and stored somewhere inside of him.

DR. FIORE: How do you feel?

TED: It's not frightening. Or is it? I'm not sure, because I feel very numb. I don't have any real emotion.

DR. FIORE: And now?

TED: They do the readings and . . . [*Pauses*] I don't know.

DR. FIORE: Let yourself know at the count of three. One . . . two . . . three.

TED: The first thing that comes to mind is really crazy. It's like a man out of some cartoon. His face is white. It's more like a human's. His eyes are smaller, more like a human's eyes. His skin's different. He doesn't have a beard. He doesn't have any ears. The skin is very smooth. There's no hair. There's two eyes, they're . . . more elliptical. The eyes are more vertical, up and down, instead of horizontal like the other beings'. He's in the room, but he doesn't show himself too clearly, and then he disappears.

DR. FIORE: Now what's happening?

TED: I'm resting. [*Pauses*] I'm still in the chair and I'm in a state of peace. Everyone around me is not doing anything particular. It seems like they're getting ready to do something else. They're extracting some blood. I see this long instrument with some finger holes on the handle part. It has a long needle. They just gently stick it in my arm and withdraw the blood.

DR. FIORE: And now?

TED: They take the instrument away. I don't know what they do with it.

DR. FIORE: Then what happens?

TED: They take me to another room and they put me on a bed to rest.

✒

Ted took a while to come out of hypnosis. He stretched his arms, shook his head as though clearing it and smiled at me. "That was really weird! I felt like I was reliving it. I could even smell odors very different from anything I've experienced before."

"I loved the way you asked the extraterrestrials so many questions. What a curious little boy you were. And you obviously felt comfortable enough with them to expect them to treat you with respect, at least enough to answer your questions."

Ted was tired from our long session, so we decided to call it a day. He enthusiastically volunteered to do some drawings for my book. He felt he could draw some of the instruments the visitors used and some interiors of the spacecraft. His parting words were, "It's going to be hard to draw the aliens. They look like a cross between an insect and an amphibian creature." Smiling good-naturedly, he added, "I'll just have to do my best and hope it's not too shocking for the readers."

"Oh My God!
They Already Know
How to Incorporate."

Gloria, a pretty woman in her late thirties, sought my help because of the stress of many family tragedies all happening within a few years.

She began by telling me that she'd been to other therapists but was uncomfortable with them because they were too orthodox. She was tired of their blaming her problems on her mother and her childhood. At any rate, she hadn't improved, and so she wanted to see a hypnotherapist to get at deep layers of her psyche.

Things had not gone smoothly for Gloria for years. At one point, about fifteen years ago, she had so many physical problems that she was hospitalized for a week of testing. She had fever and other symptoms of malaria, but the doctors could find nothing to explain her condition. It was so serious that she thought she would "fade away." She overcame her problems then by becoming a "health nut," and developing a very positive outlook.

Ten minutes into our session, Gloria looked me in the eye, as though sizing me up. "I had a really emotional reaction to a two-day seminar I took with Dr. Richard Haines. It was on UFOs.

146

Close encounters of the fourth kind." She glanced at me to see if I knew what she was talking about and to see my reaction. When she saw that I was listening attentively, she continued, "He was with NASA for over twenty years. A very credible person."

"Did you undergo any hypnotic regressions during the seminar, Gloria?"

"No, but I became very emotional. I've had particularly bizarre dreams since then, of floating out of my room and strange beings. I had nightmares before, for years actually. Dr. Fiore, are you interested in dreams?"

"Gloria, please call me Edee. Yes. Dreams are very important. I often find that they are not really dreams per se, but actually flashbacks to repressed, forgotten, experiences. Did you have a dream you want to tell me about?"

"Yes. It happened three years ago and it was so incredibly real, I've never forgotten it. I was in bed with my husband, who was asleep. I thought I was fully awake. I couldn't move. The bed was vibrating. There were several figures around me. They were hideous! Gray. Awful! Eyes that were black holes. I told them, "I'm not going to let you control me." I woke up in the morning and the dream was going over and over in my mind. It was *very* real! Less than two weeks before that dream, I witnessed a UFO and was really shaken. I know I've repressed a lot. That's why I want to work with you."

We discussed the possibility of her having been abducted and decided we would spend a future session exploring that area. There were still many things Gloria needed to discuss in laying the foundations for our therapy program. Before she left, I hypnotized her, taping suggestions for relaxation and daily improvement.

After a few sessions in which we worked on pressing issues, Gloria and I decided that we would now do a regression to a possible CEIV.

Using the hypnosis tape to go to sleep with each evening had conditioned Gloria to be very responsive to the sound of my voice. She slipped into a hypnotic trance within minutes, and I asked her inner mind to take her to the event responsible for the dream she had had three years before.

✦

GLORIA: Oh Jeez! This face, it's weird. It's not dead, but it looks dead. Ugh! It looks like a frog or toad. It's not real defined. Not smooth, except around the temple area on the sides. It looks like rolls. Like a scrub board. It's big! A big head. It's like spindly. Ugh! It said something, but I don't want to listen to it.

DR. FIORE: Let yourself remember what it said.

GLORIA: It's like angry because I was acting badly. I said I wasn't acting badly. They don't know me. How could they say I was acting badly. My right leg hurts, up by the thigh. Like somebody kicked me . . . I floated out of there. That's how I got to the sidewalk. Went right through the wall and I was on the sidewalk. [*Long pause*]

DR. FIORE: Now what's happening?

GLORIA: They're asking questions, and I don't want to answer. Jesus! I can't know everything. [*Long pause*]

DR. FIORE: Continue to speak out.

GLORIA: There's somebody there, like an attendant, like when you go into surgery. There are people around me at the end, by my left foot. They're standing there waiting. All talking.

DR. FIORE: What do they look like?

GLORIA: The ones that are giving the directions are small. The ones that help are tall. They give that look that they can't talk, even though they can.

DR. FIORE: What are you feeling and thinking?

GLORIA: I don't like it. I just want to leave.

DR. FIORE: What's being done?

GLORIA: I'm okay, but my right leg hurts. It's like being in the hospital when they give you an intravenous. They're taking my blood. They're not trying to stop me from leaving. But they tell me no one will believe me. They will think I'm crazy.

DR. FIORE: What did they say exactly?

GLORIA: "Nobody is going to believe you." I said, "Yes, they will, I'll tell a priest. I'll find a church." [*Long pause*]

DR. FIORE: Now what's happening?

GLORIA: Like I went through a wall. I'm on a sidewalk, and I'm going to go home. I'm back in bed.

DR. FIORE: Let yourself remember more about that same experience. It's all coming back to you, at the count of three. One . . . two . . . three.

GLORIA: The room smells funny. Something's blowing up my nose. It's almost like those tubes they put in you in the hospital. They're doing something. They're opening something. It's like a plastic bag . . . What's in that bag? They're hanging it up. There's that face; that face keeps passing by. [*Pauses*]

DR. FIORE: Describe the face.

GLORIA: It looks like a . . . the skin looks like the skin of a dead person. The eyes are really hollow. Really hollow. Uhhh! It looks awful. It just looks awful! But the others aren't worried about it.

DR. FIORE: The others?

GLORIA: The others that are helping them. They're humans. They don't say anything to them. They just look at each other. And after they look at each other, then the one down by my left foot does something. My leg feels like it's up. It looks like a metal bar. It's got a U on it. It comes from the side of the table . . . I can't feel it, but I know my leg's up there. There's a tube. There's a tube running somewhere. I can't see where that tube is running. I can't move.

DR. FIORE: How do you feel with that tube? Is it connected to your body in any way?

GLORIA: Somewhere. It has to be. I feel like it's my hip. I'm just looking. I . . .

DR. FIORE: What do you see?

GLORIA: There's one coming in the front, in the front of the table. I feel like I'm at a sloped angle, like my feet are up, they're elevated and I'm . . . down a little ways. Because it's hard to lift my head. It's really hard. This one just . . . came in to see how it's going. I think, just to observe. It's like this table is supported on . . . I don't know what supports it. . . . It's easy to move up and down. The tube is in my stomach. Ohh . . . Why is it in my stomach? I don't know how they got it in there. I want it off! [Pauses] There's this thing over my head. There's another tube running in it. Maybe that's the one that goes to my nose. [Agitated] "Oh, don't touch me!" I want to . . . I just want to leave. I just want that one to get away from my face. I don't like . . . Oh! . . . It's awful. I don't understand! When are they going to let me off of this? Why do they have to be so close? I know . . . they're not going to . . . they're not going to hurt. But it's so repulsive. It's like . . . It's like having dead people walk around you.

DR. FIORE: Do they give you any explanation for the tubes?

GLORIA: I said, "Is that going to help me?" And they said, "Yes." But they said it would help them do more. Then . . . huh . . . this thing that looks like . . . it has light in it . . . and it's coming down. It looks like a whole bunch of crossed wires, little squares with lights in it. It's coming from . . . And it goes to that spot on my stomach . . . and to that spot on my hip, and it's warm.

DR. FIORE: Did you feel anything else?

GLORIA: It was like a tingle. It was . . . just a tingling.

DR. FIORE: Where is the tingling?

GLORIA: All through my middle area . . . and down my leg.

DR. FIORE: How would you describe the beings that are there?

GLORIA: It's those ones that like to come to your face.

DR. FIORE: What do they look like exactly?

GLORIA: Hollow, ugh! . . . They look like . . . how do you describe them? . . . They're . . . they're . . . my height, maybe smaller.

DR. FIORE: What color is their skin?

GLORIA: Grayish, like old people or dead people, grayish, wrinkly. No hair.

DR. FIORE: What about their noses?

GLORIA: It looks like when you look at a skeleton. There's nothing there. There is a nose. They have to breathe. But there's no shape for a nose.

DR. FIORE: Do you see any nostrils?

GLORIA: Just little holes.

DR. FIORE: What about a mouth?

GLORIA: There's a mouth, but it doesn't move.

DR. FIORE: When they talk, does it move?

GLORIA: I don't know what it does.

DR. FIORE: What about the shape of their heads?

GLORIA: They're large heads; but it looks okay on them.

DR. FIORE: Do they all look more or less the same, like the same species?

GLORIA: Yes, but there are many different other people with them. I get confused.

DR. FIORE: What do you mean?

GLORIA: There's human people. There's people like us.

DR. FIORE: Are they completely like us, are they completely human beings?

GLORIA: Yes. That's why I couldn't understand why they couldn't tell me nothing.

DR. FIORE: These people who are like you, do they communicate with you?

GLORIA: Yes, they're very nice. They relax you. They ask you about yourself. It's almost, it's almost like you go out with a friend for lunch. Very casual, very unalarming. It's like they do this all the time. And then there's the other ones. And you can almost see, you can see their veins, their . . . You can see their veins, very light skin, very thin.

DR. FIORE: What color is their skin?

GLORIA: Like our flesh tone, but more transparent.

DR. FIORE: Are you saying there are ones who have gray, wrinkly skin; then there are ones who are totally human; then there's another group too?

GLORIA: Yes.

DR. FIORE: Now these ones who have the totally transparent skin, how tall would you say they are?

GLORIA: They seem to be about . . . well, they're tall, but not abnormally tall.

DR. FIORE: Can you tell what sex they are?

GLORIA: There's male and female. There's a balance.

DR. FIORE: What are they wearing?

GLORIA: They're just wearing this cover. It's supposed to protect them.

DR. FIORE: Now what's happening?

GLORIA: They were going to take something out of my left arm. I don't know what it is. I'm not dying from it. I was afraid I was going to die.

DR. FIORE: What are they doing?

GLORIA: It looks like these giant tweezers, and a white cloth. It's like a handkerchief. . . . I don't know why they were mad at me.

DR. FIORE: What do you mean?

GLORIA: Something to do with . . . too smart. I don't know if they meant I was acting smart. It's like it doesn't make any difference if I'm there. They talk . . . they don't care what you think. They don't even ask you.

DR. FIORE: What are they doing?

GLORIA: They're checking my eyes.

DR. FIORE: How are they doing that?

GLORIA: With this little tube. It's not like what our doctors use. I thought that's what they were doing. It's . . . a tube.

DR. FIORE: Does it hurt?

GLORIA: No, it makes this like buzzing noise. And they just move it back and forth. It's like a monitoring device.

DR. FIORE: Are they explaining that to you?

GLORIA: No. They just keep talking to each other, but I can't understand what they're saying. Now they're saying they're finished.

DR. FIORE: How do they say that to you?

GLORIA: They don't say that to me. They say it to the two guys who brought me in.

DR. FIORE: How many are there altogether?

GLORIA: Two that examined me, and then the two that brought me in.

DR. FIORE: The two that examined you, what are they wearing?

GLORIA: They're wearing these hooded things so you can't see them.

DR. FIORE: What do you mean?

GLORIA: It conceals them enough so you can't tell what they look like. I see one hand.

DR. FIORE: What does it look like?

GLORIA: It looks long and yellowish . . . and that's the one that's got that tube.

DR. FIORE: Do you see their eyes?

GLORIA: All I see are black holes. I think it is their eyes.

DR. FIORE: How tall are they?

GLORIA: They're like six feet.

DR. FIORE: The two that brought you in, did you see their faces?

GLORIA: Yes.

DR. FIORE: What did they look like?

GLORIA: They looked like twins, with blond hair. They looked like . . . football players.

DR. FIORE: Why do you say football players?

GLORIA: Because they were big men. They both looked alike. Not ugly, not attractive, just average, I guess. [*Long pause*] I feel like I'm going to faint. I just want to go to sleep. I feel dizzy, really dizzy. I feel really sick. Maybe if I lie on my right side I won't throw up. I feel sick. [*Squirms and puts her hands on her abdomen*] Uhhh . . . I just . . . I was going to get up to go to the bathroom. No, I'll just stay here until it's over. Then I'll wake up. They told me that it will come easier and I won't be afraid of them. I don't know why they said that. I don't care, I just don't want them to be real close to my face. But I know there's other people that's working with them. I know there is.

DR. FIORE: What do you mean?

GLORIA: People, human people, good people. They don't pick bad people. They can't. There are no bad people. Not with them. You just have to do it that way. They have to work with people that they know will help. And they know those people.

DR. FIORE: And you?

GLORIA: Me? They said I can help. I don't know how. I don't know what I'm supposed to do, but they said it'll come. Can't talk to a lot of people. I don't know what about. But the one in the robe, I want to know who the one in the robe is. He's very, very good.

DR. FIORE: Now what's happening?

GLORIA: They put me in a case after I get up from the table.

DR. FIORE: What is it like to be in that case?

GLORIA: I can't feel anything. And there's a window.

DR. FIORE: Where is the window?

GLORIA: By my eyes, so that I can see.

DR. FIORE: What position are you in?

GLORIA: On my back. It feels like it's curved, because I can feel the sides. Now I'm out again.

DR. FIORE: Did they explain why they were putting you in there?

GLORIA: To go in there and rest for a minute. I don't think it's necessarily rest. I think it's more like . . . it felt like a cleansing. It felt . . . [Pauses] The air was okay, because the difference . . . I could just feel the difference when I came out of the case.

DR. FIORE: Which air did you prefer?

GLORIA: The case. They kept the hoses or the tubes connected to my nostrils. They didn't take those off.

DR. FIORE: They [the tubes] went into the case too?

GLORIA: Yes. The air felt very thick on my arms, very thick.

DR. FIORE: When was that?

GLORIA: When the case opened. When I came out. It wasn't like when I couldn't move on the table. Maybe that's why I didn't feel it.

DR. FIORE: Did they give you any explanation for why they had you on the table and why they did these various procedures?

GLORIA: They said it just would make it easier.

DR. FIORE: To do what?

GLORIA: For me, I . . . don't know. That's what I couldn't figure out. It's almost like . . . I don't know what they were doing.

DR. FIORE: Later you said that you felt that one was very, very good. Was he there during the examination?

GLORIA: Always on my right, talking to me about my feelings, my thoughts. Very beautiful person.

DR. FIORE: What does he look like?

GLORIA: He was human, and he had light brown hair.

DR. FIORE: How was he dressed?

GLORIA: I don't know what it is. It's a tight top, and it covered his arms, and it went down all the way. It's like it was form-fitting.

DR. FIORE: He was completely human-looking?

GLORIA: Yes.

DR. FIORE: What color were his eyes?

GLORIA: Blue. And then there was a little brown on the outside. Beautiful, they were absolutely beautiful eyes. I'll never forget those eyes. He seemed familiar.

DR. FIORE: I'm going to ask you at this point to go back to your very first contact with ETs.

GLORIA: [Pauses] It's . . . red. Everything's encased in red. I don't know, it's strange. I don't know where I'm at. I'm just feeling things around me. It's all these colors.

DR. FIORE: What colors are those?

GLORIA: Reds . . . and golds and . . . then whites coming in . . . then back to red and gold.

DR. FIORE: Where are these colors coming from?

GLORIA: They're all around me. I'm waiting.

DR. FIORE: How old are you?

GLORIA: I have no age, but yet I'm old.

DR. FIORE: What position is your body in?

GLORIA: My legs . . . I'm in a curve, like a little curve, almost a little ball.

DR. FIORE: Are you a fetus at this point?

GLORIA: I think I am. I'm floating. And I get to see all these colors.

DR. FIORE: Remember your contact with the ETs.

GLORIA: They promised that they would be there. They promised. [*Pauses*] Oh my God! They already know how to incorporate.

DR. FIORE: Tell me what you mean by that.

GLORIA: They can penetrate the fetus. They can do that. They can!

DR. FIORE: Tell me about it.

GLORIA: It's not physical, not in that sense. [*Pauses*] But they can create life. They can change life. They can change life as it's developing. And they can terminate it. But then they can re-create it. [*Pauses*] They don't like termination. They can put it into a temporary status. And then help form its life. Nothing is ever terminated. That's not the whole purpose.

DR. FIORE: When you said, "Oh my God, they know how to incorporate," what did you mean?

GLORIA: Through the mind. They can reach you.

DR. FIORE: What message was there?

GLORIA: That for a while I will not know a lot, but that they would come. They would come again and they would come at the right time. And even then I wouldn't know, but they would help me search, but I would have to come on it myself. I'd have to come on this knowledge myself. They can direct me, but I still have my choice. I felt I was a part of them. [*Pauses*] That's funny, it seems . . . time with them . . . is so much different than time here. Hmm . . . Time here is slowed. It's slowed for a purpose . . . so that we can go through the entire process . . . as our immediate environment, our planet, allows us to. [*Long pause*]

DR. FIORE: Let yourself remember another important encounter.

GLORIA: There's a light. I don't know where it's coming from. [*Pauses*] I'm moving in this light. It's like a magnet. My stomach's upset, just thinking about this.

DR. FIORE: What's happening now?

GLORIA: I'm just moving.

DR. FIORE: What emotions are you feeling?

GLORIA: At first, I didn't know if it was something good I was moving toward. But whatever it was, I was drawn to a light, whether it was good or bad, and I guess it was okay. [*Pauses*] I'm in this room, but it's a room with no doors . . . but you can get in and out of it. It's a white room . . . very, very bright room.

DR. FIORE: What is the shape of the room?

GLORIA: It's like an egg. That's the only way I can describe it.

DR. FIORE: Where is the illumination coming from?

GLORIA: Everywhere, the sides, the top. It's naturally there. It's just there.

DR. FIORE: What are you doing in the room?

GLORIA: I'm reading a book.

DR. FIORE: Tell me about that.

GLORIA: There's this tool in my left hand. They said it was a tool. It looks like it's made of brass. It's light and it's long, but it's shaped like a triangle . . . but it's not sharp. And you have to point it. You have to hold it at a certain angle as you're reading this book. They say it's a learning tool. It helps you to absorb the knowledge that the book has. Now I know why they use the tool. The book isn't written in our alphabet. It's their alphabet.

DR. FIORE: Who are they?

GLORIA: The instructors.

DR. FIORE: What do they look like?

GLORIA: Actually, they're quite funny-looking. They have very, very white skin. It seems that they may be the same height I am. They've got like . . . a large top head, forehead. Like their ears are pressed against their head. You can see like little blue veins, they're so white.

DR. FIORE: What are their eyes like?

GLORIA: They look like Yodas. They almost don't look like they can be real. But they are. They look like a jellyfish. And their eyes are a yellow and a brown, but dark. Big eyes.

DR. FIORE: What shape are their eyes?

GLORIA: They look almost almond, but there's like a variation to them.

DR. FIORE: What is it you're reading? What is the information?

GLORIA: I don't know if you want to call it Arabic or Hebrew or what. But it's scrolled. And then it looks like it has some variations of Greek. It's bizarre.

DR. FIORE: As you read it with that pointer, you're able to understand the message?

GLORIA: Yes.

DR. FIORE: What is the content?

GLORIA: It has to do with learning the truth and avoiding involvement in false beliefs. There's more. Something about . . . the misconception of time. Something about the unacceptance and misconception of time. I can't make it out. I know what it is, but . . . without that tool . . . it's hard. It's almost like I've seen this page of writing before, or I may have studied it before. There's something familiar about it. [*Pauses*] Wherever they are, they want to be teachers . . . or they are teachers. Our time isn't our time. Not the time we think it is. We're not that old.

DR. FIORE: I want you to look around the room. Are you the only person in the room who's reading?

GLORIA: Yes.

DR. FIORE: And how many instructors are there?

GLORIA: Three.

DR. FIORE: And do they all look alike?

GLORIA: Yes. But they're different.

DR. FIORE: What do you mean by that?

GLORIA: They have different personalities, but yet they all help each other. It's like an equal sharing in their knowledge. Almost an enthusiasm, kind of a . . . a happy excitement. [*Long pause*] We just aren't ready to understand or accept, and so it's going to be forced on some.

DR. FIORE: Is that what happened with you?

GLORIA: They don't want me to believe . . . the ways that Man has taught . . . in his various beliefs. They said I know better. That's what the tool is for! I feel like I've been to school. I want to be left alone. I want to finish reading. [*Pauses*] I wish I could remember what they were saying.

DR. FIORE: Now you're going to remember, at the count of three, it will be crystal clear in your mind. One . . . two . . . three.

GLORIA: It's the head instructor. He put his finger on the middle of my forehead. He said that this would protect me. There's just some things that can be understood right now. And he asks if I understood what he was saying. I said, "Yes." Then I said, "I'm so sorry you can't complete your work right now. I'm so sorry that so many people are blinded." But they said that's okay. I feel so bad. They're working so hard. I don't want to leave them. They have to contact you like this. They can't do it any other way . . . not right now.

DR. FIORE: Why is that?

GLORIA: Because of Man.

DR. FIORE: Is this told to you?

GLORIA: No, I know this. Man will fight anything unknown to him. Anything technically advanced, he will take up arms against. They have tried firing a missile at one of the craft.

DR. FIORE: How do you know that?

GLORIA: There was a meeting.

DR. FIORE: What do you mean by that?

GLORIA: Those that are helping them and those that are learning. [Pauses] They won't allow other people to believe that they are real.

DR. FIORE: Who?

GLORIA: Our government, our top officials.

DR. FIORE: Tell me about the meeting.

GLORIA: It was very sad. Very sad. They feel that there are those in higher places, not necessarily good high places, maybe in different planetary structures, who oppose the work of the others. And who assist in the technology of some very destructive machinery. But yet the most destructive is Man himself.

DR. FIORE: When you are talking about this meeting, is this a meeting that you attended?

GLORIA: Yes.

DR. FIORE: Who was in the meeting?

GLORIA: The same instructor and people who have been to his classes. They're learning . . . this is funny . . . they're curious to see how we're advancing. They're curious about how and why we believe. I wanted to bring the tool, because I remembered how good it was, but I couldn't bring it. I thought I had it. Somehow they took it from me. I wanted to bring it, I wanted to show somebody that it was real.

DR. FIORE: Are you in your living room?

GLORIA: I'm sitting on the couch. I can't move. It feels like the air is very thin. Hmmm . . . I can't . . . I wish I could see who was with me.

DR. FIORE: How do you feel?

GLORIA: I was thinking . . . what a really weird dream.

◢

Once back to normal waking consciousness, Gloria leaned forward in the chair, grabbed a tissue and blotted her eyes. "You can't expect them to walk into a room and say, 'Hello, we're here to help you.' Their appearance is far beyond anything that we have physically been accustomed to, much less viewed. They have to do it the way they're doing it now, whether it's through mental telepathy, whether it's through dream states. They just have to do it their way."

"They Go in There
and Dissolve the Damn Clot!"

 "I'm feeling tingly . . . and can't move!" James started hyperventilating, while at the same time he desperately tried to maintain his composure. Within seconds, he arched his back and opened his mouth to bring in as much oxygen as possible.

"You're reliving something important, James. Let's see what it is." I got up and quickly covered him with the blanket as I pushed the chair back to its fullest reclining position in readiness for an hypnotic regression.

James, a darkly handsome physician in his mid-thirties, had sought my help a year before for a drinking problem, which we had actually cleared up in his first session. Since he lived in Southern California, he only flew up as issues arose in his everyday life. During our five visits, we had developed an excellent rapport, and so it was more like two old friends meeting on this occasion rather than a therapist and her patient.

"I guess I'm here to chat more than anything else," he said

smiling shyly. "Everything's going very well. And I'm feeling good." He talked about his use of innovative healing methods, especially electric acupressure, and his tremendous success with them.

When I had begun to describe some of the ways the extraterrestrials had healed my patients' physical symptoms, suddenly he had tensed his body and had begun to gasp for air. Some buried memory was being exhumed . . . and fast, leading me to cut short my hypnotic induction and immediately regress him to the cause of his reaction.

*

JAMES: [*Body tenses*] I feel this intense reaction, but I don't see anything yet.

DR. FIORE: Just tell me everything you're aware of.

JAMES: I'm aware of not being able to move, but I don't know why. [*Body becomes rigid*] This is really strange. . . . I feel like I'm in a metal tank, just lying flat on a metal, like a . . . table. I can see . . . [*Breathing accelerates*] some lights on the side. And . . . the things are there. I can intermittently see their forms and . . . but they're not solid forms. Ah . . . I must be a child. [*Breathing becomes labored*]

DR. FIORE: Tell me everything that's happening.

JAMES: They're moving around. Doing things. I can feel something on my head. A pressure. For a while it was relieved, now it's coming back. [*Body tenses*] I . . . I'm just lying there like a . . . I can't move, but there's something on my head, like a hemisphere over the top part of my head, and it feels like it's clamped on over my maxilla. There's a little firm pressure there. And . . . because I can't move, it's hard to swallow. And . . . [*Sighs*]

DR. FIORE: What emotions are you feeling?

JAMES: Fear. But I know nothing bad is going to happen. And I know I don't belong there. Confusion is the only word . . . the single word. And I feel both a terrible fear and a calmness simultaneously. They're doing something to my head. [*Sighs*] And I don't know whether it's energy going in. My nose is really stuffy. There's something in my nose. Now I've read these reports also, but there's something in my nose. Son of a bitch put something in my nose! Right up my nose! I'm afraid to move. [*Long pause*] They're . . . Ahaa . . . It's like an energy transfer. [*Gags*] Doesn't hurt, but I can't move my head and I can't move my body, dammit! It's kind of like . . . [*Sighs*] Okay . . . They're zapping me. There's a needle in my nose and there's energy going through that. It's as if . . . Oh Jeez . . . My frontal lobe is like . . . alive . . . the area where my frontal lobe is. [*Long pause. Body relaxes*] Now I'm feeling very calm.

DR. FIORE: Let yourself know what happened just before you became calm.

JAMES: My nose is really stuffy. [*Pauses*] The energy's stopped. The needle's out. My . . . the front part of my head is just . . . it feels alive. It's really strange. They're moving around. They're not in my vision very easily. I can feel them more than hear them or see them, but they're moving around at a control panel right over my head. They changed some switches. [*Sighs*] I . . . I feel like I'm about five or six years old, but I kind of know I'm a little older, it's really strange. Maybe eight is what I'd say. Maybe this has happened a couple of times. I can see my feet there. They're little boy's feet. I think I'm in my underwear. It's kind of embarrassing. Even though I don't have all my clothes on, it's not cold. It's just a reasonable temperature. And these things are . . . they look green. The color they emit is green, but they don't have a solid form. It's difficult to really see appendages or arms or limbs. They have a head and an oval body . . . but they do have arms. They do manipulate switches. It's very difficult to distinguish facial characteristics.

My memories of this are kind of tainted by pictures I've seen on covers of books, but that's a reasonable depiction, except they're greener, or maybe there's a greener light in the room. Either way . . . very sophisticated panels of lights. My ears are starting to get stuffy. I think there's something in my ears. They've got . . . [*Pauses*] Well, there's some probes in there too, but they feel like they're . . . that's what's keeping me still, I bet. It's like a . . . a . . . probe in each ear that's generating some frequencies that allow me to be alert. But I can't move. [*Pauses*] Hmm . . . That's all, except I'm getting nervous about it again. Something's going to happen here. Hmm . . . They're making a decision about something. It feels like . . . I feel mad because they're making a decision about me. But it's scary too. They're . . . [*Breathing becomes labored*] I have this fear, but I don't know where it's coming from. Something's not right. They're adjusting something. . . . And I think it . . . I think it hurts. It's like a high-frequency sound. I can hear my ears ringing. Maybe it's because my ears and nose are all of a sudden stuffy, but . . . I . . . [*Sighs*] Yes . . . That ringing is hurting me. They're . . . hurting me in my chest now. . . . Something's going into my chest. This is strange. [*Painfully*] Oh God! It's like they're putting needles in both sides of my chest! [*Seems to be in excruciating pain*] Oh . . . guys, I won't move! Ahh! . . . [*In agony*] I don't know what they're doing. I don't know why, but they've got these things in both sides. It's really strange. It doesn't hurt too bad, but it . . . I can feel this sharp pain. I'm afraid to take a deep breath. And it feels like a clamp on my heart. It feels like the strangest damn thing! I didn't know what it was then, but I know what it is now. They've got these needles on either side. It feels like they go right through my body. And . . . they're . . . doing something with them. [*Pauses*] Oh . . . is it a big clamp? It's inside me. Okay . . . it's easing. [*Body relaxes*] I can't tell what they did that for. Dammit! It hurt. Okay, I can breathe again. They're taking them . . . [*Sighs*] Oh . . . I feel a lot better. [*Much more relaxed*] It's really strange. I feel better. I'm just lying there semicomatose. [*Long pause*] I used to get these horrible

headaches when I was a kid. Then they went away, and I think
. . . either I got the headaches or they went away after one of
these treatments. I don't know where that thought came from.

DR. FIORE: Tell me more about the headaches.

JAMES: These headaches that I used to have, which were really, really hard, sharp, pounding headaches. I don't understand
the sequence, but they relate to what they did to me . . . and I
think the headaches went away.

DR. FIORE: Move back to anything that caused them to go
away.

JAMES: [*Chuckles*] I had a dream once. That I was floating over
my backyard. And that dream is as real today as when it happened. And that dream fits in here.

DR. FIORE: Let yourself remember more.

JAMES: I'm being . . . I can see down. I guess I look over the
side. I'm being transported up on kind of a pallet. I don't understand how it happens, but I'm moving. And I can only remember what the earth looked like before. Maybe I'm in a bubble.
I'm going right inside this big thing. Just right up. It looks like
your usual depiction of a spaceship, but it's going right up inside
this opening. There are these people. They're putting it on. It
just kind of moves on its own. They guide it . . . I can't tell,
maybe it's got wheels underneath or something, or they're
carrying it, but it's moving along. I see other carriers like this,
pallets with bubbles over them.

DR. FIORE: Is there anybody there?

JAMES: Yep. People. They're just lying there. They have little
. . . maybe a strange glow to the atmosphere inside there, but
. . . I can move a little bit and look around. Most of them look

like they're dead. [*Laughs nervously*] There're . . . just lying there without moving. . . . They're not too many, but it's hard to tell. I can see three or four immediately around me, but . . . they move these [pallets] in and then they take them out after a while and move them into another room. And . . . hmm, they're going to move mine in next. [*Pauses*] Okay. I'm in this room and I'm lying there flat, and I feel like there's something . . . going in both sides of my back. And they . . . all right, that helmet's back on . . . and . . . [*Laughs*] Yep . . . or is it the middle of my back? I can't tell. But there's a needle there. And it does something, because it hurts. I can't understand what it does. That goes on for a few minutes, and then they stop. And . . . I feel sick afterward. That one kind of aches afterward. The other one's . . . I'm not so sure that they didn't do something with my penis too. I'm a little embarrassed to talk about it. [*Pauses*] I'm sure they did, but I'm . . .

DR. FIORE: What do you think they did?

JAMES: I think they put something in it, like a rod, a little probe, or a needle or something. I don't feel that as much as I kinda . . . know that happened. [*Sighs*] It's so strange. I know those things happened. . . . It's easier for me to see myself sitting back on that little pallet afterward than . . . I guess at the time it was very embarrassing. Because that's the way I feel now.

DR. FIORE: Did they give you an explanation of why they're doing this?

JAMES: [*Pauses*] I don't understand . . . any of that. [*Laughs*] I think the answer is yes, but the whole idea was so embarrassing to me at the time that I kinda . . .

DR. FIORE: What did they say to you?

JAMES: [*Laughs*] I guess they were taking some of my sperm or something, but at the time that thought was so embarrassing to me that I couldn't even integrate it into . . . [*Laughs*] All I can say is, it's embarrassing. [*Laughs loudly*] But that's what they were doing! But I'm not old enough. It doesn't make any sense to me, that's what I keep telling them. [*Chuckles. Long pause*] And then I can see myself back in my room.

DR. FIORE: Let yourself move to the very beginning of the event that was responsible for these terrible headaches that you had as a child.

JAMES: Oh my God! . . . Oh my! . . . [*Whispers*] This is really strange, Edith. I have to give you some background on this. I don't remember how old I was, but . . . I . . . don't know why this pops into my head, but I . . . I tilted a jungle gym over on its side. I was going to be an astronaut, and I got my brother to push it. And the idea was to tumble over. And I smacked my head and had the biggest goose egg you've ever seen. My dad took me that night to a doctor, and he tried to drain it. It was a big prominent thing. Somehow those headaches are related to this. And somehow that . . . helmet . . . was treating that!

DR. FIORE: Let yourself remember exactly what happened when the helmet was put on you. It's now being put on you. Let's take it second by second. Let yourself experience whatever was happening to you.

JAMES: All right. I feel this thing on top of my head. I can kind of see it on either side. And I can feel these little . . . clamps against my cheeks again. [*Pauses*] It's like sound or . . . noise, or . . . I don't understand what's happening. . . .

DR. FIORE: What are you feeling?

JAMES: I had this . . . just tension all over and this . . . this heat, inside my head. Not hot, but . . . [*Body arches*] This goes on for a while . . . leaves me very, very tense. I don't know what happened. I don't know what that was.

DR. FIORE: Was anyone standing near you?

JAMES: I see one or sense one, right over on my right side there. [*Points to his right*] Just . . . kinda reassuring me.

DR. FIORE: What is it saying?

JAMES: Comfort and . . . a sense that I don't need to worry, that everything they're doing is okay. That it's not bad.

DR. FIORE: Do they make any references to your headaches?

JAMES: Definitely. I got the definite . . . it's almost a picture as opposed to a . . . I get this picture in my head of a . . . like a thin film that's covering the . . . top and front of my head, of my brain, and what they're doing is going to dissolve that. I mean, I know that now, but I didn't know that then, but that's the picture that's in my head. [*Sighs*] The treatment was uncomfortable, but not in a painful way. It made me, like tense all my muscles, but . . . afterward I feel better.

❧

James opened his eyes, stretched his arms above his head and sat up eagerly. "Those headaches were terrible! Really heavy duty! Then one day they were just gone. I've never known why. As a physician, I couldn't understand it."

"I think it's fascinating. I'm glad you had a positive experience. There's so much that's frightening in most of the books on abductions. It's rewarding to find these healings being done. Were there many others being worked on?"

"I saw a lot of people on those pallets!"

Since our time was up and the little light on the wall was on, indicating the next patient was waiting, we said our goodbyes. I walked James to the door. A little hesitantly, he extended his hand. Instead of taking it, I gave him a hug. "That's what I wanted," he said with a broad smile as he left.

✦

James called me a week later and said that more material was surfacing, mostly in the form of thoughts. "I think we just looked at the tip of the iceberg last time. Are you up to my flying into San Jose and our spending a couple of hours seeing what else is there?"

I blocked out some time, and it was two weeks later that I saw him next. James wasted no time in getting to the point of our session. "For years, I've been interested in UFOs, especially their purpose in being here. For some reason, I think they're interested in our awareness. Maybe they want massive crystal deposits. A friend of mine thinks they're after our fresh water, but I think it's not that simple."

"You said in your call that things are surfacing? What's been coming up since last time?"

"Nothing at all clear. Mostly dreams at night about UFOs that I can't remember. I guess it's a knowing that more has happened to me than we got during our last session."

"Let's check it out."

James slipped into hypnosis easily and quickly. I knew by now that he didn't let himself go into a profound trance, but, even though his conscious mind was right there analyzing, he let the subconscious material come to the surface with no resistance. I asked him to remember the close encounter that had had the greatest impact on him and counted to ten, with instructions to say out loud whatever came into his mind.

✦

JAMES: I have this image of people or things in the rooms of our house. And it just suddenly struck me that they've been there and I didn't realize it. They look gray and they're maybe five feet tall. And they have oval heads and oval bodies and . . . they're not, you don't see them . . . I kind of wonder if you woke up and looked you wouldn't even see them. It's really strange, they're almost not physical when you're conscious. Or maybe they don't come when you're conscious.

DR. FIORE: What are they doing?

JAMES: Standing there, in two lines with me in the middle.

DR. FIORE: What room are they in?

JAMES: In the bedroom.

DR. FIORE: In the house you live in currently?

JAMES: Yes, we just moved in six months ago. It's a very uncomfortable feeling, but I don't know why.

DR. FIORE: Just keep reporting whatever comes into your mind.

JAMES: I feel trapped, like I can't move. And I keep telling them I don't want to go. [*Pauses*] I don't understand whether it's real or a dream, but it seems like we just move right through the walls. I feel like I'm on a pallet. I'm in kind of a semiconscious state. But the strangest thing is that I'm not sure that my whole form leaves.

DR. FIORE: What do you mean by that?

JAMES: I don't think my physical form goes with them. I think it's lying there in the bed.

DR. FIORE: Take a look and see.

JAMES: No. It's not there. The bed's empty. I mean, my wife is there, but I'm not. I don't think I've been drugged, but narcotized in some way that I feel like I'm floating, but when I look at the bed, I'm not there. [*Pauses*] Okay . . . I'm going out the door . . . and into that big ship that's sitting out over the trees. I don't understand why people can't see that.

DR. FIORE: Now what happens? Tell me step by step.

JAMES: The door opens. I'm being carried in some way. It's as if I've been drugged. . . . It's not drugged, it's done with a . . . some method that leaves you incapacitated. It's a vibrational . . . device that . . . I think it takes two of them pointed at you in a certain . . . it kind of paralyzes you and leaves you feeling . . . helpless, and . . . there's no will to resist. You might as well have been intoxicated with a drug. And I feel like I'm being kind of carried. I guess they open the door. But the entranceway to the ship is kind of conventional. At least it's what you've always seen in the movies. It's kind of a ramp that's lowered, and you just go right up in the center. [*Pauses*] We're sitting . . . [*Laughs*] Strange . . . I feel like I'm sitting at a table having a discussion about our . . . I think they want to understand how we think. Maybe this is where this thought came from. I was sitting one day and had the strongest thought that these people want to contact us, but they're concerned that we're going to self-destruct if they make themselves really . . . manifest. I think that's the point of the discussion.

DR. FIORE: See if you can remember it, word by word, or thought by thought. [*Pauses*] Just report whatever comes into your mind.

JAMES: It feels like I'm sitting there trying to describe the difficulties of introducing ideas of extraordinary change into our culture. It's what I see in our day-to-day lives anyway. It's as if this one alien individual wants to . . . is arguing in favor of becoming manifest to humankind, and the other is saying, "No, they'll retaliate or perceive us as dangerous and would resort to nuclear weapons." He says he can't understand a culture that would live that way. [*Laughs*]

DR. FIORE: What is your role in this discussion?

JAMES: I'm trying to explain the way people think.

DR. FIORE: How do you feel now that you're there? At first you were resistant, taken against your will. How do you feel now?

JAMES: [*Laughs*] Halfway in awe of the situation, I mean of the . . . extraordinary uniqueness of sitting in this environment of a complex machine from another, I assume, planet. And also the awesome responsibility of both trying to explain how we are in terms that will . . . allow . . . I feel like a negotiator. The awesome responsibility of a negotiator.

DR. FIORE: How many beings are in this discussion?

JAMES: I'm kind of focused on two aliens and myself, but there are more people at the table. But they're in kind of a trance. They're just sitting there. They're not actively participating. I get the feeling they get as much information from the mental information as the words. But the other people are just sitting there. It's not an open debate or discussion. They're communicating one at a time.

DR. FIORE: When you say people, are there other human beings?

JAMES: Humans, yes. I think there are four or five. And there are two main people or aliens that I talked to. They're gray skinned and they have the same basic structure that we do, but they're not . . . they're different. There's no neck. It's hard for me to separate their head from their body. [*Becomes tense*] I get the strongest feeling that . . . difficulty in trusting these people. That's . . . without being able to discuss it with my colleagues, it's as if there's a panel, but I feel like I'm being interrogated, not in a bad way, but, I feel tremendous . . . [*Squirms*] There's both good and bad that's at stake here in terms of the discussion. They're probing for weaknesses, at the same time they're probing for the strength to communicate.

DR. FIORE: What do you feel in your body? I notice you're squirming.

JAMES: I can't explain it. I don't know. Fear. I feel like . . . [*Labored breathing*] I guess I was getting kind of irritated and began to show anger, and they . . . they won't deal with that. The way they handle that is to put you back into that . . . state of . . . whatever. You can't move. It's as if you're being strapped down, but you're not, literally. You feel enclosed in something. I think that's how they take you back to the . . . I feel like it's a tube. And then. . . . I wake up in bed. It's really strange.

DR. FIORE: How do you feel when you wake up?

JAMES: Relaxed and . . . they must do something when you're in that tube.

DR. FIORE: Let's go back into that tube. Let yourself remember, at the count of three. One . . . two . . . three.

JAMES: Okay. The whole tube is sitting on a table. There's like a cover, just goes from top to bottom. And afterward you feel . . . kind of recharged. I mean, it's not a bad feeling at all. That's the feeling you're left with, and . . . while I'm in bed, it's really difficult to remember.

DR. FIORE: Let's see if you were given any suggestions or commands not to remember.

JAMES: There's somebody standing again, at the top, just off to the side of whatever that thing is that goes over you. I get the feeling he's being very reassuring and almost talking as if he's talking to a child and telling him how important it is that nobody knows about the discussions.

DR. FIORE: Did he explain why it's important?

JAMES: He just says they wouldn't understand. [*Pauses*] This guy's someone I've spoken with several times. His name begins with an *M*. He's got a funny name.

DR. FIORE: You're going to let yourself remember his name at the count of three. One . . . two . . . three.

JAMES: Mogwan. That's the name M-O-G-W-A-N. I get the strangest feeling about the shape. I don't understand why I have so many images of their shape, unless they're . . . different. Maybe they're different. . . . This one has more of a physical form than some of them I've talked to, like at the conference table. I don't know if they're different. . . .

DR. FIORE: Could they have been wearing anything that obscured their physical form?

JAMES: That would certainly make sense.

DR. FIORE: I want you to remember. Something that obscures their body. Look at the one that doesn't have a neck, for instance.

JAMES: It's interesting, because even this fellow, this Mog fellow. I can see his lower body and his legs, but his . . . he's got kind of like a halo. It's almost as if it's a hat that extends down like a shield. Goes up above his head a bit and then down. It's like an arch he's wearing on his head. Because I can see his feet. I mean he's got kind of spindly feet and toes, and his fingers are a little longer . . . his hands are a little longer than ours. And I'm not so sure if they have only three, or four, fingers.

DR. FIORE: Take a look.

JAMES: They have three fingers.

DR. FIORE: Let yourself remember if they have given you help as to techniques to use in healing people.

JAMES: It's in the ship. [*Pauses*] They use kind of a plate, or maybe a . . . [*Pauses*] It's like a big U. And you can select the frequencies. They have both a plate and a big U. The U they use for the extremities and the plate . . . I feel like I'm sitting there in a chair discussing this stuff.

DR. FIORE: Did they demonstrate it? Or did they just tell you?

JAMES: They're demonstrating it on somebody. First an alien and now a human. What you can do is you pick up the . . . [*Pauses*] Oh, no wonder! You . . . [*Laughs*] On the screen, like a beautiful . . . television screen, you can see the different energy channels, just like they're interspersed with arteries and veins. It's like our MRI, except it shows not only tissues, it shows the energy channels, and they're . . . graphically depicted. Where they're weak, you can see the multicolors, and . . . and the ones that are . . . not flowing well, you can actually stimulate with selected frequencies. Very interesting. [*Pauses*] The incredible thing is how you can do this same thing with . . . I mean that's the key to . . . [*Pause*] We've been doing that for a long time with . . . [*Long pause*]

DR. FIORE: What are you talking about?

JAMES: Repairing those energy channels, or . . . there're techniques present now that have been handed down for such a long time. Acupuncture techniques, for example. But they've got techniques that allow you to . . . put that graphically right up on the screen.

DR. FIORE: Did they explain why they are showing you this?

JAMES: There's something that makes me very nervous about this. I think they're asking for something in exchange and I can't figure out what it is.

DR. FIORE: You're going to let yourself remember it. It's crystal clear in your mind. At the count of three. One . . . two . . . three.

JAMES: They want me to use it to . . .

DR. FIORE: They want you to what?

JAMES: They want to show me the control techniques. And I refuse.

DR. FIORE: Why do you do that?

JAMES: Because they want to use it to . . . subvert our population.

DR. FIORE: Let's go back to what they're teaching you that you are able to understand and perhaps use. Are you learning anything new from them?

JAMES: No question. It's a synthesis of ideas. But maybe it's a demonstration of how those ideas can work. In the situation I described, I think they have it, where we . . . can use it both for healing and also for control. And it's really . . . not the same techniques, but they're different applications. And it's not automatic. [Pauses] I don't understand the anxiety that this provokes, but it . . . [Pauses] I'm refusing to do something.

DR. FIORE: What is that?

JAMES: [*Pauses*] They want me to help them in some way, but I can't figure out exactly what they want. It's kinda like they're saying, "We've shown you what good this will bring your people," but there's something else I can't put my finger on that they want me to agree to.

DR. FIORE: You're going to let yourself remember at the count of three. It's very easy to remember. One . . . two . . . three. First thoughts.

JAMES: They want me to do some work with a really innocuous looking device that enhances their ability to . . . communicate.

DR. FIORE: Do you feel any anxiety when they propose this?

JAMES: Yes, because I'm not sure what their real intent is, whether it's to . . . [*Pauses*] It's a real conflict in that there's a lot of good to be shared, but also you have to be careful to not just accept the whole thing immediately, because it's not clear what their whole intent is. I just have concern that they're no different than we are in terms of different factions. And while the stated purpose may appear peaceful, there might be other motives involved. Just a simple-looking device that they claim would enhance our ability to see and communicate with them more easily. Maybe that's what they're wearing. This thing is kind of like a cone. And it emits that same kind of whitish glow.

DR. FIORE: And how do you deal with this, as they're proposing this to you? Do they want to give you one of these devices? Do they want to teach you how to make it?

JAMES: The latter. I don't know if they want to teach me or if they're asking my thoughts on how to get it accepted. If it were available. This is really strange. Marketing their device. [*Laughs*] It's not a direct question to me, but I'm aware that that's what they want. I guess I'm not in the main part of the discussion about that. I'm not brought into that. But I can see one of these things sitting there, and I know what it does. Not that it happens immediately. It's kind of like some kind of . . . stimulator, and it does that by frequency emissions.

DR. FIORE: Did they discuss any illnesses with you? For instance, did they discuss AIDS?

JAMES: Not specifically. It's more in terms of demonstrating what it takes to support these deficient [energy] systems. And I'm not really sure [whether] the thoughts that question brings to mind are directly discussed or secondary to the work I've been able to do with . . . you know, greater understanding of what's happening with people. But the work that they do . . . clearly shows an effort to support deficient systems at the same time that they try to remove the cause of the deficiency, the irritant factor, replacing the deficiency. I get the feeling that's a secondary observation, using the increased awareness.

DR. FIORE: Let yourself go back in time and space to any meeting that you had with them in which they instructed you or gave you some understanding of the body, health, disease. At the count of five. One . . . two . . . three . . . four . . . five. Just report whatever comes into your mind, whatever you're aware of.

JAMES: It's the same kind of meeting room.

DR. FIORE: Tell me all about it, how many people are there, who's there, what beings are there?

JAMES: Basically, two alien beings. [*Pauses*] One is an expert on diseases and health. And on the screen they're showing the diagrams of the studies that they've obtained on people. Different, what we call, disease states. As these people talk, what they say begins to explain centuries of concepts, more in an Eastern sense of medicine, in terms of energy flows. But the really intriguing thing is that the diagrams can demonstrate right on the screen how the energy flow changes through different organ systems with just various exposures of materials. [*Seems anxious*]

DR. FIORE: Are you feeling any anxiety right now?

JAMES: Yes, but I'm not sure why.

DR. FIORE: You're remembering everything that's happening. You're sitting there and you're seeing them change the energy flow, using different substances.

JAMES: The diagram shows how, in a very graphic way, with someone just lying there, exposures to different materials can cause changes in energy flow in our system and how that begins to happen long before the material begins to enter our physical frame. How you begin to react to things across the room.

DR. FIORE: Can you give me an example from what they showed you?

JAMES: They're bringing a plant that emits a strange perfume. [*Body tenses*]

DR. FIORE: What are you feeling in your body right now?

JAMES: I feel a lot of anxiousness.

DR. FIORE: Is anything being done to you?

JAMES: I think it brings up the memory of when this was done to me, when I'm watching.

DR. FIORE: Let yourself remember what was done to you.

JAMES: When I was young . . . [*Cries*] . . . I can remember being so scared. [*Shaking*] In the tube . . . I thought it was a coffin. I thought I was dead. I couldn't get out. I wakened and lay there for a while, afraid to scream. [*Panicking*] Ah! . . . Ah! . . . One of them's touching me on the head! Oh! . . . Their skin looks like it would feel so slimy. Ah! . . . Ah! . . . Okay . . . He's trying to soothe me. It's a he. I don't know why I know that. The words are strange, but what they say is, they're not there to hurt me. [*Pauses*] Ah! . . . [*Choking*] They needed . . . to help make it better. Talking about that accident I described before. And they were afraid to . . . totally sedate me because . . . they weren't sure how bad the damage was. And that's why I woke up. And they're sorry, that it frightened me. [*Pauses*] We've been so conditioned by the movies to be afraid and to fear them, and they're not very appealing in the usual sense of what appeals to us without their . . . mask on, they're frightful! [*Voice shakes*] Okay . . . I figure, if they were going to hurt me, they would have, so I just . . . slowly begin to relax. I think the machines they have now are much better. They look more modern than the ones they had thirty years ago.

DR. FIORE: Continue to speak out.

JAMES: I've been moved to the table again. . . . When I look at this person on the table, I can remember being there myself, and I try and tell myself that they're not going to hurt them. It's just so scary, so strange, so frightening. It doesn't really hurt. It's cold . . . my arms and legs are gently strapped in so I won't move and writhe around. That thing's back on my head, I remember that. I think that damn thing's a coaxial laser. And they go in there and dissolve the damn clot. I can't believe it! [*Sighs*] It takes a long time . . . you gotta lie there in this thing. It's pinned to my head. First they scan to see the size and location. Then there's two beams, and when they cross, it creates heat at that exact location. And it takes a long time, because as it dissolves the clot, gasses form, and they don't want to obstruct the blood flow. So, in essence, what they're doing is speeding up the process that would occur naturally, by removing the pressure much more quickly than it would have happened. And they don't have to cut, he says, because there was no immediate danger. Just to keep the pressure off. [*Pauses*]

DR. FIORE: How is this being done? Is he explaining it to you?

JAMES: Yes.

DR. FIORE: Does he explain the coaxial laser, for example? Does he use these terms?

JAMES: No. Just says that there's some beams of light that'll help take care of things. I didn't understand it before, but it makes sense now. They rotate around this big circular frame. And they stop and scan. And he's saying something about the front part of humans' brains. He says you barely have enough room to expand in there as it is, without having this extra stuff. I don't understand. They're kind of laughing. Two or three of them are laughing about that. [*Long pause*] I saw a picture of a mouse in the newspaper that they had transplanted some of the human immune system into for research, and that's what's happened to us. They're doing it to us to reproduce some problems that they've got, so that they can study ways to treat it. [*Flinches*]

DR. FIORE: What are you feeling in your body right now?

JAMES: I don't want them to take my arm. I'm holding on to my belt, so they can't take my arm. I don't want . . . I think they're going to inject something into me.

DR. FIORE: Is this happening to you as a child or as an adult?

JAMES: I think it's as a child. [*Shaking*] I'm not sure. I think it happened before, but it's . . . won't do it again. . . . [*Struggling*]

DR. FIORE: When is this happening?

JAMES: It's happening recently.

DR. FIORE: Tell me everything that you're aware of.

JAMES: I don't know what it was. They took some blood and also gave me something.

DR. FIORE: Did they give you an explanation?

JAMES: Yes.

DR. FIORE: What did they say?

JAMES: They want to know how I survived. [*Pauses*] An inoculation from twenty years ago.

DR. FIORE: Remember everything that they're telling you. Are they implying that you should not have survived that inoculation?

JAMES: Yes.

DR. FIORE: Did they explain why?

JAMES: Because it kills their people. And they had to see if the theories were right on the combined forms. [*Relaxes*]

DR. FIORE: What happened just then?

JAMES: I relaxed, and the whole thing started to make sense.

DR. FIORE: Tell me about it.

JAMES: The sedative they gave you has kind of a hallucinatory effect. It's like a mind-expander. But I think that some of us are humans . . . and aliens combined. And the ones that develop close enough to be accepted in the society get implanted.

DR. FIORE: So they need to make sure that the virus would not kill this hybrid, is that it?

JAMES: Yes. And the hybrid's really the . . . combination of the parents. But it has . . . some significant pieces added so that it'll represent the vulnerable portions of the aliens . . . what they think is the vulnerable portion in their immune systems. And they're trying to figure out how our system can adapt to it. [*Pauses*] Because their race isn't able to. [*Long pause*]

DR. FIORE: Speak out whatever comes into your mind.

JAMES: And they run correlations on so many factors that affect energy flow. And they've looked at the heavy metals. It looks like a debate . . . the research being worthless because of cofactors on the planet, the heavy-metal cofactors being one that they can't control for in their experiment. [*Laughs*] I get this image of this one . . . younger researcher trying to explain to the professor, if you will, the director of the project, that that is invalid because the subject is so contaminated.

DR. FIORE: Are these aliens having the debate?

JAMES: Yes. They're standing in the conference room, and they had been asking me about what our awareness of heavy-metal exposures is. And I told them that wasn't an area that I was really expert on. He didn't explain it to me, but it seems like it screwed up his data, that's all. [*Laughs*] I don't know why I find it comical, but maybe it's a scene you could see anywhere, in any society.

DR. FIORE: Before, you were telling me about how we could be affected by things that did not enter into our physical frame, and I asked you for an example and you told me about a plant emitting an odor from across the room. Will you go back to when this was being explained to you?

JAMES: Somebody's lying on the table and . . .

DR. FIORE: Human?

JAMES: A human. And they're being scanned. And that scan's graphically depicted in terms of the energy channels, the support structures are barely visible. The bones and tissues are like a faint outline or a background on a piece of paper, but the energy systems are graphically depicted. I guess they can do this on a limb, but not as well through the whole body, because I don't see the whole-body scans. Maybe it's too hard to put together, but when the material is brought closer to the patient, as it gets closer, one of the systems fades, as if the energy flow is not continuing as strong as it was before. It was already not as intense in terms of the intact systems represented by a nice bright color.

DR. FIORE: What colors do you see?

JAMES: Red, blue, yellow. It's the yellow one going out of this one. There's green.

DR. FIORE: You said yellow is fading?

JAMES: Yes, in this system, I don't know why.

DR. FIORE: Do you see all those same colors in the same area?

JAMES: No, they're separate. They're like cables. You can think of them as cables of different colors.

DR. FIORE: What is being explained to you? Are they demonstrating on this person?

JAMES: Yes, they're showing how different materials natural to our environment can both help and . . . it's almost as if they're demonstrating the impact of a concentrated material versus the dilution of a material. That in the natural form it may be harmful, and someone very sensitive to it in a naturally occurring concentration reacts very strongly, but if you deliver [it] in an extremely diluted dose, it has a strengthening effect as opposed to a weakening one.

DR. FIORE: Does that make sense to you?

JAMES: It does based on what I've seen subsequently.

DR. FIORE: Do they explain what is wrong with that person lying there?

JAMES: Liver.

DR. FIORE: What do they say has happened to him?

JAMES: He's dying of inflammation of the liver. And that system has become so weakened that even exposures to materials that you normally wouldn't consider toxic, he's reacting to.

DR. FIORE: Such as?

JAMES: Looks like a cactus plant.

DR. FIORE: Did they demonstrate anything else?

JAMES: They're going to use synthetically generated energy forms to treat it. I guess the question is, can they resolve this episode? But they're not sure they can. What they're asking me is why don't they stay stable?

DR. FIORE: What do you say?

JAMES: I told them it looks like the cofactors they were talking about. I'm not so sure that the virus is the problem. They don't like hearing that either.

DR. FIORE: What do they say then?

JAMES: They tell me, what would I know, I'm just a human.

DR. FIORE: How do you feel when they say that?

JAMES: I try to keep from laughing, because it's the same thing I hear from my fellow humans. [*Laughs*] I keep trying to tell them I'm not so sure there's so many differences, but they don't want to hear that.

DR. FIORE: How do you know that they don't want to hear that?

JAMES: Maybe they choose to ignore it. [*Laughs*] I just draw some glances of reproach. I'm expected to sit there quietly, I should be seen and not heard, that's it. [*Laughs*] So I'm sitting there in this chair at this table. There's a group of aliens, and there are several humans interspersed. Experts from various fields, people who have become experts in various fields that are part . . . alien, also. And by that, I don't mean they look like that, but they've got some common . . . as if they were once part of a big experiment, but the magnitude of the problem is such that they now need input, even from the experimental subjects. And they're really uptight about it.

DR. FIORE: Who's uptight?

JAMES: The aliens. I mean this is a high-priority project. And humor has no place in it, I'm told, especially from a human. And I can tell that's coming from the head of the table. It's a very authoritative comment from one of the aliens in charge. I don't know if he's in charge of the project as much as he's some kind of representative overseeing, inspecting the project. But I can tell from the glances of the other aliens that they're not in total support of his assertion that the problem isn't the cofactors, as we refer to it. On their own planet. [*Pauses*] But I guess I feel comfortable enough to . . . slip that in. It doesn't bring as much fear as it might have at one time.

DR. FIORE: What's happening to the sick person?

JAMES: It looks like he's going to die after all. They're not having as much success reversing it as they anticipated. He looks very sick, both physically and on the screen with the colors.

DR. FIORE: Do you think he might die right there on the ship?

JAMES: Yes. I've never seen that before, so it was hard for me to imagine that, but it's creating a big consternation. Some problem with getting him back. And explaining the whole issue, that creates a big problem. They don't understand why the usual reversal techniques aren't working. They ask me if I had any ideas. That's one reason I'm there. [*Pauses*] I feel a tension at the moment . . . just like I would if I were standing in front of my own colleagues trying to solve the problem. [*Laughs*] I keep telling them to get the congestion out of his liver, but I don't think we can do it. It's as if you're watching the whole system start to fail. This one's dying.

DR. FIORE: What happened to the colors you were talking about?

JAMES: They went out.

DR. FIORE: Are there any colors left, anything at all?

JAMES: Not on the screen, maybe the faintest . . .

DR. FIORE: Can you still see his bones faintly?

JAMES: Yes, the tissues are all there, the thing I'm referring to are those conduits. They look like conduits. You know, it's a graphic representation. So they look like pipes.

DR. FIORE: And what happened to them? Are the colors gone?

JAMES: Yes. There's some faintly glowing red, and maybe this light is blue, the yellow's just flicker, flicker, and then it went out. It was kinda just like watching a light bulb burn out. It wasn't ever that bright, but it's just the same thing. They don't go out totally. Maybe they're smoldering, but this guy was in bad shape to begin with.

DR. FIORE: What is the reaction of the aliens? Are they looking at the screen?

JAMES: Yes. There's a lot of disappointment and also a lot of maneuvering to figure out who's going to take care of the disposal [*Laughs*] . . . of what they consider to be a contaminated form. I mean, they think that thing is contagious. Somehow they've got a waste-disposal problem. [*Laughs*] And ideally they put it back in the place where they got it, but they're not so sure they can. . . . some transport problems because the . . . [*Laughs*] Nobody wants to be involved with a contaminated human form. In terms of taking it back. So there's a little bit of a . . . it turns into a . . . chain-of-command issue. He's back in the tube and back on the pallet. I'm not standing right there as they do this, but I know it's happening. And you've got a . . . a detail. To take it back.

DR. FIORE: They're concerned about their image?

JAMES: Two things. One, they're concerned about the apparent failure of the project and the techniques to reverse the different systems, and . . . the first thing that came into my mind was that they're concerned that they were involved, being involved with somebody who died . . . It's almost like a political event. I mean, they didn't do this, but they are very worried that they would be perceived as doing this. I get the feeling that there's two groups kind of negotiating. With . . . humans as a people. [*Pauses*] They're both demonstrating their technical prowess and also their goodwill. I think one group has generally got goodwill. I'm not so sure about the other. I mean, in terms of its impact on us.

DR. FIORE: What happens to the meeting? What happens with you?

JAMES: I'm taken back also.

DR. FIORE: When did this happen?

JAMES: I think this happened two or three months ago.

DR. FIORE: Were you given any instructions or commands that you would not remember?

JAMES: The usual.

DR. FIORE: What are the usual?

JAMES: I feel like I'm sitting in a little cubicle. And it's kind of an automated process now. I think they used to do this individually, but it's a combination of lights and sounds and like a posthypnotic suggestion to . . . or some kind of suggestion to wipe the memories out of the easy-access part of my memory. As well as the fact that if I do bring them up, if I do share them, there could be recriminations. I think that's part of the anxiety I feel as I go through talking about some of this.

DR. FIORE: Do you feel that the recriminations would be against you or them?

JAMES: I never thought about that. What they leave me with is the feeling it would hit on me. It seems like the relationship is much more relaxed, and this is almost a formality now, the suggestion part, but it leaves me feeling very anxious in discussing it.

DR. FIORE: Tell me how you were going back.

JAMES: I feel like I'm sitting in a chair. Some kind of a bubble. [*Pauses*]

DR. FIORE: And what happens?

JAMES: I get out and I'm led by one individual who accompanied me, maybe he was driving or steering or whatever you do to this thing. It kind of glides or floats. It's really strange. But I'm in kind of a buzzed-out state, so it's really hard for me to remember those details well. I might even be undergoing that suggestion period while we're moving, so it's really difficult for me to even be aware of what's happening. God, that craft is huge.

DR. FIORE: How big is it?

JAMES: Two blocks.

DR. FIORE: What shape is it?

JAMES: It looks oblong. I mean it is big! I can't understand why we can't see it.

DR. FIORE: Does it have any lights on it?

JAMES: Not now, because it's really close to the city, to the populated area. I get the feeling that I've seen multicolored lights.

DR. FIORE: Where were they?

JAMES: Around the perimeter on the bottom. It's kind of like a big elongated oval shape. And it's as if there are windows on the bottom as well as on the sides. And the lights are not directly on the very bottom, but kind of halfway between the two. I don't understand. Maybe what you see is the lights from inside coming through those windows, I don't know.

DR. FIORE: What brings you home?

JAMES: A small, round-shaped craft of some kind. It's got kind of a clear canopy in front. It's not very big.

DR. FIORE: How many people does it hold?

JAMES: I think there's just one driver, one flier. It's hard for me to tell because we're kind of in the front. I don't think it's very big.

DR. FIORE: And now what happens?

JAMES: It lands in the backyard. And I am kind of led because I'm in a semiawake state. I'm led back to my door. The doors open and they wait there while I get in bed.

DR. FIORE: Do they go into the house with you or just wait there?

JAMES: Just wait at the door. Just one.

DR. FIORE: Can they see you go into the bedroom from the door?

JAMES: Oh yes. There's a door from our bedroom. My wife stirs. And it's like he . . . he does something that kinda . . . I don't know if he's got a device in his hand or something. . . .

My wife's always complaining I don't sleep anymore. She's always saying I'm up all the time at night, that I never sleep all the way through the night. [*Laughs*] She's right more than she knows.

James came out of hypnosis and was fully alert, even though he'd been hypnotized for almost two hours. He immediately started to chuckle. "My wife has really been complaining about me waking her up, and she's a light sleeper. I wonder if she'll believe me?"

"Does she believe in UFOs? Almost half of Americans do, according to a recent Gallup poll."

"She believes in them, but this is pretty far out. I think she's ready for it, though." James glanced at his watch. "My flight leaves in about an hour, I'll have to go. I'd love to be able to run some of this by you, but I don't think USAir will hold the plane for me," he said, laughingly. A quick hug and he was gone.

I opened the sliding glass door to my redwood deck and breathed in some fresh air and watched a few leaves floating down the trickle of a creek. A bad drought had almost dried it up. I was savoring our session and wanted to skim through it again before my next patient arrived. I enjoyed James's sense of humor in the midst of such seriousness. I could just visualize him slouched down in his seat at the conference table, stifling a chuckle and making mental comparisons with the power ploys that go on at board meetings on Earth. I could imagine the silencing frown of the alien at his unwelcome observations. It had been a particularly intriguing session for me and one that I knew would benefit James in many, many ways.

"They Take My Eggs!"

 "My top priority is to lose weight. I've lost as much as ninety-five pounds at one time. Of course, I gained it all back. Last year I took off sixty pounds and regained thirty-five . . . twenty in the last two months."

Victoria, an artist in her mid-fifties, sought my help for her lifelong weight problem. Her five-feet-four-inch body was about 150 pounds too heavy.

During our first session, we covered the important areas of her life; her marriage with its frustrations, the lack of sex for many years and her struggle as an artist. Before she left, I made her a tape to use as she drifted off to sleep, suggesting that the healing force within her be mobilized to resolve her many difficulties.

I used hypnosis with Victoria in each of our next few visits and found that she was an excellent hypnotic subject. She went into a deep level of hypnosis readily and very easily established rapid and clear finger signals.

Victoria sailed into my office for our fourth session with a big smile on her face and radiating an aura of self-confidence. "I've lost eight pounds in the last two weeks. There's a real change in my way of eating. I've cut out the snack in the evening . . . and I'm not picking in between meals. I'm delighted! It's never been so easy!"

After she had been hypnotized for ten minutes and we had come to the end of our work on her weight problem, I followed a hunch and asked her subconscious mind if she had had any close encounters with extraterrestrials. Her "yes" finger popped up immediately. By a twenty-questions approach, I found that she had had a total of three close encounters of the fourth kind, the first when she was only five years old. We had time for one regression before the end of the session so I asked her inner mind to take her back to the very first encounter.

✦

VICTORIA: I'm floating, but I'm floating fast. [*Pauses*] I didn't know anything could go this fast. I'm zooming out.

DR. FIORE: Tell me more.

VICTORIA: It's real light. Real bright. All I can see is a bright light . . . and I'm just spinning. I feel like I'm spinning around and around and around. And I feel like there's something there. Something's looking at me. They're watching me, but I can't see them. This bright light's there. It's there, it's so white and I'm just spinning, and they say, "It's okay, it's okay. We're not going to hurt you. It's okay." But I can't see anything, I'm just spinning. Now we're going zooming back. I feel like I'm going backward. [*Long pause*] I'm slowing down. [*Pauses*] This hand, I think it's a hand, it touches my shoulder . . . and . . . Ah! I've slowed down and I've stopped. [*Pauses*] I'm sleeping now at home, in my bed.

DR. FIORE: You're going to remember the very beginning of this experience. Let's see where you were just before it began.

VICTORIA: I'm looking out the window at the stars. And this one star comes down. It just comes down. It just gets bigger . . . and it comes down. And I'm saying, "Twinkle, twinkle little star." [*Long pause*] But it gets bigger. It's a big star! And I just keep watching it. And now the light's real bright. Real bright.

DR. FIORE: Where is the light?

VICTORIA: At my window. And I go to the light.

DR. FIORE: How do you do that?

VICTORIA: I just kind of went. It just kind of drew me there, because it was so bright. I can't go through that window. It's closed. [*Pauses*] They opened the window.

DR. FIORE: Tell me about that.

VICTORIA: The window opened and I climbed out. I didn't fall. I just climbed out. And then we went zooming. That's when I started zooming.

DR. FIORE: Who are they? Tell me about them.

VICTORIA: I don't know who they are.

DR. FIORE: But you said that they went with you. Who are they?

VICTORIA: The people in the bright light.

DR. FIORE: What do they look like?

VICTORIA: Shadowy. Tall . . . and shadowy.

DR. FIORE: How many would you say there are?

VICTORIA: A lot.

DR. FIORE: What do you mean by that?

VICTORIA: They stand around me in a circle. That's why I keep going in a circle. They keep spinning me around and looking at me. They've got real round heads. And they don't have any hair. But they don't hurt you, they just look at you. They don't hurt you. You don't have to be afraid. [*Pauses*] "You'll think it was a dream." That's what she said. "You'll just think it was a dream." And she puts her hand on my shoulder . . . and I'm in bed. [*Long pause*]

*

I counted Victoria back to the present and, after giving her suggestions for well-being, brought her out of her trance. I asked her how she felt, because I didn't want her to leave my office still partially in a trance.

"Real kind of light. Real calm. Really peaceful."

"Have you read any books on UFOs?"

"Never. I've never read any on the subject . . . I'm so surprised!"

I reminded her that her finger signals had indicated she'd had a total of three experiences and told her that we would have to explore each one. "It's important that we deal with all buried traumas. So many times these events cause problems and anxieties in people's lives. Think of them as thorns in your flesh. We need to pull them out."

She nodded with the smile of an adventurer and, at the same time, an expression of reluctance that silently said, "I wish I didn't have to."

*

One week later, Victoria filled me in on some background material that seemed to support the probability that she had been abducted as a child. She told of waking up more than once watching a star change colors. Then it would seem that it didn't change any longer, and she'd go back to bed.

Suddenly she burst out, "They own me! My body belongs to them, not me." Tears rolled down her face. "That's why I hate my body!" She leaned forward and angrily yanked a tissue out of the box. Drying her eyes and wiping her nose and cheeks, she added, "I've been fighting an inner battle all week long. It seems that forces are pulling in each direction. I've been concentrating on surrounding myself with the white light and telling them . . . and me that I'm in power."

I suggested that we use hypnosis at that point, to see what had been affecting her during the week, what had been causing the inner battle. She quickly slipped into a trance and soon was going back in time again.

◢

VICTORIA: I'm not at home. I feel like I'm outside. I'm floating to meet this . . . And the light's getting brighter. And my head's . . . my head's heavier. He's calling. And the light's bright. [*Pauses*] And I feel a sinking feeling in the back of my head. They want to connect, and I don't want to. I never want to, but they always win. They tell me, "You know we always win." And they're pulling, and I'm going. [*Cries*] And they're saying, "It's okay." And I'm saying, "It's not." And they just keep pulling. [*Cries harder*] They've got me . . . again. [*Long pause*] But we're staying here this time. We're not zooming out. We're just hovering. We're hovering around. There's the table again. It's the table you always lie on. It's a . . . golden-glow color. And they circle around you. And you spin on this table. And as you spin, they're taking . . . what are they taking? [*Cries very hard*] They're always taking! [*Becomes calmer*] I don't know what they're taking, but they're taking my thoughts. They take my thoughts. And the light gets brighter. And the brighter the light gets, the faster everything happens. There's one that has more power than the rest. He's the one that pulls everything. Everything! "We want everything." "Everything . . . come on, everything. You're going to give us *every* . . .

thing." But I don't. That's why they get so angry at me. I keep part of me, and they get real angry at me. He tries to penetrate all of it. With . . . his eyes. His eyes beam in . . . They all beam in, but his are the most penetrating. And that's how they absorb what I know. I'm not sure why they have to know all this. "You don't have to know. Only we know, you wouldn't understand." [*Pauses*] "When does this stop?" "You don't ask questions. You aren't here to ask questions. You're here to do what we say." The back of my neck hurts again. "What are you doing to the back of my neck?" [*Cries*] "Don't do it! Please don't do it! I don't want you to do it! You make me hate you! I hate you! Don't! Don't!" They always do it. It's so hard to fight them. You can't win. They don't let you, because they won't let you go home. I can go home if I do what they say. . . . It isn't fair. [*Stops crying*] That's what they can't get from me. And that's what they keep trying to get. I never give them . . . the inner me. And they want it. But I have a stronger power . . . that doesn't give it to them. And that's why they get so angry at me. They say others let them have it. "Others can do it, you can." But I won't. I won't! My neck hurts again. They're trying again. [*Angry now*] They just keep trying, and I won't. I won't! No matter what, I won't. I've got God on my side, and I can do what I want, and they can't have that part. "Someday," they say. "Someday." He said. "Someday you'll be totally mine." And I always say, "Never!" That's why we constantly fight. That's why part of me hates the other part of me. The part he has control of. The others watch. They watch and observe. He's their teacher. I'm their subject. One . . . one always has compassion for me. And she's not supposed to. She's the one that told me it was okay when I was little. She's always there. [*Long pause*] Maybe it's always part of the plot. Maybe her telling me it's okay is part of . . . that's it . . . is part of him trying to get to me by telling me it's okay and they won't hurt me. Because they do hurt me. They hurt my body. They hurt every part of me.

DR. FIORE: How do they hurt your body?

VICTORIA: They put things in it. And they take things out of it.

DR. FIORE: Tell me more about that.

VICTORIA: They put . . . they put something in . . . that's how they control me. That's how they make me come. That's how they make me watch. That's how they call me. . . . And they do other things. They check my body, with different things to see how it functions, what it's doing. They're keeping a recording of me. It's a record of my progress as a human being. They're studying human beings. I'm one of their experiments. They want to know how we function. They find the physical. That's it! That's what I don't give them, the spiritual. I just give them the physical. And they want all of it. But you can't give that without completely losing yourself. And you have to be a strong, spiritual person to keep it. The weaker ones, they get. And that's what they want, because then they can be total, total . . . total what? I don't know what total is, because . . . I don't give in. My and's real cold, like ice. [*Pauses*] "So . . . we'll control your body . . . we'll control your body." That's what they do. They spin you around. . . . And as you're spinning, they're drawing everything they want out of you. Sometimes they use instruments, and they hurt. They're . . . they're weird. I don't know what they are. [The instruments are] always cold. The coldest is in my hand. It's something they put in. [*Cries*] They put it in so they can draw out everything. Oh yuck! They come in and out. They come in and out. [*Cries harder*] That's what they do! They come in and they use . . . they use your body. They use your body to stay alive. They come in and out, so they can watch. [*Sobs*] That's why it hurts. That's why you go back. You go back so they can change. Because if they can't get all of you, they have to change. They have to keep changing. That's why. That's why it hurts. That's why they make you hate yourself. That's why you don't feel good. You don't feel good about yourself. You're never worthy of anything. They don't want you to be . . . because then they can't be in control. So they fight you, to be in control. Oh . . . they're hating me for this. But I've got a stronger power than they have, and they're hating me for that. And I'm going to win. Because I can see this white light, and this white light always lets me know . . . I'm . . . okay. They really try to hide that, and I constantly battle them on this. Constantly. They don't want to give . . . me . . . up. And I don't want them to have me. [*Pauses*] We're battling to see who's in control. They want to be in control. In *con-trol.* "No . . . No . . . No . . . I said never, and I mean never. Never!" [*Long Pause*] The back of my head isn't hurting anymore. They're leaving. They're zooming out, and I'm staying here.

DR. FIORE: You said they come in and they go out. What do you mean by that?

VICTORIA: [*Pauses*] They come . . . when I'm off guard. They come in and out of my body while I'm there. They come in and they draw things out of my body. Then they come in and they draw more . . . things . . . out. They come in, and they come down, and they stay, and if they can't get what they're supposed to get, then I go back, and they trade. They trade energies. They trade energies. . . . in me. They all come in and out, as part of rejuvenizing energies. They draw . . . that's it, they draw the energies out of me. And at times they need it more. And as they draw out energies, I have less defense and have to fight harder.

DR. FIORE: Are you saying that they come back with you, that the others will go off and somebody remains with you in your body?

VICTORIA: One remains with me, as a controller. [*Pauses*] Oh! . . . It's what they've put in my hand. It's that feeling in my hand when my hand gets cold. One is part of me. Whatever it is that they use to control me with is what comes and goes.

DR. FIORE: Is there anything or anyone controlling you at this moment?

VICTORIA: [*Pauses*] It's like it's neutral. They were battling me all week. I kept fighting them. They don't want to lose. I can feel the pulling in the back of my neck. It's getting stronger. [*Long pause*]

✦

Despite my suggestions to feel good in every way as I brought her out of hypnosis, Victoria felt tired from the struggle and her hands were still cold. I made a mental note that there may be some repressed material associated with the regression that we would probably have to return to at a later date.

✦

When I saw Victoria in the waiting room the following week, one glance told me that things had not gone well with her. Once in my office, she sank into the chair and shook her head. "I've been really depressed all week. It was hard for me to pull out of it on the way home last time. There's something nagging at me. Something I don't want to face. I didn't want to come today. But I knew I had to."

I put her into hypnosis immediately and regressed her to the event that was causing the depression.

✦

VICTORIA: They're coming in. And I'm getting on.

DR. FIORE: On what?

VICTORIA: Whatever it is I get on. What they're on. It's just all . . . shiny and light. [*Big sigh*] I'm back on the table. Now we're going. Not as fast this time, but we're moving. It's faster. Now we're starting. They're all circling again. . . . I'm really afraid this time. It feels . . . different. Like there's been a change. It's not them, it's me. I'm older.

DR. FIORE: How old are you?

VICTORIA: Twenty- . . . five. Someone says, "Go with it. It won't hurt you. Just go with it." My legs feel . . . heavy, but the rest of my body is light. [*Pauses*] I can feel their eyes piercing. [*Pauses*] I get numb for just a little while. Only while I'm spinning and spinning and spinning.

DR. FIORE: Tell me about the spinning.

VICTORIA: I feel like I'm spinning in a circle real fast.

DR. FIORE: What position is your body in?

VICTORIA: I'm on my back and I just spin around in a circle. I feel like there's something under me, but there's nothing under me.

DR. FIORE: And how do you feel as you're spinning?

VICTORIA: Light. I feel like everything is coming out. All my thoughts . . . are just spinning away. . . . That's why it's different. The controller wasn't there right away. Now he's here. It's his time to take power. He's letting the rest see what they could do, how much they could get. He's testing to see who's the strongest. That's what he says, "Who's the strongest?" He's still the strongest. If he can totally take me over, he can stay. They want to use my body so they can stay on Earth. [*Cries*] If I don't fight, I lose. And you can't lose. This is the final test of who's going to win. [*Pauses*] I can hear my voice saying, "I'm stronger. I'm stronger. I'm stronger!" And with each time I say, "I'm stronger," the light gets brighter. It gets brighter . . . and brighter. He wants someone to be able to control me all the time, and they're arguing. [*Big sigh*] I feel far, far away. Everything's far away. I'm floating. I'm floating, and they're pulling. They're removing something. [*Grimaces in pain*] And it hurts. Oh!

DR. FIORE: Where does it hurt?

VICTORIA: I feel it in my neck, and in my arm and my legs. It's like it's pulling. Pulling. Oh! [*Cries*] Now my stomach hurts. I feel like something is holding my shoulders. And pulling my head back. They're holding me down at my waist. They won't let me go! [*Cries hard*] They're just holding me down! It's so hard. [*Breathes heavily*] It's so hard when they hold you down. It hurts! [*Cries*] It's cold, and it hurts! [*Shouts*] They pierce and they pull!

DR. FIORE: Where do they pierce?

VICTORIA: My stomach. [*Points to abdomen*] They need to know . . . Oh no. . . . [*Cries*]

DR. FIORE: What is it they need to know?

VICTORIA: How I function. They want . . . to know . . . what . . . causes . . . the reproduction. How we reproduce. They're trying to study . . . Oh! That's what they want to know . . . how we reproduce! [*Breathes hard*] It isn't the sex they want. They want the reproduction.

DR. FIORE: How do you know this?

VICTORIA: By the tests.

DR. FIORE: Do they explain this to you?

VICTORIA: She does. She says, "We have to know. It's okay." It's someone that always tells me it's okay. "We have to know." They want to find out how to reproduce us. . . . [*Pauses*] They . . . Oh! . . . That's . . . [*Cries*] . . . what they did. The probing was taking the egg. They're going to try and reproduce us. I wasn't really supposed to know. If they can reproduce us, they can come back . . . with the people they reproduce. The controller says he will win . . . the battle. Because I can't have any control over what he takes. [*Cries*]

DR. FIORE: What are you thinking?

VICTORIA: I don't want them to have any part of me. [*Cries hard*] And I really feel robbed because they took it!

DR. FIORE: What did they take?

VICTORIA: Part of me.

DR. FIORE: What part is that?

VICTORIA: They take my eggs! They knew how to probe and get them. And that's mine. Not theirs. [*Cries*] That's why they have control. And I don't want to go back. I don't want to go back!

DR. FIORE: You don't want to go back where?

VICTORIA: They took me back. When I ovulated, they took me back . . . and took the egg.

DR. FIORE: How many times did they take you back?

VICTORIA: Six . . . ten. Ten times.

DR. FIORE: Did they take an egg each time?

VICTORIA: Yes.

DR. FIORE: Did they tell you what they were going to do with the eggs?

VICTORIA: No. Try . . . try experiments. [*Pauses*]

DR. FIORE: When you say try experiments, are you reporting what you heard or what you think?

VICTORIA: What I heard.

DR. FIORE: Were they talking to you?

VICTORIA: No.

DR. FIORE: What are they going to do with these eggs?

VICTORIA: That's how they're trying to reproduce [us].

DR. FIORE: This is the female component. How do they get the male component?

VICTORIA: From the males.

DR. FIORE: What males?

VICTORIA: Ours. That they take. That's who else is there.

DR. FIORE: Who is there?

VICTORIA: A male.

DR. FIORE: Is it someone whom you recognize?

VICTORIA: No.

DR. FIORE: What's being done?

VICTORIA: They take his sperm.

DR. FIORE: Do you see this being done?

VICTORIA: Yes.

DR. FIORE: And how do they do this?

VICTORIA: I don't know what it is that they have. But they . . .
it's like a suction. They have on him.

DR. FIORE: Where?

VICTORIA: On his . . . penis.

DR. FIORE: Is this being done at the same time they're removing
your egg?

VICTORIA: Yes. Only he's, he's . . . not by me. There's another circle of people around him.

DR. FIORE: What's happening to you at this point?

VICTORIA: They're through with me and they're waiting for
him.

DR. FIORE: And what's happening to you?

VICTORIA: I'm just lying there and I'm cold. I'm cold all over.
Whatever they gave me made me real . . . cold.

DR. FIORE: What did they give you?

VICTORIA: They put something in that was so cold.

DR. FIORE: Where did they put it?

VICTORIA: In my tubes, and it was so . . . cold. Like they're
freezing. It just makes you cold all . . . over. I don't know
exactly what all they did to him. I only saw the end. Just the
suction and the end.

DR. FIORE: How did he seem to react to it?

VICTORIA: He fought too. That was the other yelling I heard.

DR. FIORE: And now?

VICTORIA: And now . . . I'm home.

DR. FIORE: Remember how you got home.

VICTORIA: Just going fast. Real fast. [*Pauses*] And then . . . the machine opens and I'm out.

DR. FIORE: Where were you?

VICTORIA: In my backyard. In San Bernardino.

DR. FIORE: Was anybody else in the machine with you?

VICTORIA: [*Pauses*] They had my daughter. They had Susie. She came out with me. We're sitting in the patio, and I'm just holding her, and she's telling me about the little blue man. That's where she got that little blue man! She's always telling me that she was talking to a little blue man, and I just thought it was her imagination.

DR. FIORE: How do you feel now?

VICTORIA: I feel . . . like they're through. I feel calm. And like it's finally over.

✒

Victoria opened her eyes as I counted her out of hypnosis, and smiled in relief. "Do you think they really do those things?"

"Budd Hopkins, an artist who wrote the book *Intruders*, reported many cases of people being used for genetic experiments or possibly for breeding purposes. Have you heard about this before?"

"No. It seems incredible. Why would they do that?" Victoria frowned and leaned forward expectantly.

"I'd rather not go into it now. I don't want to influence any further work we may do on this. Later, when we're through, you should read his book and Whitley Strieber's *Communion.* You'll find them fascinating, I'm sure."

As I walked Victoria to the door of my office, she turned and gave me a big hug. I felt relieved that we had gotten to the cause of her depression, especially since I was going on vacation and wouldn't be seeing her for three weeks.

*

Victoria couldn't wait to tell me how good she felt as we walked from the waiting room to my office. "Edee, I feel really great!" She quickly sat down and reached into her purse. "I've kept some notes for you. I was afraid I might forget since it would be a while till I saw you again." She put on her glasses and looked up. "Is it okay to read them to you?"

"Sure. I find it very helpful when people keep records. I always need to know how they do, especially on the way home following our sessions. It gives me valuable clues about what we've accomplished and what needs to be resolved. What do you have there?"

Victoria read from two three-by-five-inch cards. "I have not been depressed. I feel great. I feel that my life is going in the right direction, with new opportunities and new doors opening up more every day. I really feel in contact with my core and true feelings. I'm taking each day as it comes, with great joy and thankfulness for all the new energies around me." She stopped and her whole face lit up with happiness.

"I'm absolutely delighted for you, Victoria. You must have released some pretty powerful blocks last time. It sounds like you've got your power back as well."

"Yes. And more good news! I just saw the doctor yesterday, and I've lost fifteen pounds since I started my therapy. Without trying. That's the best part."

I got up and walked over to my desk and checked her file.

"That was about six weeks ago. Wonderful! That's a safe rate of weight loss too."

As I sat back down in my Danish rosewood chair, I noticed Victoria frowning.

"There was only one negative thing in these three weeks." She read from the other card. "On August second I was sitting outside on the patio with my ten-year-old grandson, waiting for his parents, my son and his wife, to return. It was a lovely summer evening. We were relaxing, looking at the moon and clouds. Then I saw the stars and was afraid to look at them. So I stopped looking at the sky. I have always loved looking at the beauty of the moon, clouds and stars, as an artist. Maybe there's still something, I haven't remembered." She looked up anxiously. "Aside from that one night, everything's been great."

"Tell me exactly what happened. You said you were afraid to look at the stars?"

"My eyes wanted to focus on one star . . . and yet I didn't want to. I began to feel real anxiety with this business of looking at the star. My heart was pounding. I could feel the fear mounting up with the urge to look at the one spot. I was fighting myself. A part was telling me, You have to look. There was a real battle within. I chose to turn around and think of something else and not look at the sky. In fact, it bothered me for a couple of days. And, ever since then, I haven't really wanted to look at the sky at night. Actually, I forced myself finally to look a week ago. Again, I was outside with my grandson on the patio. There was a full moon. I could look up at the stars for a while, but if any star started to twinkle, I didn't want to look at it. I felt fear, but not as strong as that first time."

"There's something still hidden, repressed. We need to deal with it," I said.

Victoria looked scared. Her body tensed and her face stiffened as she looked down into her lap. "I was afraid so. I was real depressed as I got ready to come to this appointment. I started thinking about UFOs and felt worse. I had to put them out of my mind."

After she had been in hypnosis for a few minutes, I regressed her to the event responsible for the fear she had felt on the evening of August second.

❧

VICTORIA: I just see this real bright light. It's coming toward me. It's getting brighter and brighter, and as it gets brighter, the lights keep changing in it. They twinkle red and green and blue. But there's a white light that's more penetrating . . . and they're here.

DR. FIORE: What do you mean by that?

VICTORIA: They're here and they're opening the door, and I'm going in. I don't want to go in, but they're just making me come in. They've got me by each arm and they're taking me in. And they glow in the light also. It's like it's all an illumination. I'm just not sure where I was when they got me.

DR. FIORE: Let yourself remember.

VICTORIA: It's my backyard.

DR. FIORE: Tell me about them.

VICTORIA: They don't feel like they are the same; they're not the ones I was with before. They're different.

DR. FIORE: In what way?

VICTORIA: They're taller, they're shaped different. [*Pauses*]

DR. FIORE: Tell me whatever comes into your mind.

VICTORIA: I feel trapped.

DR. FIORE: What else are you feeling?

VICTORIA: Fear . . . because they're different. Fear that it's starting all over again, only a different way. It's like I'm just, I'm just kinda . . . hovering . . . The inside's different too.

DR. FIORE: What's happening?

VICTORIA: I'm standing there, and they're just holding me. They've got a hold of me, but I don't feel the pressure. Everything's light. And I feel we're moving, but we're not moving real fast. They aren't leaving our gravity area. They're just kinda staying in this [area]. I'm not the only one they're picking up, that's why.

DR. FIORE: Did they explain that to you?

VICTORIA: No. We stop and other people get on. I don't know the others. [*Pauses*] There's something they want from us. They seem to be kinder than the others. But I'm still afraid, 'cuz I'm not sure if that kindness is a deception. They're superintelligent, a lot more advanced than we are here.

DR. FIORE: How do you know that?

VICTORIA: I can just sense it. Now my ears are ringing. And I feel tingly. But I'm not afraid. I'm not sure what's happening.

DR. FIORE: What position is your body in?

VICTORIA: I'm standing up, but it doesn't feel like I'm standing up. It feels like I'm starting to tilt . . . backward. I don't feel like there's anything holding me there. I'm just kind of being there. I feel like I'm just sort of elevated there. The other people are in the same position. We're all just kind of at this angle.

DR. FIORE: How many other people are there?

VICTORIA: I don't know. There's a row of us. I can't see the end. We're from all over, I know that.

DR. FIORE: What do you mean by that?

VICTORIA: I know we're just not all from our country . . . we're from all over the world. That's what we were doing. We were hovering and picking up people from all over the world. And now we're all lined up in this weird angle. I feel like they're taking something, but I don't know what. They're not letting us know. We're afraid and at the same time, we're calm. They've made the calmness. It's like they've got us in a spell. [*Pauses*] I feel like . . . I'm just not me. I feel like my body's there, but I'm not. But I don't know where I am. I feel like I'm looking at my body, lying there.

DR. FIORE: Where are you in relation to your body?

VICTORIA: I'm above it, looking down at it.

DR. FIORE: When you look down at it, what do you see?

VICTORIA: I'm just lying there. I don't feel like there's any life in my body. I'm just lying there like . . . a dummy. Like it's not part of me. I feel like I'm just floating up there, looking down at this row, and everybody else is doing the same thing. We're all up there, looking down at our bodies.

DR. FIORE: Look at your body and see what's happening.

VICTORIA: [*Cries out in pain.*] They're putting different rays on us. I don't know what they are, but they're zooming to different parts of our body.

DR. FIORE: Tell me more about that.

VICTORIA: It hurts when they do this.

DR. FIORE: How do you know that?

VICTORIA: Because at first . . . at first, I was there . . . when it started hurting . . . before I started floating and looking down. It's just hard to breathe. I feel like everything's being pulled out. My energy is low. My neck aches . . . my shoulders are heavy. I feel like there's nothing in my stomach . . . that everything's been taken out.

DR. FIORE: When you say your stomach, what do you mean?

VICTORIA: My stomach. The intestines . . . and my whole abdomen. It's like they've drained everything out. I feel like they've put something in that's making us glow. They can see everything and all of our functions inside. We can't see it, but they can. It's like a glowing substance. And I just feel hollower . . . and hollower.

DR. FIORE: At this point are you still in your body?

VICTORIA: Yes . . . [Long pause] Our bodies just look like they're dead mummies in a row. [Pauses] Now I feel like I'm not up there anymore. I'm starting to feel warm. I'm not cold anymore. I feel like I'm starting to fill up and that everything's working again. [Pauses] We're just lying there, and everything's coming back . . . to normal.

DR. FIORE: Describe these beings.

VICTORIA: They're taller than me. About half as much taller than me. Their bodies are shaped similar, but real thin . . . superthin, like half what we would consider normal. Almost like a skeleton frame. They're smooth-looking. I don't think they have any hair. They don't have it on their heads. Everything is real smooth. They're sort of a creamy white.

DR. FIORE: Tell me about their facial features.

VICTORIA: Real high cheekbones. Their eyes are more sunken in than ours. More round.

DR. FIORE: Tell me about their noses and mouths.

VICTORIA: The ears are kind of flat to their heads, they don't protrude out at all. You hardly see them. They don't have noses like we do. They're very . . . kind of flat, with just little openings.

DR. FIORE: And their mouths?

VICTORIA: Their mouths are larger than ours. They're wider. They're like almost clear across the jaw line, but very thin. And the same color as their skin. They're all the same color. There's no variation. Everything's the same color.

DR. FIORE: What color are their eyes?

VICTORIA: A blue . . . green.

DR. FIORE: And what are they wearing?

VICTORIA: Silver. Glowing silver. Not the kind of silver we know. It's almost iridescent . . . it's a shimmering iridescence.

DR. FIORE: Can you tell if they're males, or females, or both?

VICTORIA: I feel they're mostly male. There's a few females. But they don't do very much. It's the males that do everything. The females assist.

DR. FIORE: What do the males do?

VICTORIA: They're the ones that work on our bodies.

DR. FIORE: Do they communicate with you in any way?

VICTORIA: They just gave you an overwhelming . . . powerful feeling that you're gonna stay calm, that you weren't to be afraid. Now when all of this was happening, you felt . . . even when you were hurting and everything . . . you felt a gentleness.

DR. FIORE: From them?

VICTORIA: From them.

DR. FIORE: Did they communicate with each other?

VICTORIA: Yes, but with their eyes.

DR. FIORE: Did you hear any sounds?

VICTORIA: No. I felt they could look at each other and just communicate.

DR. FIORE: Did they use any gestures?

VICTORIA: They touched. And when they held us, the touch wasn't strong. It felt forceful, but it wasn't forceful. It was . . . like you knew that they had you . . . but you didn't feel . . . you felt harmed, but you didn't feel harmed.

DR. FIORE: After you return to your body and it's all over, what happens?

VICTORIA: Now they're dropping us off. I'm still there, 'cuz I'm waiting for them to take me next, but they're leaving others off along the way. They're just dropping us . . . all . . . back. [*Long pause*] I feel like I'm drifting now. And I can see the light again and I can see them zooming off.

DR. FIORE: And now what do you do?

VICTORIA: I don't realize I was there with them. I go into my house.

❧

One month later, Victoria came into the office obviously upset. Her whole being reflected depression.

"What's wrong, Victoria?"

"It's those UFO drawings! I got upset and disoriented doing them. I had a superhard time. I got so depressed, I couldn't finish them." She looked up at me with tears in her eyes. "Do you ever get rid of them? They'll just have me the rest of my life. Is it over? I want to believe it's over." Her eyes were pleading with me to reassure her.

"I wish I could tell you it is over, but I have no way of knowing. Probably there's still some repressed memory festering inside. If it's not over, I can help you become stronger."

She managed a weak smile. "The first pictures were a release. The UFO and the operations. It even had a calming effect. I actually felt a lot of love. But then I got into this set." She spread out some sketches on the carpet. "This one's the hardest. I couldn't draw the ship. I could see it in my mind's eye. It had a radiant haze, a glow. I just couldn't finish it. That's when I got so depressed."

"I think you've solved the riddle. Something happened on that ship that was very depressing. So it probably is over. You are just responding to past history. Let's bring it up to the surface of your mind so it won't bother you any longer."

Victoria was ready for the regression in three minutes. I asked her inner mind to take her to the cause of the depression.

❧

VICTORIA: It's their bodies in mine. They have a way of entering your body and staying with you for as long as they want.

DR. FIORE: Let yourself go to when that happened.

VICTORIA: I didn't want them to enter, and they held me down and said, "We do this to everyone, and you're the same." And they just enter you and stay there. They enter you to find out how you function, and so that they can become a part of this earth.

DR. FIORE: Get in touch with how you felt when they held you down.

VICTORIA: I felt . . . deprived. I felt like I was not me. Like I wanted to hide. That I wasn't in control. I had no say over my life.

DR. FIORE: Tell me more about this particular contact. Tell me where it's taking place and everything that's happening.

VICTORIA: It starts in their ship. With . . . blue lights all around. It's a weird blue, I can't describe the color. It's sort of a mixture of blues. And it's like their bodies enter you, and at the same time they enter you, you also feel like you're being molested sexually. But it's from within. When they enter you and they're a part of you, you just feel like you've been raped, not just physically but mentally also. And you feel like there's a constant battle of who's in control. You feel pinned down. And I don't know if the pinned down is the fear you feel or if you're being held down, or a combination of both. But you also know that when you leave the ship, that they're going to be with you.

DR. FIORE: Let yourself to back to the very part of the event that caused you to have difficulty drawing the ship. What did that drawing bring up in you?

VICTORIA: That's the ship where they took control. And I lost. I lost the battle. [*Cries*] And they took control. And they didn't let me go. [*Cries more*] And the glow, the glow around the ship is red. And no matter where that red glow is, it brings back fear, and I know they're there. Not maybe physically, but subconsciously I know they're there. They're there again. The red glow at Ann's that I saw in her kitchen is why I was so afraid. It's the first time I think I've been really awake and aware of that red glow, and I don't know if I was afraid because I just came back or because I was going to go. I could lie there and see it, and I knew I was terrified of it. And I felt if I didn't breathe and I stayed where I was at, they couldn't get me. But they didn't have to get me, because they had already had me, and they had just brought me back. I just want it to stop happening. Every time I think of the red glow, I can feel the pressure in the back of my neck.

DR. FIORE: What happens to the back of your neck?

VICTORIA: It just feels like there's a pressure right at the bottom of my skull.

DR. FIORE: What is that part of your body remembering? Let yourself know.

VICTORIA: It's remembering that there was something placed there. It's placed there and it's taken out more than once. It feels like a . . . It's a pressure that feels like it makes something stop or turn on or something. I don't know what it's supposed to do. Maybe it records whatever they want.

DR. FIORE: Are you saying that it's embedded in your flesh somehow?

VICTORIA: Somehow it's there. It's either something embedded or it's something they have that can control. But it's more powerful when they're present. It's a . . . it's like a fluid.

DR. FIORE: Let yourself remember when it was placed there the first time.

VICTORIA: The very first time I had an encounter with them. When I was little in Schafferstown, the very first time they came.

DR. FIORE: How did they implant it?

VICTORIA: That was when they kept telling me, "It's okay, it's okay, it's okay. We're not hurting you, it's okay." They try to make you believe they love you and that everything's okay. But it's not. They just want control. They apply something to find out what they need to find out. But it really hurts the back of your neck. [*Pauses*] I have never known fully what they want. Because they won't let you know. [*Pauses*] I feel a distance. Like I'm way out somewhere. Far out. And they're holding me there and just having me look down. Saying, "You want to go back, you do as we say." And you want to come back, so you have to do as they say. [*Cries a little*] Every time that door opens, when they come, you have no control. It just pulls you in.

DR. FIORE: When you say the door opens, what door is that?

VICTORIA: The door on the ship. It comes down and they draw you in. They don't come out, they just have a power that pulls you in.

DR. FIORE: Where are you when this happens?

VICTORIA: I've been in different places. At home.

DR. FIORE: How do you get from your home to the ship?

VICTORIA: This glow is all around, and the glow just pulls you into the ship.

DR. FIORE: What color is the glow?

VICTORIA: Red.

DR. FIORE: Tell me how you would get from your bedroom into the ship. Tell me exactly how that would happen.

VICTORIA: Usually I see the glow and get up and I remember I'm afraid. Then I look to see what the glow is. And then I don't remember anymore. I don't remember. I just remember the glow pulling me to the glow, and when I look at it, I don't remember anything until I'm on the ship. I can remember trying to hide from it and saying, "I'm not going to look. It's not there, it's my imagination." But something always makes me look.

DR. FIORE: Let yourself go to anything else that is causing you anxiety or depression in regard to the drawing you were doing. Anything else that was being stirred up in you. At the count of three. One . . . two . . . three.

VICTORIA: The tubes they have attached to my hand.

DR. FIORE: Tell me more about this attachment.

VICTORIA: In the tubes are different chemicals or something that they use. Each one has a different substance. And they control the substances and what they want to use from a big panel.

DR. FIORE: Where does this tube enter your body?

VICTORIA: They enter your hand on the top. They go into the vein.

DR. FIORE: Do you feel anything when this is put in there?

VICTORIA: You feel different. With each one you feel different.

DR. FIORE: Tell me about that.

VICTORIA: With some, you shake. With others, you're cold. With others, you're numb. Then you can get hot. And then with some you can't feel at all. And then they have a wire or some type of tube that's fastened by your heart, on your breast. On your navel. And usually three tubes that go into your pelvis. They control what they're doing with these with what they put in your hand.

DR. FIORE: How old are you when this is being done?

VICTORIA: I'm in my twenties.

DR. FIORE: How many times has this been done to you?

VICTORIA: Ten.

DR. FIORE: Do they give you an explanation?

VICTORIA: They need what I have.

DR. FIORE: Are they communicating with you?

VICTORIA: They're just taking what I have. They want to try to reproduce us . . . there. And become them, so they can mingle here and not be noticed.

DR. FIORE: How do you know this?

VICTORIA: They told me. That's why they're going to use . . . they can reproduce us by getting the reproduction from . . . eggs from us and the sperm from the men, and reproduce us on their ships, and that's what's scary, because you never know, and you hope that . . . you don't want to be one of them.

DR. FIORE: What do you mean by that?

VICTORIA: You don't want to be one of them. You don't want to be the ones they've reproduced. And when they're taking all of this, you wonder if you are or not. [*Cries*] But they won't tell you if you are or not. And you've got that fear that you are, and you don't want to be. [*Cries harder*] You don't know. You don't know! [*Sobs*] And you don't know if you are or if it's good or bad.

DR. FIORE: But you remember being brought up by your family, don't you?

VICTORIA: Yes.

DR. FIORE: And there are pictures of you when you were an infant?

VICTORIA: Yes.

DR. FIORE: So obviously they did not raise you through those years.

VICTORIA: That's right. But they still took me on their ship.

DR. FIORE: They took you on their ship, as they have taken hundreds, maybe thousands of people on their ships, because they're studying us. And when you became older, they wanted something from you, they wanted your eggs. But that does not make you one of them, does it?

VICTORIA: No.

DR. FIORE: Do you have the genetic qualities of both of your parents?

VICTORIA: Yes. And I've been afraid that they can make me have those, so I'd think I belong here.

DR. FIORE: Does your mother remember being pregnant with you?

VICTORIA: Yes. I am from here. [*Cries in relief*]

DR. FIORE: I'd like you to look at the very cause of your greatest fears. At the count of three. One . . . two . . . three.

VICTORIA: The fear of who they were going to reproduce with my eggs. The fear of what they were going to do with them. [*Cries*] And that they were part me, but they didn't belong to me anymore. They weren't mine. [*Cries harder*]

DR. FIORE: So what you didn't like was the lack of control over the outcome for your eggs, is that right?

VICTORIA: Right. I just wanted them to leave me alone.

DR. FIORE: And you believe that the white light can protect you from them?

VICTORIA: I believe it can, but I feel . . . this week, when I tried to protect myself from them, I had a hard time concentrating on the white light, and I was afraid it wasn't strong enough. In my mind, I kept trying to make it stronger and stronger and stronger all week.

✔

Victoria wiped her eyes with her hands and then took the tissue I offered her. "I do feel better. I'm much calmer now. I feel I can finish the drawings. I'll have them for you next time."

"Please notice if you have any problem with them. There may still be something you haven't dealt with. The proof of the pudding is in the eating."

✔

I called Victoria to see how she was doing as I finished writing up her material. I had taken off two weeks to finish the manuscript, and so it had been three weeks since we last met.

She reported that she hadn't been depressed at all. In fact, things had gone well for her, despite some stress from family problems. The weight she had regained on a vacation, she had lost as soon as she was home . . . without dieting. She feels her eating is now under control.

She had been able to easily finish the pictures for *Encounters* and while she was drawing the spacecraft, she remembered something new. As she was brought to the opened underside of the UFO, there was a very strong light that came out of it that "pulled" her into the ship.

She said in closing, "I feel resolved about the abductions. There's no fear anymore. No depression. I just have a feeling that there's a reason why I chose to have those experiences."

"To Be Back . . .
Would Be Fabulous!"

 "I've always had a deep and abiding interest in UFOs. Ever since I was a kid, I was interested in exploring beyond this earth." Dan, an attractive blond man in his mid-forties, seemed very comfortable talking about the topic that was the reason for our meeting. I had invited him to explore the possibility of a close encounter of the fourth kind.

Dan was a friend of Gloria, whom you met in Chapter Nine. In fact, he was the only person she allowed herself to confide in. She had mentioned him and his openness to the whole subject of UFOs and extraterrestrials many times during our work together. I had a hunch that he himself might have had encounters, so I asked her to have him call me if he wanted to look into his interest in depth.

"Dan, is there anything that you feel you've experienced that could be evidence of a close encounter of the fourth kind? CEIVs are when someone's been abducted or contacted. It's always fascinating to find out what a person remembers or understands before we use hypnosis, compared to what comes out later. For example, have you had any dreams of UFOs?"

"No, and I've never even seen one. That's a big frustration. I fly and I'm always scanning the night and day sky. But nothing, so far." He chuckled and added, "But I keep hoping."

"I do the same thing. I travel long distances a lot, on planes, and I usually take the red-eye. I'm always looking out the window, but I've never seen one either. Is there anything that gives you a clue about a possible CEIV?"

"I don't accept anything on blind faith. I try to remain open and objective. But it's odd. I've always had the feeling that I'm not native to here. Every time I look at the night sky, I have a nostalgic feeling, really at a gut-level, that I want to go home." Dan's voice had become softer, filled with emotion. I wouldn't have been surprised to see tears brimming in his eyes.

Dan continued to discuss his interest in flying. As a child, he spent hours building model airplanes, and, since he lived near Boeing Aircraft, he "hung around" planes as much as possible. They were the love of his young life. He started flying in high school, with a friend who was a pilot, and soon got his license.

"Do you have any interest in sci-fi, Dan?" We had just a little time left before we had to begin using hypnosis, and I felt this might give us a clue.

"I've read a lot of sci-fi, but I don't feel a kinship with it. Except one thing. It boggled my mind. I have always noticed Chesley Bonestell's work—do you know it?"

I shook my head. Science fiction doesn't hold an interest for me.

"He's a sci-fi illustrator and did covers with planets on them. This was even before Sputnik. When the close-ups came in from Pioneer and others, his paintings, done long before, were perfectly accurate. For example, he was dead-on with the colors and patterns on Jupiter. That stunned me!"

I would have enjoyed talking with Dan for hours, but we had work to do. I explained hypnosis to him, since he'd never experienced it. After a few minutes of suggestions to relax, I could see his body letting go of tensions as he concentrated on his breathing and listened to my voice. When the hypnotic induction was completed, I set up finger signals and asked him about CEIVs. His inner mind, through his "yes" and "no" fingers, told me that he had had 627 CEIVs! My policy is to keep an open mind, so I recorded the number on my notepad and then asked him to go to a particularly important encounter.

✦

DAN: I'm inside, waiting to get out. Nobody's around, just me. I'm waiting for some sort of a signal. Or an okay, a release. It's like I'm leaving an office. I go out into the corridor through the door, down to the docking base . . . Aboard a ship . . . [*Pauses*] We make dirt in twenty minutes.

DR. FIORE: What do you mean by that?

DAN: We land, from orbit, drop. And clean everything out. Nothing's standing. Nothing's left. Totally. Everything's gone.

DR. FIORE: What do you mean by that?

DAN: It was a small settlement. It's gone.

DR. FIORE: What happened?

DAN: We wiped it out.

DR. FIORE: Where was that settlement?

DAN: It was on the seacoast, small bay, flat ground.

DR. FIORE: What was your role in it?

DAN: Captain, one of the landing ships.

DR. FIORE: Do you know the reason why you did this?

DAN: Orders. I never saw the people, if there were any.

DR. FIORE: How did you wipe them out?

DAN: Weapons.

DR. FIORE: What kind of weapons did you use?

DAN: Force beam.

DR. FIORE: Do you have any remorse about doing this?

DAN: None. Duty.

DR. FIORE: This was on a seacoast. Whereabouts?

DAN: Deneb. System Deneb. Third planet. Easy job. No resistance.

DR. FIORE: Have you done this sort of thing before?

DAN: Many times.

DR. FIORE: Do you know the real purpose for doing this?

DAN: Control. Planetary control. Teach them a lesson. They're terrified of us. It doesn't take too many.

DR. FIORE: What do you mean by that?

DAN: Drop out of the sky and kill a few and leave. The rest of them come around, real quick. Kind of fun, if you don't think about it. Now I remember where I've seen that red sky before.

DR. FIORE: Where?

DAN: Curious atmospheric phenomenon, not on Deneb, not in that system. Another drop, another time. [*Pauses*] No problems, no losses. One guy hurt.

DR. FIORE: Do you sometimes have losses?

DAN: Rarely. Occasionally a mistake. Somebody screws up. Somebody dies. Nobody has the weapons we have. Occasionally they get lucky. It costs them. [*Pauses*] Hop in the bay and everybody's laughing, kidding around, cleaning their boots. Decontamination. Some of them are nasty. The guys joking about finding a planet with nothing but women. The women joking about finding a planet with nothing but guys. Everybody hungry. Go to mess. Settle down into the ship routine. Two weeks till the next one. Not much to do between them. Nobody's told us where we're going yet. It doesn't make any difference. We don't know where they send us. Not a bad life, really. Better than being on one of those planets we hit. A lot of fun on the ship.

DR. FIORE: Tell me about that.

DAN: Mixed crew. Women get wired from the combat. Keeps you busy for the first three or four days after. Then the captain usually squashes things a little bit, calms us down, gets us ready for the next one, back to training. Briefing films, tapes, precautions. Weapons status of the planet. Their level. How far along. What's dominant. What to shoot and what to leave alone. Some of them aren't humanoid. Weird. Everything thinks the same. Everything wants to live. It doesn't make any difference where you go, same story. Kind of fun.

DR. FIORE: Did you ever have any feelings for the planet Earth?

DAN: I don't know it. I've never been there. They'd know it if we got there. [*Pauses*]

DR. FIORE: What are you doing now?

DAN: Relaxing in my room, looking at tapes, reviewing them. The landing formation, seeing why that guy got hurt. See if we can keep it from happening next time. He could have been killed. The stupid shit fell out of the ship, missed the gangway. Full gear, into the ground, face first. Doesn't happen very often. New recruit. He'll fall into it. He won't forget that one. Hell of a thing to happen on your first drop. Kind of funny, watching the tape of him taking a fall. He don't look quite as good as he did when he left. Some gal someplace will like it. [*Pauses*]

DR. FIORE: Just let yourself relax deeper and deeper. We're going to move now to the first time that you were aware of the planet Earth. At the count of five. One . . . two . . . three . . . four . . . five.

DAN: Standing in the middle of a logging trail. Washington State Cascades. Looking at the Douglas fir. Watching the clouds move through the tops of the trees, smelling them, listening to the animals in the bushes. First time out. It's beautiful.

DR. FIORE: What kind of preparation have you had for this?

DAN: None. Woods behind the house. Just kind of took off, took a walk. [*Pauses*] Just walking up the trail, the road, really. They don't log there anymore. Nobody out there. Nothing around, really nice. Peaceful, quiet. All alone.

DR. FIORE: Why are you there?

DAN: Just to see what's there.

DR. FIORE: And where's your ship?

DAN: I'm a little kid, no ship, no responsibility. Just a nice summer day. Nothing to do. All day to do it. Just exploring.

DR. FIORE: Now we see you as this child. I'm going to ask you to make the connection of how you became this child.

DAN: Two different people. The child has all the memories. It's like retirement. You get a chance to do nothing if you live longer. Be at a nice pretty place.

DR. FIORE: How did you get to be this child.

DAN: I don't remember.

DR. FIORE: I'm going to ask you to remember everything, at the count of five, we'll go to the very moment when you either joined this child or you somehow are this child. At the count of five. One . . . two . . . three . . . four . . . five.

DAN: I joined him on that road. Replaced, really.

DR. FIORE: Let's go back to before you joined him, and let's see how you got to be on that road.

DAN: Drunk. Horribly, horribly drunk. Good party. Next morning . . . tour the bridge. Say goodbyes.

DR. FIORE: Then what happens?

DAN: Just me today. One at a time, pick your planet. Pick an easy one. Everybody's laughing.

DR. FIORE: You say that you were drunk?

DAN: The night before, terrible hangover.

DR. FIORE: Where did you get drunk.

DAN: On the ship, officers' mess . . . Confusion, drinking.

DR. FIORE: What kind of ship is this?

DAN: Class M. Large. Battlecruiser; fourteen drop ships; 3500 people. Armed to the teeth.

DR. FIORE: Where are you from?

DAN: [*Pauses*] Try and remember home; it's been a long time.

DR. FIORE: The first ship, where does it travel?

DAN: Space.

DR. FIORE: And then you landed in the state of Washington, on the planet Earth, is that what you're saying?

DAN: Never touched down.

DR. FIORE: I see.

DAN: No need. The ship's too recognizable.

DR. FIORE: How did you get from that ship to the loggers' trail?

DAN: No need for physical transport. The body never leaves the ship. The mind.

DR. FIORE: Part of you, the mind, goes?

DAN: Right.

DR. FIORE: Do you know the purpose of going to that particular area?

DAN: Retirement.

DR. FIORE: Did you know that you would be joining the boy there?

DAN: Sure.

DR. FIORE: Was this all planned beforehand?

DAN: Yes.

DR. FIORE: Go to the very moment when you see that boy for the first time.

DAN: From behind. He doesn't know. He couldn't see me anyway.

DR. FIORE: Do you know the boy's first name?

DAN: No.

DR. FIORE: But he has been selected, this has all been planned?

DAN: He's my choice.

DR. FIORE: You chose him?

DAN: No. At random. Looked around.

DR. FIORE: Now you've seen him from the back, tell me step by step what happens.

DAN: I replace him.

DR. FIORE: What happens to him?

DAN: Gone.

DR. FIORE: How is this done?

DAN: I don't understand it.

DR. FIORE: Have you ever done this before to anyone?

DAN: I've seen others.

DR. FIORE: What do you mean?

DAN: Other retirees.

DR. FIORE: Other retirees do this?

DAN: Yes.

DR. FIORE: So you take over this boy's body, is that it?

DAN: Yes.

DR. FIORE: Do you have all of your memories from before?

DAN: You lose them, they fade with time.

DR. FIORE: Do you have his memories?

DAN: Yes.

DR. FIORE: What kind of reaction does he have when you enter him, when you take over?

DAN: Fear, then he's gone.

DR. FIORE: What does it feel like for you to be in this particular body?

DAN: Strange, very strange.

DR. FIORE: Tell me about it, in what way is it strange?

DAN: It's small. It's not strong.

DR. FIORE: Was your body much bigger?

DAN: Yes, adult. Seems funny, it's so soft. [*Pauses*] Things look so pretty, though. I made a good choice. Good thing too. Can't be reversed.

DR. FIORE: Now what happens?

DAN: Thinking. It was a lot of fun. Wondering what's ahead. Wondering what it's going to be like here. No choice now. Just go ahead, do it. Wondering if it's a great idea or not, this method. Can't change your mind. It's kind of funny, sure changed that kid's mind, permanently. Now I'm him. I'm stuck, and no way out.

DR. FIORE: Do you have some instructions or some game plan?

DAN: No plan, just play it as it comes. No instructions.

DR. FIORE: Was there some purpose in your being in this partic-ular place, on this planet?

DAN: No, it's just easier to get rid of retirees, than pensioning them off on the state. No welfare. It's funny, here they take care of everybody; can't get used to that.

DR. FIORE: Are you planning to go back sometime?

DAN: No. That won't be. They told me, only if needed. Un-likely. I wasn't that valuable. Probably be here forever.

DR. FIORE: What are you doing now?

DAN: Go home, go back where he lives.

DR. FIORE: How do you know where he lives?

DAN: I have all his memories.

DR. FIORE: Tell me about your first minutes at his home.

DAN: Open the door, walk in. My mother's standing there in the kitchen. Seems kind of funny. She seems nice. We get along all right. It's going to take some time for the memories to fade, become a kid again. Smells funny in the house. It's different. There's a dog. [*Pauses*] Kind of a lost feeling. [*Pauses*] I find my room. It's okay. I plop down on the bed and just relax, go to sleep.

DR. FIORE: Move to when you wake up.

DAN: Strange surroundings. Real strange. Hungry. I go out, she fixes me something to eat. I go out and play. [*Pauses*] The ship's gone, everything's gone. Put that behind me. Just forget it.

DR. FIORE: Now what do you do?

DAN: Go out and play. Find a friend or something. We go down by the creek. Mess around. Have fun.

DR. FIORE: Does anyone notice anything different? Do they seem to react to you in any different way, to indicate that they know something has changed?

DAN: No. They couldn't know.

DR. FIORE: Why is that?

DAN: I have all his memories, all his patterns, and mine will fade.

DR. FIORE: How do you feel about the fact that yours will fade?

DAN: I'm sorry. I think maybe it wasn't such a great idea. I had a lot of fun. Did a lot. Saw a lot of places. Miss some of my friends. That's supposed to go away.

DR. FIORE: Is his body any different from yours, basically?

DAN: No. The same.

DR. FIORE: Are you saying that you had a human body before?

DAN: Yes.

DR. FIORE: On that ship?

DAN: Yes.

DR. FIORE: Move ahead, to a time when, as this new person, Dan, you had your first close encounter, at the count of five. One . . . two . . . three . . . four . . . five. Just report everything that comes into your mind.

DAN: There's nothing, I can't see anything.

DR. FIORE: How do you feel?

DAN: Sweaty, tingly. Tight chested.

DR. FIORE: It's all coming back to you, crystal clear.

DAN: I hope not.

DR. FIORE: Every detail of that first encounter.

DAN: I can't quite make it out . . . meeting with someone.

DR. FIORE: It's coming clearer and clearer into your mind.

DAN: He's not human, he's familiar. I'm not afraid, except for what he's going to do.

DR. FIORE: What is he going to do?

DAN: I'm not sure. He's not nice.

DR. FIORE: What do you mean by that?

DAN: He's not one of those we like. Treacherous. Hard to deal with. Wants information.

DR. FIORE: How old are you at this point?

DAN: Eighteen. I want information from him. He just laughs, won't give it to me.

DR. FIORE: Just speak out whatever you are aware of.

DAN: I don't have the information he wants. Very risky. Accidents can happen. Seems stupid, all he's asking.

DR. FIORE: What is he asking?

DAN: I only remember that it seems so dumb. Probably a test. There's nothing here he wants. [Pauses] These people are backward. He must be just testing. He leaves me alone. It's a good thing nobody here can see him, they'd have nightmares for a month. He's not an air-breather. I wonder why they sent him. Strange. Frightening. I hope they don't send him back. They told me they'd leave me alone. Something must have gone wrong. I can't remember enough about it to do anything. I can't even remember how to build a goddamn weapon. It's awful. Can't defend myself. I don't want to have that experience again. I'm glad it's over.

DR. FIORE: What happened?

DAN: Just interrogated.

DR. FIORE: And where are you now?

DAN: Standing someplace, at a school crossing.

DR. FIORE: It's all crystal clear in your mind. You're remembering everything.

DAN: On the sidewalk in front of the school. Waiting for the bus. Nobody around me notices anything. Everything's fine, back to normal.

DR. FIORE: Where were you when you were interrogated?

DAN: Not sure.

DR. FIORE: Let yourself remember the very beginning of this interrogation, of this encounter.

DAN: Mental interrogation.

DR. FIORE: What's the very first thing you notice?

DAN: This face in my mind.

DR. FIORE: How do you feel when you see that face?

DAN: Oh shit! It's not supposed to happen.

DR. FIORE: So you're remembering.

DAN: They said they'd leave me alone. I want to go back. Not with this guy. [*Pauses*] Maybe if I give him the right kind of lie I can get out of it. I don't have the information he wants anyway.

DR. FIORE: What kind of information does he want?

DAN: It seems stupid.

DR. FIORE: What is he asking you?

DAN: I can't remember.

DR. FIORE: You're going to allow yourself to remember, at the count of three. One . . . two . . . three.

DAN: He did a good job. He was good at what he did. I can't remember. I don't know what he wanted.

DR. FIORE: Why do you say he was good at what he did?

DAN: He took the memory with him.

DR. FIORE: Do you feel that maybe he created amnesia in you?

DAN: No, he just took the memory, that part.

DR. FIORE: Now you're going to go to the very next encounter, at the count of three, whatever form that encounter takes. One . . . two . . . three. First thoughts.

DAN: My old captain, friend, familiar. Good person. He apologizes. For being there. Just a chat. Against the rules. The other side's worried. That's why the questions seemed dumb. They're paranoid.

DR. FIORE: Is he explaining this to you?

DAN: He's asking me what he asked. And I'm telling him. But I don't remember what I told him. That part's gone.

DR. FIORE: Do you want it to be gone?

DAN: No. I want to remember it.

DR. FIORE: Then you'll be able to remember it. You see, they can't take the memory away.

DAN: They can take the memory. Just as I replaced the child. The memory can be erased.

DR. FIORE: Did you tell your captain what he asked?

DAN: No, I didn't. I couldn't tell him.

DR. FIORE: Does your captain give you any instructions?

DAN: Not to talk to them again. I laugh and tell him that I have no choice. He laughs and tells me to get drunk, I'll feel better. And goes away.

DR. FIORE: How did you make this contact with him?

DAN: Mental. I'm in bed.

DR. FIORE: How soon after the first contact is this?

DAN: A couple of weeks.

DR. FIORE: Now move to your very next contact.

DAN: I don't think I want to remember that one.

DR. FIORE: Why do you say that?

DAN: Just not a good memory.

DR. FIORE: Is it frightening?

DAN: I don't know if it's frightening or it's bad or wrong, or . . . what. Just doesn't want to come, and I don't want it to.

DR. FIORE: Okay, that's fine. You're in charge of what you remember and what you don't want to remember. Let's move you to a memory of an encounter that's perhaps more recent, that you do want to remember, one that you will allow yourself to remember, at the count of three. One . . . two . . . three.

DAN: I open the front door, and there's one of them standing there. I never met this one. He's humanoid. I know the type. I'm not afraid. They're not violent. Intellectuals.

DR. FIORE: What does he look like?

DAN: Silver. The suit. It's not really that way. They need protection. He comes in. We sit and talk. Old times.

DR. FIORE: Does he realize that you've replaced the boy?

DAN: Yes. He knows me. I don't know him. He's been reading records.

DR. FIORE: What do you talk about?

DAN: He's asking me what's going on. What I'm doing. How I like it. I'm begging him for the secrets that I used to know. He won't tell me. I can understand he wouldn't give me the weapon. I'm trying to get him to tell me. It's so simple. I can't remember. So damn simple a child could build one, and I can't remember. I can't remember the damn way to put the thing together, and he's not helping me.

DR. FIORE: What is the purpose of that weapon?

DAN: It's not a weapon.

DR. FIORE: What is it?

DAN: It's the drive for the ship. It's simple, so simple. And I tell him I think I can come up with everything I need here. And he won't tell me. He just laughs and says, you made your deal, you're stuck. And I tell him I'm not stuck or they wouldn't keep coming back. It's pointless to argue with those people.

DR. FIORE: Why is that?

DAN: They're too intelligent and they're way ahead of you.

DR. FIORE: What does he look like?

DAN: If you peel off the suit, it'd be brown. Rather large eyes, small mouth. Pretty nose. Slight build.

DR. FIORE: What color is his skin?

DAN: Brown. Doesn't tolerate temperature extremes well.

DR. FIORE: Is any part of his skin exposed, or is it covered?

DAN: It's covered. Just holes for the eyes. They're not really holes. They've got . . . covering across them, just to protect them.

DR. FIORE: What color does his skin look like with the suit on?

DAN: Silver.

DR. FIORE: But underneath it's brown?

DAN: Underneath it's brown, medium brown.

DR. FIORE: What else do you talk about?

DAN: Women. Differences.

DR. FIORE: Do you feel there's more to it than just a social get-together?

DAN: There always is with those. They only socialize with each other.

DR. FIORE: What does he want from you?

DAN: He seems to be interested in my attitude toward . . . my feelings about being here. He's probably some sociologist on a field trip. I tell him that. He laughs. They never give you a hint whether you got it right or not. You could guess dead-on. They never tell. Makes me nervous after a while. He's staying too long. I'm afraid somebody's going to walk in. Then he gets scared. Sees I'm nervous. And scared. Accuses me of setting a trap for him. I invite him to leave. Then he goes. A little paranoia. He's worried that the rest of the family's going to come in and find him. I tell him just sit there and I'll go get them. They'd love to meet him. Against all the rules. Can't do that. Don't think the wife could handle it anyway. The kids would love it. I don't feel him take any memories when he goes. They're pretty good, though. Huh . . . They don't usually come and go through the front door. Strange . . . Seems funny . . . Treat him like anybody else. Back in the old days, he wouldn't have even talked to me. Brings back the old feelings. I'd like to go back.

DR. FIORE: Let's move on to another encounter, a recent one.

DAN: Same one, only this time less chat. Same guy.

DR. FIORE: What's happening?

DAN: Been messing with the computer, and he's taking some printout of some program. He doesn't need it. It's a toy for him. Won't do anything for him.

DR. FIORE: What computer is this?

DAN: Personal computer at home.

DR. FIORE: What's he taking?

DAN: He's taking printouts of my programming. It's silly. I use it in my work. Probably just doing it for a laugh. He says it'll help him. Not unless he's going to retire here or what. Then he's gone.

DR. FIORE: How did he get there?

DAN: He didn't use the doors this time.

DR. FIORE: What was the date when this happened?

DAN: Twenty-fourth . . . August . . . '88.

DR. FIORE: Move to another encounter.

DAN: I don't know how I got here, back aboard the ship. Party time. People I haven't seen for a long time.

DR. FIORE: What's it like for you?

DAN: Like being alive again. Everybody's laughing at the way I'm dressed.

DR. FIORE: What are you wearing?

DAN: Blue jeans, cowboy boots. They made me take them off to prove my feet weren't that shape. Lots of people. Good friends. Lots of war stories. Good party. Lots of pictures. Some of the old drops. They save the one where the guy falls off the ship. He's a captain now. [*Pauses*] We get a tour of the ship, just for old times.

DR. FIORE: Same ship?

DAN: Same ship. Same one I served in.

DR. FIORE: Tell me about the tour.

DAN: Start with the bridge. All different people. Crew's changed. Look out through the windows. I remember what it was like. Just traveling. Sit up on the bridge and talk. Just watch the stars. Drop down through the ship. Past the old quarters. Down into the bay. Then home. I wanted to stay. I just wish they'd let me stay. I'm getting tired of being jerked around.

DR. FIORE: Is there any chance of your joining them again?

DAN: Possible. Possible. Mention drops coming up. Needed the experience. Don't have it anymore. Memories are gone. I don't know if I could get them back. [*Pauses*] I spend time with the captain. We talked in his quarters for hours.

DR. FIORE: What do you talk about?

DAN: I want to come back. He wants me to. Against the rules. Can't do it. He'll look into it and let me know. [*Pauses*] Talked about the big drop out on the far side. Sounded like old times.

DR. FIORE: What do you mean by drop?

DAN: Swing into orbit. Set up. Load up. Open the bays, let enough landing ships out to do the job. Drop down through the atmosphere.

DR. FIORE: Are these drops always hostile?

DAN: Always. That's what makes it so much fun.

DR. FIORE: How many ships are involved in the big drop?

DAN: Four or five ships.

DR. FIORE: How many men are in each ship?

DAN: Thirty-five hundred. All class M. Go for it. All fourteen, each ship.

DR. FIORE: Fourteen smaller craft in each ship?

DAN: Yes.

DR. FIORE: And how many personnel in each smaller craft?

DAN: A hundred. One hundred people on that ship, take care of anything.

DR. FIORE: The big ships hold 3500 people?

DAN: Yes.

DR. FIORE: How big are they?

DAN: A mile and a half long, approximately.

DR. FIORE: What shape are they?

DAN: Basically, hard to describe.

DR. FIORE: Are the big ships circular or disc shaped?

DAN: No. That shape won't work in the atmosphere.

DR. FIORE: Are you interested in the big drop the captain talked about?

DAN: Yes. Sounds like a good time.

DR. FIORE: What will happen?

DAN: Showed me reconnaissance photos. Have to take on about three cities at a time. I don't know what these people did. Must have been bad, because they want that place clean.

DR. FIORE: Do you know what planet that was on?

DAN: No.

DR. FIORE: Do you know what galaxy it's in?

DAN: Same galaxy as Earth, other side. Out on one of the arms. I don't think Earth has a name for it.

DR. FIORE: When will it occur?

DAN: It's coming up. There won't be any resistance. Big operation.

DR. FIORE: Would they make a drop on Earth?

DAN: No, they won't. There's no need to.

DR. FIORE: Why is that?

DAN: Earth is of no significance.

DR. FIORE: Tell me more about that last experience, that encounter.

DAN: I had a couple of drinks with the captain. Says they want somebody to coordinate it. I ask him why he didn't. He says he was told to ask me. I ask him how he's going to do it, since it's against the rules. He says he doesn't know. We're getting a little drunk and a little confused at this point. I think we're getting a little fuzzy. All I can think of is that it sounded like fun. I need the excitement, to feel alive again. Then the discussion's over.

Nothing's resolved. Go down the corridor. Down a deck. And I'm home.

DR. FIORE: How do you get home? Let yourself remember that.

DAN: Through the door. Close the door behind you, and you're there.

DR. FIORE: How do you get from that ship to your own home?

DAN: I don't know how it works.

DR. FIORE: You're going to let yourself remember.

DAN: I don't think I ever knew. It's too technical.

DR. FIORE: Were you taken on another ship?

DAN: No, there's no transport. You simply walk in the door and close the door behind you. When you close the door, you're there.

DR. FIORE: When you're there, do you remember what you've just experienced?

DAN: Briefly. I remember it's unnerving. Sudden change of scene. I didn't realize I hated to travel that way.

DR. FIORE: Let yourself remember another encounter on the ship.

DAN: Just once in a while, the parties. They played some tapes of some of the things I was involved in. Showed the pictures. Got a chance to relive the old days. That was fun.

DR. FIORE: Let yourself remember if you've ever had any close encounters on a different ship.

DAN: Shore leave. [*Pauses*] Lots of different places. Different races. [*Pauses*] Not too much visiting between the ships. Most of the time too far out. Only when you come back. Too many people to know them all. [*Pauses*] Don't talk too much to the other people on the other ships, no chance, no opportunity.

DR. FIORE: When did this happen? Did this happen after you assumed the body of Dan?

DAN: No.

DR. FIORE: Before.

DAN: Yes.

DR. FIORE: After you took on the body of Dan, the identity, have you had any other close encounters with other types of extraterrestrials?

DAN: Just the intellectual and the treacherous ones. Those are the only two that I've seen.

DR. FIORE: Are you ready now to remember that encounter that you avoided before?

DAN: I don't like that one. I don't like that one at all.

DR. FIORE: Let yourself remember a little something about it.

DAN: If I had the right weapon, I'd kill him.

DR. FIORE: What was he like?

DAN: All I remember is the protruding face, oversized teeth. A coarse fur. Grease. Stink.

DR. FIORE: Where did this encounter take place?

DAN: I don't know where it took place.

DR. FIORE: Did it take place in your home, or on the ship, or outside?

DAN: I think this one was mental. That one couldn't ever come down here.

DR. FIORE: Why is that?

DAN: He'd never be able to fit in, never blend. He just couldn't do it. He's too strange. He wouldn't want to anyway.

DR. FIORE: You've run into that type before?

DAN: Yes.

DR. FIORE: Was that before you came into Dan's body?

DAN: Yes.

DR. FIORE: Will there be any drops on planet Earth? Or have there been in the past?

DAN: No, not to my knowledge. Earth is backwater, it's the outback. It's a retirement planet.

DR. FIORE: Do you feel like there's many people here who are retirees?

DAN: Probably quite a few.

DR. FIORE: In your last encounter with the intellectual type who wanted the printout, did he want actual paper from your printer?

DAN: Yes.

DR. FIORE: And why did he want it?

DAN: I have no idea why he'd want it. It doesn't seem to make any sense. Of course, with them, you never know.

DR. FIORE: Was there something unusual you had printed out?

DAN: No. It was just basic language programming. He doesn't even need programming. I don't understand why he would even want it. Maybe a curio.

DR. FIORE: He was there in your room?

DAN: Yes.

DR. FIORE: Did he sit down at the computer?

DAN: No, he just stood beside me. Watched me work. Asked me to print it out, so I did.

DR. FIORE: Did you give it to him?

DAN: Yes, there's no harm in it. He can't do anything with what he got. At least not that I know of.

DR. FIORE: You've seen the cover of the book *Communion*?

DAN: Yes.

DR. FIORE: Does that face look familiar? Does it look like anything that you'd recognize?

DAN: Similar, but it's very elongated. Eyes are much too big.

DR. FIORE: Is there anything else you want to remember?

DAN: I could spend all night going over the ship, I love it.

DR. FIORE: Why don't you describe the ship some more. Where did you sleep?

DAN: A bed about the size of a single bed, adjustable, at an angle, so you could read. Screen on the wall. So you could watch entertainment or reviews, whatever.

DR. FIORE: Was there other furniture?

DAN: Yes, same kind of things. And . . . storage cabinet. If you walk in the door, it's to your right. Bed straight ahead. View screen on the right-hand wall. Storage cabinet in the right-hand corner. Locking drawers. Very plain, maybe ten by twelve.

DR. FIORE: What are the walls like?

DAN: Painted, feels like steel.

DR. FIORE: You said painted?

DAN: It's painted over.

DR. FIORE: What's on the floor?

DAN: Carpet.

DR. FIORE: What color is it?

DAN: Dark brown, cream-colored walls. Whole ceiling illuminated. Adjustable switch by the door, and one by the bed.

DR. FIORE: When you're on this ship, how long is your tour of duty?

DAN: A year.

DR. FIORE: And then what happens?

DAN: Rotate back to base, shore leave, then another year.

DR. FIORE: Is that on your home planet?

DAN: No. It's a station.

DR. FIORE: In space.

DAN: Yes. Trying to remember how long. It's been a long time.

DR. FIORE: When you're on this ship, are there women, as well as men?

DAN: Oh yes.

DR. FIORE: What's the function of the women?

DAN: Same as the men. Fight. Any duty the man does.

DR. FIORE: You were talking about having a party, with alcohol.

DAN: Yes.

DR. FIORE: What kind of food do you eat?

DAN: I'm trying to remember.

DR. FIORE: Just try to remember a meal, sitting down to a meal. Maybe it's a special meal.

DAN: I'm trying to remember eating in my quarters.

DR. FIORE: Is that where you ate?

DAN: Yes. Not always. I'm just trying to remember sitting on the bunk, eating, a metal tray with about eight compartments cut into it, like a stamp, like an aluminum-foil tray.

DR. FIORE: And what utensils do you use?

DAN: It's like a fork, sharp on one edge, for cutting. And . . . food's pretty similar, looks a little bit different.

DR. FIORE: Do you eat meat?

DAN: Yes.

DR. FIORE: Vegetables or fruits?

DAN: Yes, vegetables, some fruits. Some special treats. Takes a lot to feed them.

DR. FIORE: What do you mean?

DAN: It takes a lot to feed a ship that size.

DR. FIORE: Do you have sexual contacts between the men and the women?

DAN: Every chance we get.

DR. FIORE: Is there any homosexuality?

DAN: Some.

DR. FIORE: And how is that seen?

DAN: Tolerated. Not favorably, but tolerated.

DR. FIORE: Is there any problem with contraception?

DAN: No.

DR. FIORE: Why is that?

DAN: Medicines, injections.

DR. FIORE: How often is it given?

DAN: Every tour.

DR. FIORE: Just once?

DAN: Just once.

DR. FIORE: When you're back at the home base, do you have sexual contact with the crew?

DAN: Yes. It's part of the normal routine.

DR. FIORE: Do you have one partner, or do you have many partners?

DAN: Individual preference. Some pair up. It's not a good idea. You get too attached. They get killed, and you go nuts. You'll become ineffective. Doesn't work.

DR. FIORE: So it's discouraged?

DAN: It's not discouraged. Most people just assume it's not going to work, they can't get that close to somebody.

DR. FIORE: How are they killed?

DAN: Somebody screws up on a drop.

DR. FIORE: What percent per drop have some kind of injury?

DAN: Drop a hundred in, somebody might stub their toe. Occasionally you lose one.

DR. FIORE: How many drops do you have, say, per year?

DAN: One every two to five weeks.

DR. FIORE: What is the biggest drop that you were ever involved in?

DAN: Two ships.

✱

When Dan came out of hypnosis, it was nine o'clock and black outside my window. The lighting was dim in the room, and we both had skipped dinner, so there was a feeling of it being later than it was. My day at the office is usually over at five, six o'clock at the latest, so it was an unusual feeling to be there at that hour.

Dan stretched and rubbed his eyes as though waking up from a nap. I asked him how he felt.

"Like a thoroughly dangerous person until I realized exactly where I am. The regression put me back into a different mind-set. It's not one you carry around with you, except in a situation where you are allowed to kill, and where you are rewarded for it. It's your job, being a soldier."

"Dan, were you ever in that situation in this lifetime? Were you in the service?" So many of his terms sounded like Navy jargon to me, that I was sure he would reply in the affirmative. In fact, because of terms like "bridge," "bay," etc., I had wondered at one point if he weren't retired from a professional career in the Navy.

"No, thank God! I'm glad that I never got into the service here, because I knew intuitively, even long before this session, that I would have enjoyed it too much. I don't know if I would have been able to make the transition from one minute you're killing somebody in some field in Asia, and three days later you're back on the streets in America. I don't know if I could have done that."

He commented on how his conscious mind had constantly critiqued the material that was coming forth. (I quoted him at some length in Chapter One.) My favorite line was, "It's a very strange feeling, like your mouth is operating on its own, and your mind is saying, 'Shut up, you idiot!' "

I reassured him that he had done an excellent job of just letting it flow. I felt that his conscious-mind analysis hadn't interfered at all.

"It was an interesting experience. I didn't know that I would still be aware of my body, as much as I was. I was amazed at the physical reactions to the memories."

This intrigued me and added to my impression that it was not just one big fantasy.

"There was great tensing of the muscles. Like the fight-or-flight reflex. This feeling that you're sweating, but you're not."

"Did you feel any anxiety?"

"Yes. But much to my discredit here on Earth, I felt a lot of fun too. A lot of joy at making the drop, going in, hitting the dirt, going out, and feeling alive and like this was great fun. And that's not exactly your Saturday night entertainment in San Jose, California." He laughed heartily.

It was time to stop for the evening, but we decided to get together one more time to see what else we could find.

✹

Two weeks later we met again at the end of the day. I wanted to have plenty of time available in case we needed it. The last time he'd been under hypnosis for almost two hours, which is long for one sitting.

"Dan, how did you feel when you left here?"

"On a real high. I was very comfortable with it. It put everything into place, nice and neat. Everything's explained now. I don't worry about where I came from or what I'm doing here." Dan seemed relaxed and excited at the same time. Our session had obviously been a very positive experience for him.

"Have you noticed any changes in yourself? I know it's only been two weeks, but sometimes these regressions lead to rather dramatic results immediately."

"One of the smaller changes has been not worrying about things nearly as much. They don't seem as important as they used to. I'm more able to deal with crises that are going on around me. I seem to be a more objective observer, rather than a panic-stricken participant. I think that, coupled with having some of the answers, has given me more self-confidence. I'm a little more assertive than I was, simply because there's not this great sense of having something to lose. To sum up, I think that one of the major changes is an increase in self-confidence."

I was curious about how his self-confidence could have been so enhanced. I suspected his identifying with who he had been before he took over Dan's body was the obvious answer, but I was interested in his insight into the change. "What do you feel caused you to feel more self-confident?"

"It's due to his character. There was *no* lack of self-confidence. I don't feel an arrogance, but rather a surety in his own mind of a near invincibility. And he never had to deal with anything that he couldn't overcome through superior force or any other means. I think realizing that side has filled in the self-confidence a lot. I know I came out of here just really hyped. I really enjoyed it. I felt good. When I talk about it now, I still get tingles up and down the spine, and it still fills me with a sense of power and strength." He looked up at me gratefully. "It was great. I don't think, when we separated last time, you realized how much it had done for me."

I felt extremely happy that he had gotten so much out of the session. I knew his material was really exceptional and different from the other cases I'd be presenting in *Encounters,* and I was more than glad that it was so rewarding for him.

As I was covering Dan with the blanket, I explained that his body temperature would probably drop when in hypnosis. He suddenly remembered something. He was already in a reclining position, so I asked him to sit back up and not let it wait for later.

"I'm not sure, Edee, what this means, but I think it has to do with what we've been working on. When I'm asleep, my body temperature and my heart rate and my respiration will drop way below normal levels. If you were to touch me, I would be quite cold to the touch. It's scared the living chickens out of the wife a number of times when she touched me in the middle of the night. She couldn't wake me. And she was afraid I was gone. She told me she put her hand on my chest to make sure I was breathing. I was, but very slowly. In that stage, if I'm awakened, brought out of it suddenly by a calamity or a sudden loud noise, I can't see for two or three minutes. I'll run into walls. I can barely coordinate to walk. It's almost like I'm so deep asleep that it just won't come back. But it never bothers me. It's never given me any difficulty or problems. It is so restful." Finishing, Dan looked almost blissful. Then he glanced over to me for an explanation.

"It sounds like you're out of your body at those times. The physical body goes almost into a state of suspended animation while your energy is being used in your other body. The other body's called by various names, mainly an "astral" body, because even in ancient times, it was understood that this body was capable of traveling through the stars, while the physical body remained where it was. This traveling is called, "out-of-the-body" travel or astral projection. You're right that it's related to what we found out last time, because you did remember visiting the spaceship and the space station. So you probably did it in your astral body."

Again, I pushed Dan's chair back to its fullest reclining position. I made a special effort to tuck him in with the blanket, since his body temperature would undoubtedly drop more than most people's do when they're under hypnosis. I wasn't expecting him to leave his body, but I wasn't taking any chances of his being chilled, if he did, as has happened before with some of my patients, while in a particularly deep trance.

Once he was hypnotized, I asked his inner mind to take him to an especially significant event. I wanted to leave the suggestions fairly undefined in order not to miss something important to him. I counted him back in time and space and asked him to speak out whatever came into his mind.

❧

DAN: I'm kneeling next to an open hatch, with another man, looking into the side at the machinery. Neither one of us knows what's wrong. We're trying to figure it out. I can't come up with the answer. Something's wrong with the ship. It's not working right. We're worried about being stranded. Neither one of us is an engineer. Can't repair the silly thing. We're under pressure of some sort. Need to get out of there. We're struggling to fix it, do something with it. Neither one of us understands what. I can't seem to quite get it done.

DR. FIORE: Is there anyone else there with you, on the ship?

DAN: It's just us at the hatch. On the outside. The ship's on the ground.

DR. FIORE: Where is it?

DAN: It's in a forest.

DR. FIORE: Do you know the name of the planet you're on?

DAN: Something like Markel. It's getting dark. We give up and close the hatch and go inside. Some success; it lifts. We make it back. Laughing at our success. But we didn't even know what we were doing. Complicated things.

DR. FIORE: What did you actually do?

DAN: Reached in and . . . just tugged and pulled, twisted and wiggled things around, looking for loose tubing, connections. Must of wiggled the right thing.

DR. FIORE: How did you feel when you felt the ship lifting off?

DAN: Apprehensive, scared. It might not lift all the way, or it might not continue. It's the only way out, though. Take a chance. Go for it. Have a couple of drinks aboard the ship, when we get back; try to relax, calm down. Close call.

DR. FIORE: How long did it take you to get back, in Earth time?

DAN: Ten minutes.

DR. FIORE: Let yourself remember another encounter, one that's still having a negative impact on you, at the count of five. One . . . two . . . three . . . four . . . five.

DAN: Interrogation with one of the violent ones. Stupid questions. No way to know the answers, from my position. Keeps pressing.

DR. FIORE: What kind of questions are you being asked?

DAN: Where are you living? What are you doing here? Questions I shouldn't answer. Not to him. Too dangerous. Can't trust him. I'm afraid he'll see through it. He shouldn't be here.

DR. FIORE: Where is this taking place?

DAN: Seems to be in front of where I went to high school.

DR. FIORE: How old are you when this is taking place?

DAN: Fourteen.

DR. FIORE: Tell me more about the interrogation.

DAN: It's like a test. He's not one you mess with. No answers. Don't want to give him any answers. He's mad. Can't really do anything now. Breaks it off. Leaves me standing there. Shouldn't talk to them.

DR. FIORE: Tell me about that.

DAN: Vicious. Untrustworthy. The worst. A race of killers. Born that way. Useful and troublesome.

DR. FIORE: What do you mean by useful?

DAN: They have their uses. Troublemakers. Difficult to control. I'm defenseless here. He really shouldn't even be here. I don't know how he got here. I'm glad he's gone.

DR. FIORE: Let yourself remember another contact that's having an effect on you.

DAN: Conference on the ship, talking with the captain. Old friend. Sitting in his cabin. Comfortable. Feels good to be there. No, I can't stay. Sorry about that. Laughing. Just kidding with each other, remembering old times. He's human. Just like me. We're discussing the troublemakers. He doesn't know about the contact. Finds it upsetting, it's been too long ago to do anything about it. No more trouble. It's all over. They won't be back for a long time. It finally became too much trouble. To put up with it. Talk late into the night. Lots of stories. Good times. He says good night. Walks me down the corridor. Into the room and closes the door behind me. And I'm back.

DR. FIORE: How do you get back?

DAN: Just close the door.

DR. FIORE: What happens between the time you close the door and the time you get back?

DAN: I just change positions.

DR. FIORE: Once you're back, what do you remember?

DAN: Just a warm feeling.

DR. FIORE: Where are you when you get back?

DAN: Back in my house.

DR. FIORE: What are you doing there?

DAN: Walking down the hallway.

DR. FIORE: How long would you estimate you've been gone?

DAN: All night, ship's time.

DR. FIORE: Go back to the beginning of that encounter and get in touch with the very first thing you experience.

DAN: Dizziness as I go through the bedroom door, brief dizziness. As I walk out into the hallway, brief dizziness.

DR. FIORE: And then?

DAN: Then aboard the ship. And then back down, halfway down the hallway, I'm aware again.

DR. FIORE: How much time elapsed altogether, in Earth time?

DAN: Maybe fifteen seconds, walking down the hall.

DR. FIORE: And how much time in terms of the ship's time?

DAN: Eight hours.

DR. FIORE: Just continue to report everything that comes into your mind, as you remember more and more of your encounters.

DAN: There's a friend at the door, the front door. One of the intellectuals. Comes in. Social call. Just to say hello.

DR. FIORE: What is your reaction?

DAN: Glad to see him. Good to hear . . . any news of the ship. He's in a hurry to leave. I want him to stay and talk some more. He says next time. Goes. Disappointed.

DR. FIORE: Why was he in a hurry this time?

DAN: Busy. Duties.

DR. FIORE: Where were you when he visited you?

DAN: Front room.

DR. FIORE: Was there anybody else there in the room with you?

DAN: No.

DR. FIORE: Let your mind help you to remember another encounter, an important one that is still affecting you in some way.

DAN: Talking with the captain. On a possible recall. Makes me hope. Nice to think it might happen, so I might get back. I'd be doing something I really like. No schedule. No timetable. It's coming up. They want experience. They want people. Makes me feel good.

DR. FIORE: What is he saying about a recall?

DAN: Talking about the big operation. Possible. Needs a lot of people. I'm falling all over myself trying to volunteer. It's important enough to break some rules to do it. No promises. Just a maybe. I'm anxious. Want to be involved. Telling him that. Who knows? They'll let me know.

DR. FIORE: Did he say how many ships would be involved in the drop?

DAN: Four or five.

DR. FIORE: How many planets would be involved?

DAN: Just one. This time the whole planet. Major action.

DR. FIORE: Did he tell you the name of this planet?

DAN: No. Have to go to base to regroup. Standing on the bridge looking at the base. Beautiful, just hanging there in the blackness. Other ships all nosed in all around it. Huge. Beautiful sight!

DR. FIORE: How long is it?

DAN: It's a couple of miles across. The whole ship's up against the outer ring, nose first. Quite a sight.

DR. FIORE: What shape is it?

DAN: Large . . . almost disc shaped . . . thicker in the middle than at the edges. Circular. Ship's nosed up against the outer rim. It's pretty.

DR. FIORE: Where are you when you're watching this?

DAN: Standing out on the bridge of the ship, looking in toward the center of the station.

DR. FIORE: Has it been decided that you will be recalled?

DAN: No. They'll let me know. No word.

DR. FIORE: What are you aware of now?

DAN: Bridge. It's all quiet. Everybody's busy below. Just one or two people on the bridge. Just relaxing, nothing to do. Just enjoying the view. Back home again.

DR. FIORE: Let yourself know the date when this happened.

DAN: August fifteenth.

DR. FIORE: What year?

DAN: It's '87.

DR. FIORE: Let yourself know if they have informed you as to whether you're going to be recalled or not.

DAN: No. No, still waiting. No further word. I just hope they didn't go without me.

DR. FIORE: What would happen to your life here if you went?

DAN: Just take this body, everything, as it is.

DR. FIORE: Would you just disappear, be a missing person?

DAN: Right.

DR. FIORE: How would you handle this with your family?

DAN: It wouldn't be important. A few minutes of worry. I wouldn't be important anymore.

DR. FIORE: Would you return to Earth again?

DAN: No. This would be it. Memories come back.

DR. FIORE: Who is making this decision?

DAN: Command leaders.

DR. FIORE: What outcome do you want, in terms of the decision?

DAN: Only one! I want to go!

✦

Once he was back to normal waking consciousness, I asked Dan how the regression had been for him.

"It was difficult dealing with the memory of the violent ones. But I realized we got even, and I won't have that problem again. I got that understanding from the captain. So I know that it's been taken care of. They're not going to be a problem for anybody for a long, long time. They're not going to be able to get into space for generations. So I don't have to worry about that, nor does anybody else, which makes me feel better. Last time, that kind of bothered me. It had drifted in and out of my mind since then."

Going along with the material that had emerged, I was concerned about the possibility of Dan returning to space. I knew he had a wife and children. He also had a specialized job in construction management and an expertise that few others could match. "Dan, what would you do if presented with the chance to go back?"

"I want to go back. It's not that I don't love the wife and children and all that sort of thing. It's just that it's so far superior to be there than to be here. And I know that if I were there, I'd be involved in something so grand, that what happens here means nothing. Means nothing! To be back, to be able to do that again, would be fabulous!"

"How would you arrange it with your family, Dan?"

"A couple of months ago, the wife and I were standing out back, looking up the stars. It was a nice clear night. And I told her, 'Someday I'm going back.' And she said she'd really like to also. And I said, 'No, you don't understand. Someday I'm going home.' And she said, 'I'd like to go up there.' But she doesn't consider it her home, and I do."

"Did you know any of what we uncovered tonight, then? Or did you just have a very strong feeling?"

"I couldn't have possibly had any idea. I just always had this very strong feeling that that was where I belonged, that that was home. And I can't think of any other possible reason to say it to my wife, other than to prepare her."

"And to prepare yourself too."

"Yes! I'm ready!"

"They Call Themselves
the Planters."

Diane Tai is an exceptional person. She's been a gifted psychic since childhood. When I mentioned to a mutual friend that I was writing *Encounters*, she told me I should have Diane in the book because she's probably been a contactee for years. I called Diane, and she graciously agreed to come over to my office for a regression as soon as possible.

Diane arrived early for our appointment. She is a beautiful woman, just over forty, petite, with curly dark-brown hair and sparkling brown eyes. Her flowing white cotton dress and brilliant blue beads added to the general impression of her being special. She has had to cope with a serious physical condition since she was a child. She was diagnosed as having spinal muscular atrophy, a genetic disease. The doctors she's consulted through the years are amazed, first, that she is alive and, second, that she can walk and is actually quite active and mobile. Her sister died of the same disease at the age of nine, never having walked. So Diane has overcome many obstacles.

After a few minutes of social chitchat, we got down to business.

Diane had mentioned during our phone conversation that she had had a particularly exciting thing happen after a dream nine years ago, while she was still married to her former husband, so I decided this would be a good place for us to begin our investigation into a possible close encounter of the fourth kind.

"Edee, this kind of thing is always happening in my life. You won't believe it. Oh yes, you will, but nobody else would!" Diane laughed and continued, "I just talked to my ex-husband today, whom I hadn't spoken with for two years. He said, 'I was just thinking about you yesterday and today you call.' And then I said, 'I'm going to see Edee about this UFO thing. Remember that incident that happened and you laughed at me?' And he said, 'Oh, my goodness. I was just thinking about that yesterday, and here you're telling me about it today.' So I thought, We're either telepathic or something's going on here."

Knowing Diane, I wasn't in the least surprised. I've also experienced that sort of thing many times myself. I wanted to know about the UFO incident. "What happened, Diane. Tell me about the dream, and you said on the phone that something special happened after it?"

"On a Wednesday night, I think it was about nine years ago, I had a dream that a UFO was over my house. I had awakened from the dream, sat up in bed and told my husband, 'The UFO is here and they're over the house and I have to pack and get ready to go.' I was getting out of bed, and Dick said, 'It's a dream. You're okay. Go back to sleep.' He laughed at me, and I was half-remembering that I was in this spaceship. So I realized it was a dream and went back to sleep. The next day I was talking to my son, Ronnie, about it, and he and Dick were laughing and teasing me all day, saying, 'Here comes the UFO.' That night, Thursday, we were all watching '20/20,' when the first words out of Hugh Downs's mouth were, 'This is "20/20." A UFO was sighted over Cupertino, California, last night.' I thought, this is not true! I must be dreaming. I remember sitting there, and Ronnie and Dick turned and looked at me like I was an alien." Diane was really laughing at this point. She composed herself and continued,

"He went on to explain that it was an official sighting and had been picked up on radar at the San Jose Airport."

"Diane, we'll regress you to your so-called dream in a few minutes, but for the record I'd like to know more about your psychic abilities. When did they start?" Often psychic sensitivity is a consequence of CEIVs, and I was trying to get an idea of how long she might have been a contactee.

"I had an eye operation when I was seven, so I had bandages around my eyes while I was healing. They had taken the eye out and done the operation on my muscles because I was cross-eyed. It didn't take long before I realized I could see other things without my vision."

"You mean you could see things that weren't there?"

"No. My parents would try to test me, 'Okay, what's the neighbor got on today? Who's here, Diane? What do they look like?' I could see a lot of things. I was using a different sight. My parents didn't understand these things. They were simple people and they just thought it was fun. And it was."

"Thank heavens they didn't squelch your development. That's what usually happens. Parents are threatened by children who are different, so they wash their mouth out with soap or tell them they're lying. I've heard some pretty pathetic tales. That usually drives those abilities underground. If they ever surface again, it's usually in adult life. When did you next notice something special?"

Diane thought for a few seconds, and then her face lit up with a mischievous grin. "In junior high I began to have these strange feelings that I was communicating with an alien. I was about thirteen, maybe fourteen. And the psychic ability was really getting strong at that time. I didn't even know what the word 'psychic' meant. Sometimes I would look at the kids and say, 'This is going to happen to you.' And it would. So I went to school and I started to tell them I was talking to this woman from another planet who was giving me all this information about the planet, and she also knew things about other people. And they'd say, 'Well, what does she know about me?' And I'd say all these things. And finally it got so big that everybody was talking about it. You know how things can go fast in school. One day my gym teacher had me stand up in class and she said, 'Today we're going to ask Diane about this planet, and she's going to talk to her alien.' And they were asking me all these questions. And I don't know where the answers were coming from. I just stood there for an hour answering questions and looking at the kids and saying, 'This may happen to you,' and 'This is coming in your family.' The things started coming true, so they had some PTA meetings about me, because a lot of the children were upset. Some people said I was a witch. They called my dad down to the school and told him I would have to leave, if I didn't stop. I carried it to extremes just before that. I drew my eyebrows way up and made my face up like the woman I saw. I would just sit quietly and talk to the woman in my mind. I could see her and what she looked like. She said she was hundreds of years old. They all lived hundreds of years on her planet. So that was quite interesting. But my father got really upset with me and said how embarrassed he was. He told me I had to knock off that stuff and stop making up all these stories. So that was the end of that."

"That's too bad, but understandable, Diane. Let's get back to what we'll be starting with today, your dream of the UFO nine years ago. Did anything happen after that '20/20' show?"

"After that UFO incident, I began to realize that possibly what I'd thought or felt as a child might also be true. Maybe I had been contacted. Then I started to hear a lot on television, and I felt that possibly those contacts could have been real. Whenever those things happened to me, it was always something good. It was never fearful or negative. I would get a lot of comfort."

"Do you feel you have been contacted since you were a child?"

"One interesting thing comes to mind. One time in Washington, D.C., I was about twenty, and I was standing with a man, talking in the parking lot of my apartment. We were looking at the stars. It was a beautiful night. We were looking up and talking about something else, and we saw a UFO. I mean we saw it! This was not imagination or anything. It was red, glowing, and it was moving in straight angles across the sky. It would stop and move, and stop and move. We watched it for about five minutes, and then it zoomed away. So I went in and turned on the television set. I was shaking, because I thought, Oh God, the UFOs have landed! There was a news bulletin that came on and interrupted the channel and said, 'A UFO has just been sighted over Washington, D.C.' And I thought, Oh my God, we really saw this thing. He said, 'Details on the eleven o'clock news.' And you know, they never mentioned a word about it, not a word. So the government, I guess, covered it up."

I got us each a glass of water. It was good to stand up and stretch a bit. I told Diane about Timothy Good's book that had just come out, *Above Top Secret.* He had spent years collecting data on the worldwide cover-ups of governments of their own investigations of UFO sightings.

As soon as Diane had finished her water, she leaned forward excitedly. In a conspiratorially lowered voice, she said, "Now another thing I'm going to tell you, Edee. Darn, I wish I had those letters! One day, about four, five years ago, Paul [Diane's husband] came home and he was shaken. He said, 'I want to show you something that came in to the company by mistake.' It was addressed to a different company, Technical something; his is Technical Analysis. We opened it up, and it was letters from an Air Force colonel to Barry Goldwater and some other people. And there were these letters back and forth about how this colonel had seen UFOs. He knew of other Air Force people who had seen UFOs, and why wasn't some of this information out, and what was going on at some Air Force base in California where they had a UFO and some alien bodies. This was all in these letters. There were all these different letters back and forth, and copies of letters. Paul said, 'I'm really scared about this. I don't know what I should do.' And I said, 'Oh, this is wonderful! I can't wait to show it to this one and that one.' He took the letters, and I never saw them again. He said he got rid of them."

I was totally fascinated by what Diane was telling me. I had known her for years and knew she was telling me the truth. It would be completely out of character for her to be making up a story about this. Also, since it was so recent, I felt that her memory of it was probably accurate. Further questioning brought out

that there were about seven letters and that Barry Goldwater
knew all about the issue. Paul had figured out to whom the letters
should have been sent originally and had mailed them on without
making copies.

I would have loved to have seen those letters and for them to
have been made public. We had gotten off onto an intriguing
tangent. But it was now time for us to see about Diane's "dream."

Diane meditates daily, does regressions herself and, under hypnosis, gave birth naturally about two years ago to a beautiful baby
girl. I helped her with the birth by giving her hypnotic suggestions. It was a peak experience in my life. I knew Diane was an
exceptionally fine hypnotic subject. Within a few minutes, Diane
was ready to be regressed. I asked her to go back to the night
about nine years ago when she had had the dream of a UFO. I
counted to ten and asked her to report whatever came into her
mind.

*

DIANE: I'm in bed, I can feel the bed and the room. Dick's
there, he's sleeping. This is the first time I remember this, but I
get up and I go out to the backyard. I thought I heard something.
So I go out to the backyard. It's very, very quiet. And what I
heard, now I can hear it . . . it's humming. It's a hum. So I
thought it was the pool, maybe the pool was on. [Pauses] The
next thing that happens is I start to feel very, very heavy. There's
this heaviness coming over me. My whole body feels kind of
funny and heavy and numb. And I look up and I see this light,
just a light. So I think, well maybe it's a helicopter, a light from a
helicopter. It's shining down on my face. And then I feel this
numbness, so I'm afraid. [Pauses and frowns]

DR. FIORE: Tell me everything that you're aware of.

DIANE: I feel afraid. I don't know what's happening to me. I'm
in this light, and I can't see out of the light. I don't see around
me. [Long pause] Now I see okay. There's been a gap somewhere, because now I'm walking in this large ship and there's

these . . . about twenty black people, sitting down in the ship, on this, almost like a bench.

DR. FIORE: How are they dressed?

DIANE: These black people are dressed in a Western American style. They look very confused and disoriented. And there's this man . . . now I see him beside me, but he's tall, and I said to him, "Why are all these black people here?" And he said, "Well, these people were sent down into the most difficult of circumstances, like poor ghetto places, for a very high service there. These are different souls." And I'm really confused, I don't understand what he's saying. And now we're going into this room. Oh, I understand. . . . Okay, there's a time difference. I'm really there for a long time, but when I'm put back, the time hasn't changed much. I don't understand this difference, but it's like we've left the atmosphere and we've come back.

DR. FIORE: You're going to go back to before you're in the ship, and you're going to take it moment by moment, without any gaps. You're going to allow yourself to remember everything that you experienced.

DIANE: The numbness first and the heaviness. It's like I'm lifted. I can't stop it. It's like a magnet, and I can't stop it. It's pulling me away. And I think maybe I must be dying. Because I'm going . . . away from the ground. [*Pauses*]

DR. FIORE: What emotions are you feeling as this is happening?

DIANE: Confusion. Like am I going to be okay? Am I going to see God? Or am I dreaming? Maybe I'm dreaming. But it happens very quickly, and I'm in this room. It's a strange room and it's got a very strange metal all around it. Now I can see this room. It's almost circular and it's small and I'm seeing it better now. I see these blue lights, about eight or ten blue lights on the ceiling and they're turned on . . . they cover the whole ceiling. They go through the whole room. And something's happening from these lights. It's like my body feels . . . the air smells funny. The air I'm breathing has a sweet smell to it. [Sniffs] Almost like honeysuckle. And I'm alone. It seems like I'm here a long time, but I guess not.

DR. FIORE: What are you doing?

DIANE: I woke up on this table. And . . .

DR. FIORE: What position are you in?

DIANE: I was lying down on this table. On my back. And it's cold. I look around. Now I don't have . . . I don't have on the same clothes.

DR. FIORE: What do you have on?

DIANE: I have on these . . . it's like a white, almost like a white pair of shorts, and it ties right here. [*Points to her waist*] And a little top . . . that ties here and here. [*Points to the center of her chest*] I don't understand this, I really don't. The door is opening. It goes inside the wall. And there's this very tall man with dark hair. And I think he's a doctor. For some reason, I think he's a doctor . . . I don't know why. Now I've been here for a while, I don't know what happened. So I said to him, "Can you make my muscles grow? Can you help me to get over this disease?" [*Long pause*] Now we are walking down this hallway. . . .

DR. FIORE: How did he answer you?

DIANE: He says, "The body is not as important as the spirit. Your spirit is already well, and your body will follow. And you're here. We're watching our children." That's all he says, "We're watching our children."

DR. FIORE: How do you feel when you hear that?

DIANE: He's so special. He's so wise. When he talks, it's very low and very soft. And comforting. And he touches so nice. I don't have to be afraid of him. But the black people are a little afraid. They're the first people I see. "And they're up there," he said, "to refresh their minds." I don't understand what he means. But they've been planted . . . their souls have been planted in specific places of high need.

DR. FIORE: Are they in the same room with you?

DIANE: No, I was alone. I asked him, "What are the beautiful blue lights?" It's almost like a violet-blue. And he said, "We put everyone here first so that their bacteria won't hurt us." I don't understand that, but it's like a cleansing room. When you first come up, you come in here . . . and it's like you're sleeping and you're breathing and these lights are killing something. And he said, "We checked you." I don't know what happened. That's why my clothes were different. They took my clothes away, my pajamas. And it's warm out. It's cold in that room, but it's warm out in the corridor, where we're walking. We're going to some other place.

DR. FIORE: Where are the black people?

DIANE: They're sitting, waiting to go in this room. Not the blue-light room, but there's another room. There's so many of us, there's a lot of us up here. This must be a huge ship.

DR. FIORE: How many would you say there are?

DIANE: The corridor that I walk through is filled with people. There's like twenty here, and over here there's thirty or forty. And we're being . . . it's like this contact is made every so often, to give us strength and to see how our bodies are doing physically. I don't understand. We're part of this group that comes into the physical body that sometimes has trouble adjusting to the vibration of the physical form. And it's like, it's . . . we have to learn to stay focused.

DR. FIORE: How do you know this?

DIANE: That's what they're telling us.

DR. FIORE: Who are they?

DIANE: They call themselves the Planters. They go to different parts of this world and different parts of other worlds to check up on their . . . it's like we're distant cousins. It's like we were planted here thousands of years ago to start the colony. And there were different planets that planted different things here. It's not like an experiment, although I'm starting to feel like one. He says, "No, no, no." I feel not as evolved as they are. And I feel a little uncomfortable that I'm not on their level, like my dog might feel around me or something. I'm feeling that I hope they'll be kind, because they're so far advanced. I want to be like they are, but I'm not on that level. I'm just still growing. They can do so many things. They can . . . they can materialize themselves. They can levitate things. They can travel in this ship by making this ship change form and then beaming it on this laser beam of light to another destination. And that's how they go from planet to planet. And when they take us out of orbit, we go . . . we go away. I see the earth through this little window . . . it's green. But the time is stopped. And when we come back, it's just a few minutes difference. They can do anything. They're so incredible!

DR. FIORE: Tell me what happened to you. You're walking down the corridor, and you see the black people and the other people, and then what happens?

DIANE: They said they want . . . they must keep making contact, because certain people . . . policemen and doctors and healing professions and psychics, social workers, and people who care, those people are drawn to try to change the negative force that is on a self-destruct cycle . . . the people who don't care about pollution and don't care about the natural way of the planet. And the others are waking up, and they want to try to counter that, to save the planet so we don't destroy it through some ignorance of the others. So he's saying to me that I need to pray for communication. There is a part of my brain, somewhere in the middle of my brain, that enables me to tune in to a different frequency. Be careful how I use it. Never think a negative thought toward another, for that thought is energy, and the higher the vibration of the one using it, the faster the energy can be created in the physical form. We're all in this big room, and we're listening to this man talk. "Go out and be of service. And talk to us. We are always here. You will hear us, and you must come from time to time." For this . . . it's like a renewal somehow in this room. . . . I don't understand what we go through, but it's a renewing process to help us deal with this dimension. Sometimes the chemical imbalances can throw us off, if we're not getting the right light foods. The energy waves from the televisions and the radio frequencies can disrupt us. It's too much going on. It's like we can't make our brains quiet, so we become agitated and irritated. The only way we can protect and balance is turning on that little thing in our head and changing our frequency. This enables us to help transcend time and space, to see the future, to see the past, and to help bring about healing within an individual's mind and body. When they came here, and it was like 40,000 years ago when they first came . . . they took up many people.

DR. FIORE: Is this being explained to you? And if so, is it being explained to you individually or to all as a group?

DIANE: As a group.

DR. FIORE: And is one person explaining this or are there several?

DIANE: No, there's just that one "doctor," I call him, but I don't know why I call him a doctor. When they bring you up, they do something in your brain.

DR. FIORE: Let yourself remember what was done to your brain, at the count of five. One . . . two . . . three . . . four . . . five. Just report everything that comes into your mind.

DIANE: [Pauses] It's hard.

DR. FIORE: Don't try. Just let yourself remember. Remember where you are when this is being done and what's happening.

DIANE: I'm back on the table. [Pauses] And I'm awake, but I can't move. There's this, almost like an X-ray machine that goes from the top to the bottom. I said, "Are you going to take blood?" And they said, "No, we don't have to do that." [Pauses] "What are you looking for?" "We're looking for the way that you have evolved in physical form over the thousands of years." "Did my soul evolve with the body?" And I'm not understanding how the connection is made between the soul and the body. If the soul comes in a body, that body begins to form, like a response from the thought of the soul. And the vibration of its environment and that's what makes you look the way you do. And they're interested in my reproductive system. Especially. They want to make sure that there's not a weakness for a new generation. They're speeding up production of something in my brain. It's like a radio turned on that hears frequencies, intercepting thoughts, intercepting your music, the way a radio does when you turn it on, and that's the way you explain it. It's almost like a needle, but it's not. It goes in through the top of my head, into my brain somewhere. It's not really painful, but there's something going in there. And then I feel . . . I feel calmer. And they told me I would have another baby. And I said, "But I've had my tubes tied." And they said, "No, that doesn't matter. You will have a healthy baby." And I keep asking them to heal my body. I keep asking them, "Please, can you make my muscles grow?" They said, "You will not get worse. Eat foods with the highest vibration on your planet; they will nourish you. And you must talk to us. Talk to those of the light. That's who we are. And when you feel the light, you will get your nourishment. Bathe in the light. That is the force of love." And I feel this heat in my body, in my reproductive system. And it's like starting from there and going out. It's in my ovaries. I don't want to go home. I want to stay here. Because I feel lighter and I walk so easy here. I feel like I weigh fifty pounds less, and I said, "On the planet, I feel heavy. I can walk here, I can bend down and get up." But I cannot go. I can't go with them.

DR. FIORE: How do you know that?

DIANE: My vibration is not up to theirs. I can't yet disappear and reappear, the way they can. He says we will all do that, eventually, and the more we pray in the light . . . this accelerates our vibration. That is the key to our evolution . . . is that contact with God, who created the universe. And those who have gone before us who walk in this light of love and service. So communication is the key to our evolution, through quietness, just being quiet and feeling that part of the brain inside the middle, asking it to turn on, like a radio, and then waiting to receive our information. All things are known through that receiver. Those who don't do it become pulled down to the force of a lower vibration, and they'll become angry and hurtful. You must awaken that part of the brain. They say, "Turn that on and join the light, and then help others to awaken their light as well." We all then hold hands and affirm our missions, and we would be strong together.

DR. FIORE: Who holds hands?

DIANE: All the people in the room from all over our area, the Bay Area. They work this area today. And they only come back every so many years, it feels like. But this trip is the biggest one. They seem to be concerned about the bombs and the lack of love between countries. And so people have to be stronger in order to little by little, raise the vibration of the planet.

DR. FIORE: How do you know this?

DIANE: That's what we've learned, and we feel it in our hearts. They say that the animals are also part of this. We are to the animals, as they are to us. They're in our care. And if we can love those things that are evolving toward the light, that will enable love to come to us more, as well. How can we kill our animals and destroy our nature? If we can learn these lessons, we can go on into a different vibration where we will be able to drop the heaviness of physical form and travel among the stars, free of disease, free of aging. [*Long pause*] We all want to stay, but we wake up. I wake up in bed, and I remember only part of the dream.

DR. FIORE: Let's see how you got from the ship to your bed. Let yourself remember at the count of five. One . . . two . . . three . . . four . . . five.

DIANE: I'm standing on this disc. It's a circle about four feet by four feet, and the ship seems to be very high up in the sky. I mean, I can see the outline of California, I'm so far up.

DR. FIORE: Are you in the ship at this point?

DIANE: I'm in the ship, and we're standing on these discs, and then I feel that numbness again and I see that bright light again, and then I'm in my bed. And this metal thing I'm standing on in the ship is very, very dense. It's a different feeling, of a metal I've never stood on before. And I don't have any shoes on and I'm in my pajamas.

DR. FIORE: Let yourself know how you got from wearing the shorts to wearing your pajamas.

DIANE: [*Pauses*] The pajamas were waiting for me in this large open area, where we all come into to go back home. That's where our clothes are, and we just put them on there. It was so warm in the ship. It felt like it was eighty-some degrees, and we didn't need to have a lot of clothes on. Only in that blue-light room, it was cold. It was very cold there, but the rest was very warm, almost like the sun was shining on you.

DR. FIORE: Let yourself remember if you were given any suggestions that you would not remember.

DIANE: I don't remember that.

DR. FIORE: Okay. Approximately how many people were in the room where you were all together?

DIANE: In the room where we were holding hands, there seemed to be about fifty or sixty people.

DR. FIORE: Did you recognize anyone?

DIANE: No. And there was . . . in that corridor, a lot of black people, all together.

DR. FIORE: Were these same black people together in the room where you were all holding hands?

DIANE: Yes, they were there, and when I looked at them, they were the most beautiful people. Their eyes were so beautiful, and they seemed so wise. They were evidently in more distressed areas of our area, and they were working with people who had really gotten out of balance. They were very religious and very filled with such joy in the face of what seemed to be a lot of obstacles to overcome. So I felt very good where they were. They were beautiful spirits. And they needed a lot of extra encouragement.

DR. FIORE: Were you given any information about your specific role?

DIANE: We all seemed to be taught that we were here to show others how to awaken that part of them inside their brains that helps to communicate with the light. I remember asking if the light had to do with the earth and it was the universal light. In other words, there seemed to be one light for everybody, and even them [the extraterrestrials]. Even though the planet was still young, they had come and had children with some of the people, so some physically were a little more evolved. But the light was for everybody, and it would renew and strengthen on all levels, no matter what the evolvement was. So it seemed like there was a central point for this light that radiated out to the planets. And that light is high consciousness . . . of thought that is pure in every sense of the word. We call it God on this planet. They never mention too much about specific religions or anything like that, just universal light. It was in each of us. And all we had to do was ask for it to waken and to grow. That's all we had to do, nothing else. [*Long pause*]

DR. FIORE: Go back in time to when you were a little girl, to the very first time when you met with the woman, with the extraterrestrial who guided you, at the count of five. One . . . two . . . three . . . four . . . five.

DIANE: Right now I'm fifteen, and my sister, Denise, is lying on the bed. And she's ill. She's almost nine. She says to me, "Diane, who is that lady standing there?" But I don't see her. And she said, "She's so beautiful, I've never seen anyone that beautiful." I could sense something, but I didn't see anything. And I just held her hand and said, "It's okay, Denise." And then that night she died. And I kept thinking about that woman she saw. Who was she? Now that, that's fading away, and I'm going back

. . . I must be . . . six or seven. I'm in my room. Upstairs, alone. [*Pauses*] And there's . . . there's somebody in my room and I start to feel afraid. And I wonder if it's the bogeyman that my baby-sitter said would get me. But there's this light, and I don't understand why I see this light in the corner. It gets brighter. There's almost like an outline in the light. I can't see the face. I just see this outline of this woman with dark hair. She has her hands out. And so I put my hands out. And when I put my hands out, with my palms up, my hands start to tingle. And I think she's very nice. And she's smiling. And I feel the tingling in my hands. [*Smiles*] And then I also feel the warmth in my head. And then she's gone. And she never said anything to me then.

DR. FIORE: Let's move to the time when somehow you are informed that she is from another planet, that she is an extraterrestrial. At the count of five. One . . . two . . . three . . . four . . . five.

DIANE: I'm in Mount Ranier. I have to walk to school a long way. It takes me almost an hour, every day, back and forth. Something happens, I don't remember where. This woman . . . it's as if she begins to merge with me. For a short time. To feel the earth energy. And when I look in the mirror, it's almost like I see her too. So she's there, sometimes out of me, and sometimes she comes in me.

DR. FIORE: What is your reaction to this?

DIANE: When she comes in me, I start getting A's in school, because it's easier when she's there. And I also can see into people easier. It's as if I feel their thoughts. I begin to ask her questions about our planet. And I'm talking to her when I close my eyes when I sit in the park. And she tells me all these things. But I didn't listen to some things she told me.

DR. FIORE: Why is that?

DIANE: I was telling everybody about her, and some people were laughing. And I feel very bad about that. And they didn't want me to talk about it to everybody.

DR. FIORE: Whom do you mean?

DIANE: Those people on the . . . where she came from. I wasn't supposed to say all those things, because people laugh, they don't understand. And I did get in trouble, like she said, but she said not to worry about it, that they would know someday. And she was only there a short time, and then I didn't see her anymore.

DR. FIORE: How long was she with you?

DIANE: It seemed like maybe a month.

DR. FIORE: Let's see if you ever were taken anywhere, into a ship or anything of that sort, during your contacts with her. Let yourself remember.

DIANE: I remember now. I had forgotten this, but now I remember. I'm in this big funny kind of see-through tube, and I'm standing up. And when she decides to join with me, we get into this tube together. And when she left, we got into the tube again, and then she was gone.

DR. FIORE: How many times did that happen?

DIANE: It feels like I went up twice, once when we went in the tube, and once when we went back into the tube, and she left.

DR. FIORE: Let yourself know what happened just before you got into the tube, and where the tube was.

DIANE: [*Pauses*] Well, it's in a ship . . . the tube is in a ship.

And . . . I can't remember how I got there, but I think it was when I was walking.

DR. FIORE: You're going to let yourself remember, it's very clear in your mind. You're going to take it step by step and remember everything. At the count of five. One . . . two . . . three . . . four . . . five.

DIANE: Okay . . . I'm waking up now, and it's late at night and everybody's asleep and I hear a humming. So I'm going out to the backyard, and it's very clear; there's no clouds. And I'm wondering where is the humming. It's louder and louder. And then there's that light again. It's the same feeling like before, the numbness and the light getting brighter and then everything around me getting darker . . . and then I'm in the ship.

DR. FIORE: Is this the first time you've ever been in the ship, or does it feel familiar?

DIANE: No, it's the first time. I feel like I'm dreaming. It feels like I must be . . .

DR. FIORE: What's happening to you?

DIANE: [Pauses] I said, "Am I in a dream?" I'm only thirteen, fourteen. "Oh no, child, this is true." There's another man, but it's not the other one, the doctor. He's different. He takes my hand and we go down like little corridors that are short and circular. I feel lost very quickly. I don't know where I'm going. Now I see this woman . . . dark hair, dark eyes. Very straight hair. No curls. Very white face. Her skin is so white and pure. And then we hold hands. And she said, "Do you remember me?" And I remember her from when I was little. And she talks different than everybody else. I can hear her talking even though she doesn't move her mouth. The others, they talk to me, but she thinks to me, and I can hear her. So she must be special. [Long pause] That's when . . . I begin to change.

DR. FIORE: Where are you at this point?

DIANE: I'm just holding her hand, but I can't remember . . . everything's going black after that. I can't remember what happened.

DR. FIORE: You're going to let yourself remember. It's crystal clear in your mind at the count of three. One . . . two . . . three. Just speak out whatever comes into your mind.

DIANE: [*Long pause*] I'm in the theater. It's almost like that other auditorium we all went to, but it's a little different. It's longer, and there's this big screen. It's like a movie. I don't know why I'm looking at this screen. All these things are flashing so fast on the screen, one after another, words and pictures, and words and pictures. And I'm just supposed to look at it. And it's almost like, as fast as it's flashed on the screen, I know it. I'm just watching it. I don't know how long I'm there. There're several people there, looking at this screen. Now the lights are on, and . . . and I'm back on this different table, and they move this funny thing up and down my body again. They're looking for something, but they don't really tell me anything. They just go up and down my body with this machine. And again, they're interested in my ovaries. Because I can feel that heat, when the machine stops there.

DR. FIORE: When did they do this examination?

DIANE: The first time I went up. I didn't say too much, like I did when I went up the other time. Then I said many things. But when I was little, I just sat there mostly and watched. And the beautiful lady didn't talk that much to me, she just looked at me and smiled, and I could feel things.

❧

Diane came out of hypnosis feeling a little groggy. She had been under for just short of two hours. She was tired, but very interested in what had emerged. There were many unusual aspects to her work; the female alien "possessing" her for a month, the information she had been given, her many contacts over the years. I suspected that there also were many more we had not delved into. It had been a delightful experience working with her and one that she felt had enriched her life. Additionally, it had answered some questions she had had for years. She left feeling good, and feeling good about what she had learned. In fact, we both felt uplifted.

14

"I Went Through
Those Venetian Blinds!"

🖊 "I was extra sensitive. Every time I read a newspaper, saw a TV news show, or heard people talking, I would pick up on parts of the conversation that would start what I call the nagging. I would have this overwhelming desire to say, 'But you're wrong,' or, 'I need to correct you.' 'If you do this, a hundred years from now, this is what we're going to have.' So I started drinking."

"To try to cope with it?"

"Yes. I found that when I drank, I could be normal. I could have a social relationship with people. I could listen to their babblings and conversations and be a part of it, and this other thing didn't bother me."

🖊

Fred had come to my office just after I had finished writing *Encounters*. A colleague, Josie Hadley, had told me about him over dinner one evening about a month earlier. He had seen her several years before and had benefited greatly from hypnotherapy. During their work together, he had related to her a remembered close encounter of the fourth kind. That in itself was unusual. She and I and other hypnotherapists with whom I had discussed the topic found that abductions usually became known only with hypnosis. Josie gave me his name and suggested I contact him.

Fred and I couldn't meet sooner because he was in Europe, and when it was possible for us to get together, the finished *Encounters* manuscript had already been sent to my agent and editor. But I felt that it would be very interesting to include him in the book, because he had recalled the abduction experience without the aid of hypnosis. I planned to interview him and then check his remembered account against the material that emerged with hypnotic regression. If it proved to be as unique as I suspected, it would be well worth adding his chapter at the last minute.

✦

The nagging that Fred had referred to was a consequence of his remembered CEIV. At this point, fifteen years later, it no longer troubled him. In fact, it appeared that very little troubled this dynamic businessman and author. At fifty-three, he seemed the picture of health and was full of surplus energy. He talked so rapidly, I was glad I had a reliable tape recorder to back up my verbatim notes.

"Fred, before we get into the details of the abduction you told Josie about, I'd like to know if you have any evidence of having been contacted before, maybe when you were a child."

"Something happened to me in the Boy Scouts when I was eleven or twelve years old. We were out hiking at a Boy Scout camp in Riverside County in Southern California. We were walking along, and I heard a voice saying to me, 'Gregory. Have you noticed that Gregory's not with you?' And I looked around and he wasn't there. And I hollered out to the guys, 'Where's Greg?' 'Oh, he'll be along.' And I said, 'No, there's something wrong.' And then we all laughed and joked about it a little bit. But it concerned me, and I went back the way we had come. There was a ledge, and I heard this noise, crying. And I went over to the ledge. I saw Greg. It was a good eighty-foot drop. And he was hanging on to a dead mesquite bush. He couldn't move. And he said, 'Help me, help me, Fred.' I helped him get up. He got up and he said, 'I was scared to death. I was afraid if I yelled out I would fall. And I was afraid if I did anything I would fall. All I could think about was that I was going to be here forever.' And that night when we were sleeping, or one night during that week of camp, was the first time those people were around."

"Do you remember seeing them?

"Sort of. But I'm concerned that this is being fabricated in my mind because of the Mountain View incident, which happened later."

"Something gave you a warning about Gregory being missing. That in itself is remarkable, whether it has anything to do with aliens or not, Fred."

"In my growing-up years of junior high and high school, if I was with a group of people socially, adults or children, it made no difference, if I spent some time with them, I would sit there in my little mind and say, I know what's going to happen to them. And my father, the typical Italian father, would say, 'Don't think. What are you doing there sitting and thinking?' But that was a very minor type of thing. This perceptiveness helped me in the beginning of my career in sales. I could sit with someone, a customer, and he would discuss with me something that was going on in the business, and I'd say, 'Well, if you do that, this might happen. Of, if you expand the business, have you taken into consideration what that's going to do to your existing customers?' But it wasn't as powerful then as it was after the Mountain View encounter. That's when it really started coming in strong!"

"What happened to you? Josie told me you apparently had a close encounter that you remembered without hypnosis. Is that right?"

"Right. Well, I'll tell you about it. One night after a meeting, I had gotten home, was quite tired and went to sleep. During the night, I was awakened. I looked around and there was nobody in the room. The bedroom faced the street. It had a large window, an eight-by-six-foot window, with those old-style venetian blinds. Remember the wide ones, two inches wide, that were so hard to clean? The blinds were open. I was lying there and I started to move. This is the one thing about the whole experience that I have never been able to fully accept or understand. And I probably never will. I went through those venetian blinds! I was absolutely terrified. I went through them. They didn't open. The window didn't open. I literally went through those blinds. To this day, it astounds me! The next thing I saw was a sign saying Church Street. There is a Church Street in Mountain View. Then I saw the building. GTE Sylvania had a light, inflatable building that was kept up by two large fans on each side, and I was over the top of that building. I could see that building, and that's what gave me my bearings. That's how I knew I was still in Mountain View. And I'm looking down at those buildings and down at the Sylvania complex and the Central Expressway. I was thinking, oh my God, what if people see me? I'm nude. Then the next intelligent memory I have is being inside the building. At that time, I thought it was a building. It was a large round room with these people walking around, the aliens."

"Did you know they were aliens?"

"Oh, absolutely!" He laughed and continued, "In the beginning I thought I was inside that inflatable building, and these people had clean-suits on. But I thought, either there's a whole bunch of five-feet-one-inch people working in this building or . . . These things were going through my mind. But this UFO group wanted me to give them technical data. But I had no technical . . . I'm not a technical person. But I'll describe the room to you. It was round, and you couldn't see any light, like a light bulb or a lamp or a chandelier or anything. It had sort of like this backdrop all the way around, with fluorescent-type tubes or something on the other side. That's where the light in the room emanated from. And it was in gray tones. You're seeing color, but everything looked like tones of gray and black, like a very soft black-and-white photograph. And they put me on a table, and that's when I started getting nervous, and I said, 'What are you doing?' We were communicating in a strange way."

"Were you speaking out loud to them, Fred?"

"I was, but they weren't. But I understood everything they were saying to me."

"Were they communicating telepathically?"

"I guess so, because I heard them, but I didn't hear them. My ears didn't hear what they were saying, I did. And, of course, they had those outfits on. They have to wear those, the prophylactic outfits. That's what makes them look weird."

"So you talked to them?"

"Yes, we talked. Of course, I'm an inquisitive person. When they put me on the table, I told them I didn't want to. I asked them what they were going to do, and they said, 'We're not going to hurt you.' And I said, 'I don't want to be on this table. Can't we go sit somewhere?' There's no chairs. 'Let's go sit somewhere.' 'Well, no, we have to do this. We have to take care of this first.' I'm paraphrasing this, but that's what they said to me. And I said, 'No.' That's when I realized that what I said didn't make any difference. That's really hard to deal with, when you're a person who likes to sense that you have control of your life, and you've spent thirty-eight years of your life making decisions in relative freedom, practicing some self-government. But you're practicing it on yourself, self-discipline. To have someone else say to you, 'You haven't got the choice. We have to do this.' There is no choice. That's the hardest thing, Edee, to experience. You have no choice. Well, then they brought a clear Plexiglas dome down. I was lying on my back. I could see through it. I could see everything that was going on. They had some things they used to reach inside. And they were messing with me, but nothing hurt. They were messing with my genitals and my nipples and my teeth." Fred chuckled, "My nipples! It was weird!"

"Were you still nude?

"I don't wear anything to bed. It's one thing to be that way in your bed, it's another to be that way in public. By the way, that's another interesting point. When I was looking down at the building, I was looking down for people. I wanted to shout, 'Hey look at me.' Until I got in front of Sylvania. Then the first thought was that they might see me naked." He looked a little sheepish and smiled. Then, growing serious, he continued, "So they're working on me."

"You're on your back and there's a Plexiglas cover over you, Fred?"

"Yes. A Plexiglas-type of thing. They had a way of manipulating tools inside of that chamber. They could put their hands in, down at the bottom, because I felt that. Not their bare hands, but they could put them in, and they were messing with my feet. I don't know exactly what they were doing. They were looking at me. And then, just like that, the air left that chamber. It was a total vacuum. Caught me completely by surprise. I couldn't breathe. My chest wouldn't move. I was absolutely panicked!"

Fred's hands gripped the arms of the chair. His breathing stopped momentarily. Then he took a deep breath and continued, "She said to me, 'Don't worry. It's going to be okay. This isn't going to last long.' I couldn't talk, but I was thinking, You've got to stop this or I'm going to die. I'm a human. I'm a human. And she was saying, 'So are we.' Then, when that stopped, whatever that vacuum was, there was the greatest feeling, to be breathing again. That it was over! It was like a great physical release for me." His body relaxed and he smiled in relief. "We talked after that. I could tell the males from the females. The females had breasts. The woman, the one who seemed to spend the most time communicating with me, said, 'Of course I have a vagina.' And I said, 'Why did you say that?' And she said, 'Well, you're wondering if we have . . . if we are like you are. I'm just like you and just like everybody else. We're the same. We have children, but we don't have families. We think sometimes that you are children, because of the way you portray us.' And she explained to me why they wear the uniform. It keeps them immune from everything. They may have something. I'm not a doctor, but they may have some bacteria or virus in their system that's perfectly okay for them that could kill us if one of us got it or it spread amongst us, and vice versa. So they wear these outfits. They're white, and they have like sunglasses that are right on the uniform. They're dark, but you can see the eyes in there. You can see the mouth. These uniforms were really tight on their skin. I was trying to figure out how they were breathing, why they weren't suffocating."

"Fred, you must have seen the picture of the alien on the cover of *Communion*. Do you feel that he's of a different species, or do you feel he looks that way because there's a uniform that's covering him?"

He shook his head and rubbed his hand over his mouth. "This is my opinion. That's the way the uniform is. I saw that, the artist's rendition on the cover of *Communion*, and I've seen other renditions. That's the way you and I would look if we had one of those suits on."

"Do you think the reason they don't appear to have hair is because their heads are covered?"

"I don't know whether they have hair or not. But, for instance, most of your hair is on the top of your head, and if you had that outfit on, your hair would be bulging inside of it, and there was no bulging. It was tight, all the way down. I could tell the age of those fellows. I could sense they were in their late twenties, early thirties. And I could tell she was pretty and very feminine. Yet when they were away from me in the room, talking in some other areas, from the rear they all looked the same, except for a little difference in the woman's figure. We discussed the similarities between us and them. There is no difference except for height. They're just like us. They have eyes and teeth, and they eat food, and breathe air and things like that."

"And you know that from the conversation?"

"Yes. I really learned a lot. They treated me like I was a child."

"The sequence is that they brought you in, then they put you on the table, then they talked to you afterward?"

"When I first came in there, the conversation was very curt, polite but curt, sort of reassuring. Then they went through this messing with my body. After that, it seemed to be more like we're talking now, except I was lying there talking. I'm talking, they're not talking, okay? And another thing, Edee, when I was inside the case, whatever it was, we could still communicate. In other words, they either had a microphone in there or they were using whatever it is they use. Which reminds me, she seemed to be the one who was doing most of the talking. Everybody else was kind of busy. Have you ever had an operation?"

"Yes."

"You know how it is when they first give you the gas or whatever it is they give you. You see people walking around doing things, and you wonder what they're doing. It's very similar to that. A lot of activity. Nobody's just sitting there."

"How many people were there?"

"In that chamber, in the beginning there were about a dozen and at the end there were probably five, including her."

"Were all of them interacting with you? Were they all doing things related to your presence?"

"I think so. There were some of them over there working on a table, and there was some equipment. That is when I saw their backs. But my sense is that everything that was going on had to do with me. She was the one who began the conversation about oneness and how we've got them wrong."

"I'd love to know more about that in detail."

Fred chuckled and leaned back in the chair, crossing his arms behind his head. "I guess I started my usual wisecracking, typical salesman. I was making comments to myself, but she heard them, can you understand that? I had thoughts about her. Of course, she picked up on them. Then she would respond to me, you know, very professionally. But I could tell when she was feeling humorous. When they were talking back and forth, I could sense the humor. By the way, I couldn't understand what their conversations were at all. I don't even remember if it was verbal or mental, except I knew they were talking. She would talk to them and then talk to me, or he would talk to me and then talk to somebody else. And I'm getting it when they're talking to me, but not getting it when they're talking to someone else. Yet I knew they were talking, they were communicating."

"But it seems you could pick up that they were being humorous with each other."

"Yes, and with me. And our kind of humor. The real emotion of humor. Then she said, 'You've got it all wrong.' I don't, but she meant people. She explained, 'We're not invading anybody. And we're not here to stop people from causing a nuclear holocaust. All the different things that you think about us are false. We're the ones with the problem.' And that's when I came unglued. 'We're the ones with the problem. We want to know more about where we came from so that we can resolve this problem, the oneness problem.' As best I understood it, they're technologically and intellectually ahead of us, but the things that make up the elements of a human are the same universally. The emotions, the feelings, the bad as well as the good, the quest for power, for domination. We're all linked that way. She said they had reached a point where they had eliminated almost any form of discrimination, prejudice or conflicts, because of years and years and years of working the way we're working toward this goal, one race, one nation, one world type of thing. Those are my words, not hers. They don't have religious conflicts. They don't have wars. They haven't got affirmative-action programs. They don't need them. We didn't need them either then. But using that to illustrate, they don't have race wars and KKKs and all that kind of stuff. But what they've done to themselves is that they've lost their identity. They've lost their individuality. There's an emotion in her when she's discussing this with me. And what they're leaving with me is, first of all, I wasn't picked because I have anything special about me. Those people in that laboratory didn't know how the selection process worked."

"What do you mean by the selection process? How were you selected?"

"Yes. I mean, it's not that I might be smarter than someone else or more available, or dumber than someone else. That wasn't their decision to make. They had these random selections that were going on. According to her, they had been doing it for a couple of years at that point. So we talked, communicated about this oneness thing. And they see our conflicts from an admirable point of view. They don't see anything wrong with people having differences in beliefs or philosophies of life, but as the essence of individuality. So what has happened with them is they lost their identity, their individuality and their uniqueness. Maybe they have lost the sense of destiny and of individual achievement, all

these individual things that we take for granted." Fred took a
deep breath and leaned forward. "You can imagine what it was
like for me, after having that experience. I had some prejudices
before, and they were gone. All of a sudden, I looked at some
people whom I had held in a prejudice, and now I said, this is a
unique person. I can't be who I am, if he's not who he is. Because
if he and I were the same, I would lose my identity, my individuality."

"That's pretty powerful thinking, Fred." I was mentally planning the regression we would be starting soon. I asked Fred for
more details about the sequence of events.

"It seemed like we conversed for a long time. I was very comfortable. I was not self-conscious of the fact that I had no clothes
on. I wished it could have gone on longer. But I thought that
must be what it's like to be raped, because someone else controls
your body, and there's nothing you can do. Nothing! But I didn't
feel that way afterward, when we were talking. Then it was like
just talking, like we're talking, sharing ideas and things like that. I
have this thirst to know more, to know as much as I could. And
some I forgot, by the way. It comes back to me every once in a
while. Then, Edee, I don't know when I left. I do remember
being back in bed and saying to myself, Oh God, you just had a
nightmare. And I fell asleep. When I woke up, I remembered it.
But I went around during the first week almost in a state of
euphoria." He frowned and continued, "With the exception of
when I was listening to people saying things that I knew were
taking them in a direction that was dangerous, dangerous in relation to the understanding I had from the aliens, of what they
considered danger to be. So I started to be one of the boys." He
shook his head resignedly.

"What do you mean by that?"

"Started drinking and denying the thing. I got ahead of myself,
Edee. I was going to say that first week was euphoric, but after
that I really felt violated. I felt that I had been personally violated.
And it took a long time to get over that. That's a weird emotion.
On the one hand, there's the excitement of the experience and

what it has done, and at the same time, feeling that you really have been abused."

"Do you feel that there are any other negative consequences of that incident still affecting you? Any symptoms or vulnerabilities that you would consider negative changes?"

"Yes." He paused and scratched his head. "It's this uncanny ability I have to make projections. It's a plus and a liability."

"Fred, are you still drinking excessively?"

"The alcoholism's not an issue anymore. That was dealt with successfully through hypnosis. By the way, one more thing of interest. It's New Year's Eve, and my wife and I and another couple are on Front Street in Lahaina, in an open restaurant, looking out to the ocean. New Year's Eve is a big celebration in Hawaii. There was a bit of a storm, and the power went out, and we're sitting in the restaurant with a minimum of fifty people, plus people walking up and down the street, celebrating. I looked up and saw a UFO. Actually I saw three of them, in formation, and I nudged my wife. I said, 'Look!' And she said, 'I'll be darned!' And she turned to our friends and said, 'Hey, you guys, there's three of them up there!' And they looked up and saw them, and then we talked about it for a little while. And we said, 'We saw some of those when we were in Scotland.' And this was just a casual, midnight-snack conversation amongst four people. I would estimate there were a minimum of sixty thousand people who were awake at that moment on the island of Maui. Some of them must have been looking in the sky. We were the only ones that saw them, as far as we know. Because I didn't see anything in the paper the next day. There was nothing on the radio about it."

"What did the UFOs look like?"

"These were what I call the triangle-style, because you can see the three engines on the bottom of the ships emitting exhaust and fire. So it looks like three triangles flying in the sky. But since it's dark, you can't see the shape of the ships, all you're seeing are the engines, but they were flying in formation. What you're looking at when you look up there are three little round balls of fire in the shape of a triangle, flying in a group of three. In our type of formation, the V-formation. Isn't that cute?"

"Fred, our time is slipping away. Let's do the regression now."

Fred was a naturally good hypnotic subject. His work with Josie had enhanced his ability to slip easily and quickly into an excellent trance. I asked his inner mind to take him to his first close encounter with the visitors. After a brief pause, he began speaking slowly, in a higher, childish voice.

◢

FRED: I'm in the Boy Scouts. I'm eleven years old. We're on a survival trek, having a ball, singing songs, talking about the girls over at the camp on the other side of the mountain. And Gregory's not there.

DR. FIORE: What makes you think of him?

FRED: I don't know, we're just all together on the trail, having a ball. I don't even know him.

DR. FIORE: Go to the very moment when you think of him.

FRED: I had to go find some sticks. That's how we cook. No forks or anything. We gotta learn how to survive. We have to get these sticks, birch, hardwood. There's not much birch around. And I was out scrubbing around, and there was a guy sitting there on a rock.

DR. FIORE: What do you think when you see him?

FRED: "Hi! I'm looking for birch." He has black hair, white skin, black eyes. Kinda skinny. [*Whispers*] Not much bigger than me.

DR. FIORE: How is he dressed?

FRED: He has on a shirt and pants and shoes.

DR. FIORE: He's just dressed normally?

FRED: Except he's really white. He needs sun bad.

DR. FIORE: Are you startled when you see him?

FRED: No. The guys are around. I could holler out. I don't think that's real hair. It looks like somebody painted it on there. No beard, no hair on his face. No smile either. "What do you want?" "You're special." "Why me?" [*Whispers*]

DR. FIORE: Go back to the very moment you saw him, and take it second by second.

FRED: There's all this mesquite and tumbleweeds and stuff, and I'm trying to find some hardwood to make my utensil out of. And I come walking around, and there he is, sitting there. [*Pauses*] "What do you want? What do you want me for? Oh God . . ." [*Cries*] "I'm not going to hurt you. Everything's going to be fine." And before the day's over, I'll know that we've talked to each other. He's going to prove it to me. "You're going to make me some kind of Captain Midnight?" "No. . . . We need you to help us. You're going to help us. And you're not going to say anything to anybody." "How do you know that? I'm going to go tell Mr. Foster." "No you won't." [*Whispers*] He's not any bigger than I am. [*Long pause*] Now he's gone. What a weirdo! [*Cries*]

DR. FIORE: What are you feeling?

FRED: I waited until he was gone before I cried. [*Cries*] 'Cause he scared the shit out of me.

DR. FIORE: Do you know why he was scary?

FRED: No. [*Trembles*] I don't know what's going to happen, and he said I would. And I'm scared. It's all stupid stuff!

DR. FIORE: Let's find out what happened. Move ahead in that same day to the next significant event.

FRED: We're on our survival hike. And I notice that this kid, Gregory, isn't there.

DR. FIORE: Move to the very moment when you notice that.

FRED: Holy shit! Aha . . . The guy is over there on the other side of a tree. Spooky. And I see him and he sees me with those little beady black eyes. And I look and there's no Gregory. And I have this feeling that Gregory's in trouble. I told the guys.

DR. FIORE: Move to the moment when you had the feeling that Gregory is in trouble.

FRED: I'm looking right into those little black eyes, right in those eyes, yeah, yeah. . . .

DR. FIORE: What thoughts come into your mind?

FRED: Gregory's gone, Gregory's going to die. I've got to check. Then the little guy's gone. And I say, "Aren't some of you guys going to go with me." They say, "No." And I went back. And I heard him, like whimpering. And Greg's big. And my first thought was, I'll bet he's down there. And what am I going to do if he's down there? I can't help him. He's going to pull me over if I stick my hand down there. I looked over the edge, and there his face was, right there. I could almost reach him, and he's crying. He says, "Help me, Freddie." And I look around and the guys are gone, and I can't find the little beady-eyed guy either. And I finally figured out how I could help him. I wrapped my legs around this massive tumbleweed. It was sticking in my legs. And I got ahold of his arm and his neck, fricking near choked him. [*Long pause*] I got a badge from Mr. Foster. But I don't want badges and stuff. I can see Mr. Foster standing up there with his little badge, chewing everybody's ass out. "You always take a count before you leave," he said.

DR. FIORE: Now move to the encounter that you call the Mountain View incident. Let yourself remember it exactly as it happened.

FRED: [Pauses] I'm looking down at everything. I'm looking at me. I'm looking at me lying in bed.

DR. FIORE: How do you feel as you're doing that?

FRED: Silly. Yes . . . Not bad-looking. I'm trying to hide from . . . going through those venetian blinds, because I know that's going to happen. [Whispers] Oh no! [Pauses] Okay, take me where you want me. Take me. [Long pause]

DR. FIORE: Continue speaking out.

FRED: I'm scared to death. I'm floating. I had pizza after the meeting. Maybe it's the pizza. I'm floating, and I'm naked. And there's the House of Pancakes . . . Payless. I'm over the top of the Leisure Arms. Wow . . . El Camino, the Chevy Dealer. There's the building. It's kept up by air, you know. Like a balloon. Church Street. [Long pause]

DR. FIORE: You're going to let yourself remember this exactly as it happened.

FRED: I'm scared. I'm inside. I know I'm inside, but I can't see anything, and there's people here. Oh boy! The lights! I'm on the table.

DR. FIORE: How did you get on the table?

FRED: I don't know.

DR. FIORE: Let yourself remember.

FRED: It was black, like going inside of an armadillo shell. And now, here I am. But I'm smarter this time. It's not like I thought it would be. I'm not living it. I'm seeing it like a movie.

DR. FIORE: From what vantage point are you seeing it?

FRED: I'm on the table, but I'm standing here. Very nice, clean place, circular. No direct lighting anywhere. Gray. It's like being in a black-and-white movie, but it's not. Equipment all around the room, a lot of space. Small people.

DR. FIORE: How tall are they?

FRED: Four feet eight to five-two. And everything's clean, spotless clean. No pictures anywhere, no calendars, nothing. Trying to see the gauges. I got the message I can't go over there. I'm to stay right here. But I'm outfoxing them. Because I'm standing up, looking down at me. Now I can see what they're going to do. She knows everything that I think of and everything that I'm saying. I am not going to spend my life as a living test tube. No matter how good it might be for me. And I'm getting hot. It's hot in here. [*Whistles*] "Could you cool it down a little bit?" "No." "I'd like to get up." They're not going to let me. I feel kind of foolish. And now, all I want to do is get it over with.

DR. FIORE: What's happening?

FRED: They put this cover over me that's made out of some kind of clear like glass. God, I feel naked! No clothes. And now they're messing with me.

DR. FIORE: What do you mean by that?

FRED: They have some way of getting inside here with probes. Poking at me. Poking at me! I'm not circumcised. [*Laughs*] It's embarrassing.

DR. FIORE: At this point, do you feel you're in your body?

FRED: Yes! Boy, oh boy! Is it hot in here! Phew! . . . "Oh, thank you, thank you, thank you." [*Whispers*] I gotta help you. They're taking it off now. Just—white! Tight to the skin. Outfit. And those girls have got nice bodies. Small, but nice. I feel like a fool, because whatever I think, I know they're hearing. [*Pauses*] And we should not be that way about them. They are just like we are, just smaller. And that could have happened in any galaxy in the universe. It all depends on how people breed, whom they select for their mates. And the head is normal, maybe a little bit bigger. So don't expect any new great mystery. [*Laughs*] And they do it! And they have babies. And . . . yes, the fingers are small.

DR. FIORE: How many fingers do they have?

FRED: Four and a thumb. And it's warm. I can feel it through the uniform. It's just small.

DR. FIORE: What's small?

FRED: They're just small. [*Long pause*] Yes . . . I feel very good. I wish I could just stay here for a long time. Taste, smell, taste, smell, taste, smell. [*Whispers*] It's like the inside of a scuba mask. That's what it tastes and smells like, the inside of a scuba mask.

DR. FIORE: Go to the feeling of the vacuum that you described before.

FRED: I beat it this time. I outsmarted them. When I knew they were going to do it, I beat it, somehow.

DR. FIORE: How did you know what they were going to do?

FRED: Because I've been here before. I know how they operate.

DR. FIORE: How did you beat it?

FRED: I closed off. This is gonna kinda screw things up, I'm afraid. Can't have one without the other. Can't have the sharing without the vacuum.

DR. FIORE: Where do you get that idea?

FRED: From her. I feel like a little kid, trying to beat my mommy at something and I got caught. So it's going to come back down. It's going to come back down. [*Whispers*] Shall I just give in to it? [*Pauses*] Oh yes. They don't use anesthesia. They don't use that kind of stuff. They can put you in this, and they can just hack away and do anything they want. And when it's over, you feel good instead of sick. [*Pauses*] I can't get away from the table. They won't let me. [*Long pause*] I wish I knew why it was me. I wish I could be of more help. And I wish I could bring this little lady back to my apartment tonight. [*Smiles*]

DR. FIORE: How did she respond when you had that thought?

FRED: She laughed. Have you ever heard a person laugh and not seen the mouth move? Quite an experience. Isn't it funny how we develop concepts about things and people and all that, and then when you get right down to it, everything is so logical. Like humor. He's . . . oh, the guy down at the end where my feet are, I'll bet if I got that mask off, he'd be that little beady-eyed guy. [*Pauses*] They really don't want to hurt anybody. They really don't want to mess up things or alter the course of our lives. That's why they stay up here the way they do, instead of landing somewhere. They don't trust . . . the nature of man, because they are like us. They know that the people would get ahold of those things and they might use them for the wrong reasons.

DR. FIORE: Is that what they're telling you?

FRED: Yes. And I'm a simpleminded man, and that's why I'm here. I thought that was pretty unique to us Americans, and that's why I'm here. I want to know how I was selected. They say they have no choice, that that's taken care of before they get here. [*Pauses*] I wish we could do some things together. I'd like to take them to a football game. [*Shakes his head*] They've already been to a football game.

DR. FIORE: How do you know that?

FRED: They've seen everything.

DR. FIORE: How do you know that?

FRED: She told me. "We can travel at the speed of thought. And if you would just think about it logically, you would understand." And they eat food.

DR. FIORE: Did you see that happen, or did she tell you that?

FRED: She told me that. I can't see anybody eating. I can't see how they could eat anyway.

DR. FIORE: What's happening now?

FRED: There's a round like door over on the wall. There's like a uniform stretched around the door. They climb into the uniform from outside, so that when they're into the room, the uniform is around them. And there's this guy helping them. Then they shut the door, and then the next time somebody comes in, the same thing is repeated. They put this white uniform around the door, the way you'd put a balloon on a whistle. And the other side is similar. The door is gray. And when they open that door, when they go out, they leave the uniform inside.

DR. FIORE: Now what's happening?

FRED: Cholesterol. I don't even understand what that word means. My first exposure to the word cholesterol.

DR. FIORE: Who mentions that word?

FRED: The guy at my feet.

DR. FIORE: What does he say to you?

FRED: He says, "Cholesterol!" It's negative. It's . . . ewww . . . cholesterol!

DR. FIORE: What is he implying?

FRED: Like he's saying, "Ewww . . . gonorrhea. Yuk!" He's not saying gonorrhea, but he's saying cholesterol in the same . . . way. It's disgusting to him. [Long pause] I'm feeling like I'm waking up. I just had the wildest dream of my life! That's what it was. It's nothing more than a dream, an illusion. Because there's absolutely no way in the world that I can go through those venetian blinds.

DR. FIORE: Go back to just before you wake up.

FRED: Cholesterol.

DR. FIORE: What happens next?

FRED: Cholesterol. Then she puts her hand on me, and it's warm.

DR. FIORE: What part of your body does she touch?

FRED: She's touching my stomach. And . . . I don't know what he's doing down there. My feet are kinda gross. Doesn't seem to bother him. I want to know if we're ever going to see each other again.

DR. FIORE: Whom do you mean when you say that?

FRED: The girl and . . . I'm not really supposed to say "girl," you know.

DR. FIORE: Did she say not to use the word "girl"?

FRED: Yes, and "man" too. But I don't know how else to communicate. Think. And I really want to know what this is going to do to my life.

DR. FIORE: What do they say to you?

FRED: There will be no harm, and that it will be good. That woman was right. They had been with me before. And there'll be no harm, and I'll be wiser. I was chosen. They don't know how. I mean, they do what somebody else tells them to do. The people who are chosen are people who will not exploit the experience. Can you imagine that word? Exploit the experience. How in hell are you going to exploit it? And I'll be taken when my work is done.

DR. FIORE: What does that mean to you?

FRED: I don't know. I say, "What do you guys think about God, G-o-d?" [Pauses] They have God, same one. But there hasn't been a Jesus there.

DR. FIORE: Is that what they told you?

FRED: Yes. And all the elements are the same. Minerals, and the chemistry of the body, the uniqueness of the human.

DR. FIORE: Did they tell you where they're from?

FRED: No.

DR. FIORE: Did they tell you what galaxy they're from?

FRED: This one. "Do you know if there's any more [earth's]?"
Yes. There's more earths, not E-a-r-t-h, in this galaxy.

DR. FIORE: What does that mean to you?

FRED: There's consistency of creation in the universe. And that
maybe I should have spent more time in my science classes.

DR. FIORE: Is that what they told you?

FRED: No. That's what I said, and it brought a laugh. There's a
black guy and a white woman who're married, and they went
for two days.

DR. FIORE: How do you know that?

FRED: She just told me.

DR. FIORE: Who told you?

FRED: My friend here. She was trying to make me feel better
about not doing well in science. I guess I better start reading
books about this stuff, huh? I don't know anything about those
people. I'll find out later.

DR. FIORE: Continue to speak out.

FRED: I'm just getting to feel better all the time. I'd like to spend
a little time with the guys, but she seems to be hanging on here. I
feel like they're not going to let me off this table. And I'm lying
here thinking that I'm in control of the situation, and yet I have

no control. My friend here, at my feet, tells me that they don't rule my emotions. They don't rule each other's either. And that . . . that would be the ultimate disaster for anybody. They're just like we are when it comes to that business. Water. Must have water and oxygen and food. "And I need to know how you can communicate the way you do, because I think that would be a wonderful thing." And I am told that outside of the experiment, they communicate just like we do. I mean noise comes out of the mouth. They don't speak English, but we could learn their language. "Why do you keep it so warm in here?" "Your bodies have to be warmed up." "Tell me what it looks like over there." And that's the simplicity of it all, no methane gas floating around in the sky. They have oceans, salt, and water and clouds, everything.

DR. FIORE: Now what's happening?

FRED: [*Smiles*] I want to hold them. That's an earthling emotion. "But I really would like to give you guys a hug. Because I believe that you really are who you are, and you really are here for the reasons that you've told me, and I'd like to give you a good old-fashioned hug." And I'm sitting up, and he's saying, "Don't leave the table." And I'm hugging him. You can almost feel right through these things. Nice hug. And she's telling me to remember to look for the logical, simple things to find the answers and stuff. And I said, "How can I go home without getting off the table?" I see little flashes. Vividly! Like shooting stars or something, and . . . I'm lying in my bed.

DR. FIORE: Are you back in your home now?

FRED: Yes.

DR. FIORE: How do you feel?

FRED: Great.

✱

Fred took a while to come completely out of hypnosis. There was something obviously still bothering him. "I realized with the Gregory incident that nobody else was going to either believe me or help me. I started back down the path. I don't know how, but I knew he was in trouble. It was like a dream. I heard him sobbing, but I couldn't see him. I knew he was down on the side of that ledge, somewhere. My first reaction was to pretend that I didn't hear him. To pretend he really wasn't there and to run away, so that I wouldn't have to help him. The reason I didn't want to help him was he might pull me over." Fred smiled guiltily. "Maybe the real reason was that I didn't want to accept that the beady-eyed man was real. I didn't want to accept that he could arrange Greg's accident." He turned in his chair and looked out the window at the creek. With his back to me, he said. "But most of all, I didn't want him to single me out."

After a few seconds of silence, he rotated the chair back and looked deeply into my eyes. There were tears welling up in his. He stared down at his lap as though weighing something in his mind. Then, seeming to have resolved a conflict, he looked up at me again and smiled broadly. "I guess they have. And I'm glad they have. I wonder what's next?"

"... The Signs and Symptoms That Are Indicators."

As you were reading in the preceding chapters how thirteen people experienced their close encounters of the fourth kind, you may have noticed certain features that many accounts of abductions had in common, as well as some features that were unique to a particular case.

In order to help you assess whether you have had a close encounter with extraterrestrials, I'll describe the signs and symptoms that are indicators. It is not necessary to have experienced all of them, sometimes just one important indicator can give you a very strong clue about the repressed event. Often, that one may be only the tip of the iceberg.

1. One of the most telling signs of a CEIV is the phenomenon of missing time. As you can imagine, the experience of being removed from one's home or car, for example, and then transported into a craft, the subsequent meeting with ETs and being returned, takes time. It is a very common finding that there is a gap, usually of about an hour or more, though sometimes less.

One of the very first cases I studied involved a loss of about one and one-half hours. Two women were in their car when the CEIV occurred and were surprised to find that time had elapsed, though they had no memory of what had happened in the interim, and also to find that their vehicle was on a road going in the opposite direction from their destination. They had been abducted, car and all, and deposited in a remote area.

Missing time is usually noticed after day or evening abductions, which took place while the person was awake, as contrasted with the frequent CEIVs that begin while the person is sleeping and therefore has no concept of time.

2. As you may have seen in many of the cases you've read about in *Encounters*, nightmares or dreams of UFOs or aliens (or monsters with large eyes) were later revealed to be memories of actual happenings. ETs often give hypnotic commands to contactees that they will only remember the experience as a dream. Sometimes they give suggestions that the event will not be remembered at all, but the mind tries to heal itself through the dreaming process, so the flashback is remembered as a dream upon awakening. Take seriously even one dream, especially a nightmare. *Write it down as soon as you awaken. Do not wait!* Dreams, no matter how vivid, have a way of evaporating.

3. Sleep disorders are often strong indicators for many reasons. If you consistently wake up at a certain time, for example 1:43 A.M., you can be reasonably sure that something traumatic happened at exactly that time. If you are unable to go to sleep easily and naturally, it may be that your subconscious mind is seeing to it that you do not put yourself in a position for the traumatic event to be repeated. That's the subconscious's job. Likewise, sleeping very lightly may be a way of avoiding vulnerability. However, as you have seen, it certainly doesn't matter whether a person is asleep or not for an abduction/contact to take place. But the subconscious mind does not operate with the same logic as the conscious mind.

Of course, sleep disorders may be due to many causes that have nothing to do with CEIVs, and if disturbing, should be treated by competent medical and/or psychological specialists.

4. If you wake up during the night or in the morning with

unusual bodily sensations, even once, you may be experiencing the aftermath of a CEIV. Actually, this telling sign may occur other than on awakening. Remember Sandi from Chapter Two? She "came to" from her CEIV on her living-room couch in the evening. The most common bodily sensations are tingling, numbness, dizziness, heaviness and paralysis. These are often accompanied by disorientation. All of these sensations are temporary. Take note of them, especially if you experience this sign in addition to others. But be warned: Like sleep disorders, these sensations may be due to physical conditions requiring medical attention, perhaps urgently.

5. In a few of the cases in this book, and in others that I did not include, individuals found unexplained marks on their bodies. These were due to procedures done during an examination and/or operation or treatment. Scrapes, fine red lines, little scooped out marks, bruises which suggest that blood was drawn are all frequent indicators of a CEIV. Nosebleeds, bleeding from the ear, finding blood on the sheets that cannot be explained are signs that should be noted. These may be due to insertion of tracking implants. One of my patients reported she had a little extra "cartilage" at the base of her nose, almost between her eyebrows. Medical tests could not determine what it was. She suspected it was some sort of tracking device that had been inserted by the visitors. And remember the case of Tom of Chapter Five. He also found something had appeared in his nose overnight.

6. ETs are monitoring and watching people throughout the world. If you suspect that they are monitoring you, you could be correct. On the other hand, many emotionally and mentally troubled individuals believe they are being monitored by the CIA, FBI, the television or aliens.

It appears that the visitors communicate with us by telepathy (mental talking). We are told to go outside, to drive to a deserted area, to look into the sky, etc. Unfortunately, the issue again becomes cloudy, because many emotionally and mentally disturbed people feel they are being communicated with and controlled by others, including extraterrestrials. These paranoid ideas come from within themselves and have no basis in reality. Also, to add to the confusion, CEIVs and subsequent communication and monitoring can lead to emotional/mental imbalances. This is why I have emphasized the need for finding a competent therapist or investigator.

7. Many abductees/contactees report seeing UFOs repeatedly. Even one sighting can be the remembered part of an abduction, the major part being repressed. However, if you often see UFOs, it is quite probable that you have had one or more CEIVs.

8. Some people remember their CEIVs clearly, exactly as they would any other significant experience. Most only remember the event vaguely, even doubting that it actually happened. If you remember anything at all resembling the encounters you read about in this book or in others, you are probably recalling an experience that actually happened.

9. As you saw, for example in the cases of James (Chapter Ten) and Ted (Chapter Eight), healings took place. In about one-half of the cases I've been involved with, there have been healings due to operations and/or treatments. Sometimes the cures are permanent. At other times, the conditions recur. There can be many other reasons for spontaneous cures or improvements of physical conditions. But if you have noticed a healing or inexplicable improvement, and you see other signs of a probable CEIV, you may have had help from the visitors.

10. Reactions of fear, anxiety, unusual bodily sensations (tingling, numbness, heaviness, etc.) to pictures of, movies or documentaries about, of discussions of UFOs and CEIVs are very clear indicators of abductions by aliens. A friend of mine noticed she felt faint and her heart started beating wildly when she picked up a book, *Communion*, at a local bookstore. As an experiment, I showed her the cover of the Time-Life book *The UFO Phenomenon*, and she was again overcome by anxiety. A later regression under hypnosis revealed a CEIV.

I'll now give you a checklist of the ten most common indicators of CEIVs.

1. Missing time
2. Nightmares and/or dreams of UFOs and/or aliens

3. Sleep disorders
4. Waking up with unusual bodily sensations
5. Unexplained marks on the body
6. Feeling monitored, watched and/or communicated with
7. Repeated UFO sightings
8. Vague recollection of close encounter(s)
9. Unexplained healing
10. Fear of and/or anxiety about UFOs and/or ETs

While the foregoing are the most common signs of a CEIV, there are many other less frequent indicators that I'll briefly touch on now.

When people are abducted or contacted, they are often told of a mission or task that they are to carry out immediately or in the future. Since the experience is repressed, the feeling of needing to do something important nudges at them, yet they do not know what they are supposed to be doing.

A number of fears, all related to the buried traumas, present problems of varying degrees of seriousness. Fears of needles, being kidnapped, UFOs, monsters, aliens, creatures with large eyes—like owls—the dark, certain places in the home or outside, and many other fears and aversions, have been traced to CEIVs.

People often develop psychic abilities (telepathy, precognition, clairvoyance, etc.) after CEIVs. Since these experiences may have occurred very early in childhood, it is not unusual for these individuals to feel they were born that way.

Seeing a beam of light or balls of light in the house is often the remembered part of a CEIV. Sometimes people just remember waking up with the room full of light.

If you have found yourself outside at night without remembering how you got there, it could very well be that you had just been returned from a CEIV. Or, if you've felt an irrepressible urge to go outside at night, you could have been given a telepathic command to do so by aliens.

It is commonly found that UFO buffs or others with an intense interest in ufology and CEIVs are contactees. Leo Sprinkle, Ph.D., known throughout the world for his research into the contactee phenomenon, discovered only recently through hypnotic regression that he himself was a contactee. I believe that most researchers and therapists specializing in this area have been contacted or abducted.

As I mentioned previously, any anxiety reactions experienced while reading this or any other book on UFOs and CEIVs is a strong indicator. What is happening in this case, as with any reactions of anxiety in relation to this topic, is that you are actually partially reliving the original traumatic experience during which you felt anxiety, maybe even terror.

✿

Now that you know the signs and indicators of repressed close encounters with extraterrestrials and have determined that you've experienced one or more signs yourself, you are ready to discover if you have had a CEIV and, if so, what happened during it. The next chapter gives you a simple technique you can use in the privacy of your own home to explore this amazing possibility.

16

"You Can Discover
Your Own Close Encounters."

By now you realize that your subconscious mind has a perfect memory. *Everything* you have ever experienced is recorded in your subconscious memory banks exactly as you perceived it. The inner mind can be seen as your own personal computer. With a computer, you can access files. With your subconscious mind, you can retrieve memories. Therefore you can discover your own close encounters of the fourth kind. Later in the chapter, I'll show you a simple, time-honored method for exploring forgotten memories.

You have seen in previous chapters how people under hypnosis recalled and, at times, vividly relived experiences that they were totally unaware had happened. Repressed memories, those that the conscious mind cannot access, sometimes spontaneously surface in dreams or meditation. On occasion, something will trigger them and they will break through to conscious awareness on their own. The trigger is usually something strongly reminiscent of an aspect of the buried event: a picture, an account, smell, place, anything so similar to what has been repressed that the forces keeping it forgotten are overcome.

The *only* method that I consider safe for you to use on your own is a form of dowsing, using the pendulum. The pendulum, as a dowsing tool, has been used over the centuries for many different purposes: to find missing people (by holding the pendulum over a map); to ascertain the health of the body; to find gold, silver and other minerals; to discover underground water, etc. There are many theories about why and how it works. I personally feel that it taps in to a part of our subconscious mind that is omniscient. In exploring your own possible close encounters, you will be using it as a means of accessing your memory banks.

However valuable and remarkable the pendulum can be, it is *not* infallible. At times, the answers obtained are wrong, misleading or contradictory. However, I and other UFO researchers have found it to be very helpful for exposing repressed sightings and encounters. When you use it, consider the responses as probabilities, not as gospel. It helps, in terms of validity, to double-check, by going over the same questions again on another day and seeing how closely the answers match. Remember, you are using your subconscious mind, and your conscious mind may be interfering. For that reason, *it is imperative to remain as neutral as possible, to leave emotions out,* as you are questioning your inner mind. Also, do not allow a conscious answer to remain in your mind. Take the position of really asking a question, not trying to confirm a preconceived idea. You may be very surprised by the answers you receive.

By using a pendulum, you can discover whether you have ever seen a UFO and especially if you have had one or more encounters of the fourth kind.

Most bookstores and/or shops that specialize in metaphysical subjects and/or crystals or minerals have pendulums of many kinds and different sizes. Some are made of quartz or other attractive minerals set in gold or silver so that they can be used as necklaces. Others are made from various woods or metals. I have an assortment of pendulums that I've collected over the years. One of my favorites is a small clear quartz crystal suspended from Indian beadwork that covers one end.

It is, however, very easy to make your own pendulum in a

matter of minutes. All you need is a string or heavy thread between six and ten inches long. Tie a button, bead, ring, pendant, or even a small cross to one end of the string. Any slightly heavy object may be used, but it is better to use one that is symmetrical. Once you have an adequate pendulum, sit at a table or desk, hold the end of the string between your right thumb and index finger if you are right-handed (left thumb and index finger if left-handed). Rest your elbow on the table or desk. *Without consciously* moving the pendulum, think the word "yes" and will the pendulum to move back and forth in front of you. When you nod your head indicating "yes," you are moving it in the same plane or direction as the desired swing of the pendulum. To establish the "no" response, use the same technique. *Without deliberately* moving the pendulum, think the word "no" and will the pendulum to swing from right to left, or left to right, in a side-to-side movement, just as when you shake your head "no."

At first, the pendulum may not budge. Keep thinking "yes," and imagine it moving back and forth. Soon it will easily and freely swing back and forth in front of you as you think "yes," and from side to side as you think "no." When this happens, you are ready to ask your subconscious mind questions.

While you are establishing the pendulum responses, remain calm and patient. *Know that you can do it!* If you do not succeed the first time, keep trying. Everyone can eventually develop this technique. Once you have the signals working for you, you will have a wonderful tool for exploring your own subconscious mind!

If you use the pendulum on more than one occasion, start each session by reinforcing the yes and no responses. I have used it innumerable times, and each time I get it swinging strongly in the yes and no responses before I begin.

If you become upset while working on your list of questions, stop for a while. Calm yourself. Do something else, and later, or on another occasion, try again. If you are entirely too upset to continue, you have already answered a major question by your reactions. You probably have had one or more encounters and should seek help. The Appendix lists organizations and people who can work with you.

I have designed a list of fifty questions, which follows. You may use these questions or write out your own. If you use the ones here, place a sheet of paper next to you and write the numbers corresponding to the questions, 1 through 50, down the left-hand side. You will record your responses, yes or no (Y-N), next to each number. At the top, you may want to record the date. Then, if you later double-check the answers, write the new date next to the new answers. That way you can compare the responses on each occasion. If you do seek additional help with your exploration, the dates may be important.

I suggest that you have another sheet of paper handy for questions or thoughts that occur to you as you are reading and answering the questions on the list. Another way to go beyond my list is to remember any questions that came up in your mind while you were reading *Encounters*. You may want to reread it, all the while very carefully monitoring your reactions, physical, mental and/or emotional. From these responses, you can compose your own questions.

1. Have I ever seen a UFO?
2. Do I have a subconscious memory of seeing a UFO?
3. Have I had a UFO experience that I do not remember with my conscious mind? (More than one—two, three, etc.?)
4. Have any dreams actually been memories of a CEIV? UFO sighting?
5. Was I alone when I had the UFO experience(s)?
6. Was the experience(s) traumatic? (Emotionally? Mentally? Physically?)
7. Did the experience(s) involve ETs?
8. Where was I first contacted by ETs? Outside? Inside? (Backyard, bedroom, living room, etc.?)
9. Was I taken aboard a UFO?
10. Was I examined physically? (Genitally?)
11. Were instruments used in the examination?
12. Was a needle(s) inserted into any part of my body? (Navel, head, nose, ear, etc.?)
13. Was a "medical" treatment done?

14. Was an operation performed?
15. Were lasers involved?
16. Did any treatment or operation help me?
17. Was I cured of a physical problem?
18. Was I questioned?
19. Did the ETs speak?
20. Did the ETs use telepathy? (Communicate without speech.)
21. Was I given an explanation for the abduction/contact?
22. Was I given information?
23. Did the ETs look like humans?
24. Were they over five feet tall? (Under five, four, three feet?)
25. Were there ETs of different sizes involved?
26. Were there different kinds (species) of ETs involved?
27. Was there more than one ET involved? (Two, three, etc.?)
28. Did the UFO encounter (or first encounter) occur before I was twelve years old? (Five, four, etc.?)
29. Did the last encounter occur less than one year ago? (One month, week, etc.?)
30. Was I told of a mission I was to carry out for (or with) the ETs? (Now? In the future?)
31. Did the encounter last more than one hour? (Two hours, three, etc.?)
32. Was hypnosis used?
33. Was I told not to remember the experience?
34. Was I told not to remember the examination?
35. Did the ETs put a tracking device or object through which they can communicate with me in my body?
36. Have I received telepathic messages from ETs?
37. Are any of my problems (fears, phobias, anxieties, etc.?) due to experiences with ETs? With UFOs? Both?
38. Does my subconscious mind know if someone else I know (brother, sister, mother, father, spouse, friend, etc.) has been involved in encounters with ETs? UFOs?
39. Have I developed any psychic abilities as a result of the encounter/contact?
40. (For women) Have any of my eggs been removed by ETs? (If so, before, after fertilization? More than once—twice, three

times, etc.?) (For men) Was an instrument inserted into my penis? Was sperm removed?

41. (For women) Have I had a sexual experience with an ET? Intercourse? If so, did a pregnancy result? Was the fertilized ovum removed? Naturally aborted? Was the fetus brought to term, born? (For men) Was I forced to have intercourse with a female ET? (Once, twice, three times, etc.?)

42. Have I received information about or visions of future events?

43. Have I received information about or visions of planet Earth changes?

44. Have I received information about or visions of future political and/or social changes? Personal changes? Scientific changes?

45. Am I a human-alien hybrid? An ET?

46. Have I been incorporated by an ET? In the past? Now?

47. Have my experiences with ETs shown them to be hostile? Uncaring? Scientifically objective?

48. Have my experiences with ETs shown them to be loving? Compassionate? Concerned about the welfare of planet Earth?

49. Have I been seriously damaged or hurt in any way by my experience with ETs?

50. Have I benefited in any way by my experience with ETs?

If any thoughts, images, bodily sensations, etc., came up as you asked and answered the questions, be sure you recorded them. These may be excellent clues to, and even bridges into the repressed material that you can use later while working with a qualified UFO researcher or therapist.

If you have uncovered one or more close encounters of the fourth kind, you have confronted something that undoubtedly has been affecting you in many ways. Just by tapping in to it to this extent, you may very well have released the "charges" associated with it and freed yourself from its negative impact. In which case, you should notice across-the-board positive changes in yourself. If not, then you do need to get in touch with a hypnotherapist competent in this field and/or a UFO abductee/contactee researcher. (See Appendix.)

There are also a growing number of support groups for abductees and contactees. The Rocky Mountain Conference on UFO Investigation (annual contactee conference) is a way for people who have had encounters to get together, have counseling, hear speakers and generally share their experiences. You can find out more about it by contacting Leo Sprinkle, Ph.D., Institute for UFO Contactee Studies, 1425 Steele St., Laramie, WY 82070.

"... The Evidence Can No Longer Be Squelched."

Are close encounters of the fourth kind real or are they fantasies? This is a question that has bewildered people for centuries. It is intriguing to read the accounts from ancient times of the wee people, gnomes, fairies, angels and mysterious folk who kidnapped or helped humans.

In the 1950s, when Major Donald Keyhoe's book *Flying Saucers Are Real!* came out, there was great controversy about UFOs that lasted for decades. Only in the last ten years or so has it become blatantly obvious that governments around the world have been doing their best to cover up the UFO phenomenon, including their own investigations into it. In order to accomplish their goals, they have discredited witnesses and silenced experienced air-traffic controllers and pilots, even our astronauts. The cover-up surrounding this exceedingly important topic makes Watergate look like child's play. The net effect is that citizens are still confused. However, the cover-up is not working! As I mentioned earlier, approximately one-half of the people in the United

States believe in UFOs and one out of eleven thinks they have seen them.

Not only do people believe in the existence of UFOs, many accept that thousands among us have been abducted by extraterrestrials. And as more books and reports are published, the evidence can no longer be squelched.

As a therapist, I have been impressed with the very positive results of regressions under hypnosis to CEIVs. People who have undergone one or more regressions have experienced profound changes in their lives. Often symptoms of many years' durations, such as phobias and depressions, were immediately resolved when the patients remembered being abducted and traumatized. In my opinion, the only way these severe problems could have been eliminated by regression is by an *actual* event having been dealt with and the negative energy associated with it discharged. Besides these exceedingly obvious changes, there were frequently minor positive improvements, leading to a general enhancement of people's lives.

Even in those people whom I worked with more as an investigator than as a therapist, and even when the encounters had not been traumatic, I found positive changes following regressions. The case of Dan (Chapter Twelve) is an excellent example of this point. He felt very little anxiety during his regression. In fact, it was a thrilling experience for him. He noticed immediately after our first session a definite improvement in his self-confidence and a wonderful inner peace of mind that he had not felt before.

I believe the experiences that I have reported in *Encounters* are real, that they actually happened very much as they were remembered. By that I mean that the experiences were remembered as they were originally perceived. There were CEIVs, and any distortions or misperceptions were part of the confusion of being in a totally unfamiliar situation that was traumatic. Additionally, the visitors very well could have deliberately done things, used devices and/or given hypnotic suggestions to erase memories or to have what was experienced distorted in certain ways.

Because my main concern is to help people, it is not important to me if the patients/subjects report correctly the color of the aliens' skin, for example. What is important is that the negative effects of encounters be released through regressions.

It has been fascinating for me in working with abductees/contactees to learn that the extraterrestrials can incorporate, either temporarily or permanently. Incorporation, the actual taking over or possession of a human's body by an alien, was temporary in Diane Tai's case and permanent in Dan's. From the accounts of my patients/subjects, it also appears that there are human-alien hybrids living among us. I'm sure that more about this will be revealed in the future and will prove to be very exciting.

One of the most interesting findings that emerged from this work was the many healings and attempts to heal on the part of the visitors. Even when lasers were not yet being used by Earth people, the extraterrestrials were using them on humans in their spacecraft. I wonder if some of the modern developments in medicine, technology and space exploration can be credited directly or indirectly to the intervention of our space friends. Remember telepathy! Wouldn't it be interesting if our top scientists were being helped with their research and development?

I feel that the discovery of visits to our planet Earth by beings from other worlds and their interactions with humans is the most exciting and significant happening of the twentieth century.

Appendix

Organizations

J. Allen Hynek Center for UFO Studies. (CUFOS)
1955 John's Dr.
Glenview, IL 60025

> Dr. Hynek was respected as one of the United States' leading UFO researchers. Since his death, the center continues to investigate reports of UFO sightings. It also publishes the *IUR (International UFO Reporter)*, a bimonthly journal for UFO research, edited by Jerome Clark.

Mutual UFO Network (MUFON)
103 Oldtowne Rd.
Seguin, TX 78155

> Walter Andrus, Jr., Director. This organization has the largest membership of any UFO organization. It publishes a journal and conducts an annual conference for international exchange of UFO information and research.

National Investigations Committee on UFOs
P.O. Box 5
Van Nuys, CA 91401

> This information center publishes books and a newletter based on alleged contacts with a Venusian.

Guardian Action Publications
P.O. Box 27725
Salt Lake City, UT 84101

> This organization offers a free catalog of UFO material. They claim to be channels for the Space Command, extraterrestrials supposedly orbiting around our planet.

335

Fortean Research Center
P.O. Box 94627
Lincoln, NE 68509

> This group investigates UFO reports and other metaphysical miracles.

Institute for UFO Contactee Studies
1425 Steele St.
Laramie, WY 82070

> This organization counsels people who feel they've had a close encounter. It sponsors an annual contactee conference each summer.

The New York Center for UFO Research (NYCUFOR)
134 W. Houston St., Suite 1
New York, NY 10012
(212) 995-0384

> Michael Luckman, the director, sees this organization as a vehicle for disseminating information about UFOs and extraterrestrials. Conferences, lectures, media presentations are the main emphasis. However, there is a referral service for those seeking help with problems arising from their abductions/contacts.

Church of the Seven Arrows
4385 Hoyt St., 3201
Wheat Ridge, CO 80033

> Rev. George Dew is a shaman and pastor of this church. He and his coworkers use shamanic and modern psychological techniques to help abductees.

Publications

The MUFON Journal
103 Oldtowne Rd.
Seguin, TX 78155

> Walter Andrud, Jr., is the director of MUFON. The journal contains articles about international information and research.

Flying Saucer Review (FSR)
P.O. Box 12
Snodland
Kent ME6 5JZ
England

> Edited by Gordon Creighton, FSR is published quarterly (U.S. $30 subscription, plus $10 for airmail). The journal features photographs and articles by an international network of UFO researchers.

UFO Magazine
1800 S. Robertson Blvd.
Los Angeles, CA 90035
$15.00/Bimonthly, six issues

> This newletter gives information about UFO news and related items of interest.

Quest: The Journal of UFO Investigation
106 Lady Ann Rd.
Soothill, Batley
England
$25.00/Bimonthly, six issues airmail

> This magazine contains articles on the latest worldwide UFO research regarding sightings and government reports.

Fate Magazine
3510 Western Ave.
Highland Park, IL 60035
(312) 433-8100
$1.50 per issue/Monthly

> This magazine often has articles about UFOs, personal accounts of both sightings and abductions, as well as summaries of the latest theories and information.

The Star Beacon
P.O. Box 174
Delta, CO 81416

> Edited by Ann Ulrich, this newsletter presents information about UFO abductees and contactees and related topics.

Contactee: Research of UFOs by Direct Observation
P.O. Box 12
New Milford, NJ 07646

> Published quarterly by Ellen Crystall, this newsletter provides information about UFO abductions, contacts and related topics.

The Star Network Heartline
P.O. Box
Poway, CA 92064

> Edited by the Rev. Diane Tessman, this newsletter provides channeled information (Tibus) about "star people" and New Age prophecies.

White Star
P.O. Box 307
Joshua, CA 92252-0307

> This newsletter provides channeled information about Earth changes and prophecies about UFO/ET encounters.

Hypnotherapists Working With Abductees/Contactees

Aphrodite Clamar, Ph.D.
30 E. 60th St., Suite 1107
New York, NY 10022
(212) 988-8042

Beverly J. Carter
4491 South Yates
Denver, CO 80236
(303) 794-7626

Ann Druffel
257 Sycamore Glen
Pasadena, CA 91105
(213) 256-8655

Stephen Field, Ed.D.
800 Oak Grove, Suite 207
Menlo Park, CA 94025
(415) 325-46788

Edith Fiore, Ph.D.
20688 Fourth St.
Saratoga, CA 95070
(408) 867-1100

Josie Hadley
2443 Ash St., Suite D
Palo Alto, CA 94306
(415) 321-6419

Richard Haines, Ph.D.
P.O. Box 880
Los Altos, CA 94023-0880

Tisha Hallet
450 San Antonio Rd.,
Suite 27
Palo Alto, CA 94306
(415) 857-0638

James Harder, Ph.D.
2800 Hilgard St.
Berkeley, CA 94709
(415) 848-6043

Barbara Levy, Ph.D.
317 Eureka St.
San Francisco, CA 94114
(415) 826-2250
(415) 751-3971

Linda Marie Martin
152 Olive Springs Rd.
Soquel, CA 95073
(408) 479-3493

Jeffrey Mishlove, Ph.D.
48 St. Francis La.
San Rafael, CA 94901
(415) 456-2532

Raymond Moody, M.D.
205 Tanner St.
Carrollton, GA 30117
(404) 834-6393

Sharon Moss, Ph.D.
2947 Eastmoreland
Oregon, OH 43616
(419) 691-4926

Jean Mundy, Ph.D.
33 Windward
East Hampton, NY 11937
(516) 267-8896
and 105 West 13th St.
New York, NY 10011
(212) 741-1278

June Parnell, Ph.D.
2219 Rainbow Ave.
Laramie, WY 82070
(307) 742-3394

Alice Rose, Ph.D.
4651 Roswell Rd., Suite
I-8013
Atlanta, GA 30342
(404) 255-7051

Patricia Shaw, Ph.D.
225 S. Meramec Ave.,
Suite 506
St. Louis, MO 63105
(314) 863-3588

Richard Sigismund
1557 9th St.
Boulder, CO 80302
(303) 447-9170

June Steiner
987 University Ave., Suite 6
Los Gatos, CA 95030
(408) 395-9209

Jo Stone, MFCC
P.O. Box 2828
Los Angeles, CA 90078

Sue Street, Ph.D.
University of South Florida
St. Petersburg Campus
140 7th Ave. South
St. Petersburg, FL 33701
(813) 893-9129

Keith Thompson
P.O. Box 5055
Mill Valley, CA 94942
(415) 388-9008

Mary Ellen Trahan, Ph.D.
205 Tanner St.
Carrollton, GA 30117
(404) 834-6393

Norma Triggs
10 Willow Creek
Richardson, TX 75080

Thomas J. Zinser, Ed.D.
2041 Raybrook SE
Grand Rapids, MI 49506
(616) 957-3168

Suggested Reading

Andrews, George. *Extra-Terrestrials Among Us.* St. Paul: Llewellyn, 1986.

Berlitz, Charles and W. L. Moore. *The Roswell Incident.* New York: Grosset & Dunlap, 1980.

Druffel, Ann, and D. Scott Rogo. *The Tujunga Canyon Contacts.* Englewood Cliffs, N.J.: Prentice-Hall, 1980.

Editors. *The UFO Phenomenon.* Alexandria, Va.: Time-Life Books, 1987.

Emenegger, Robert. *UFO's: Past, Present & Future.* New York: Ballantine, 1986.

Flammonde, Paris. *UFO Exist!* New York: Putnam, 1976.

Fowler, Raymond E. *The Andreasson Affair.* Englewood Cliffs, N.J.: Prentice-Hall, 1979.

————. *Casebook of a UFO Investigator.* Englewood Cliffs, N.J.: Prentice-Hall, 1982.

Fry, Daniel. *The White Sands Incident.* Louisville, Ky.: Best Books, 1966.

Fuller, John. *Aliens in the Sky.* New York: Medallion/Berkley, 1969.

————. *The Interrupted Journey.* New York: Berkley, 1966.

Good, Timothy. *Above Top Secret.* New York: Morrow, 1988.

Hopkins, Budd. *Intruders.* New York: Random House, 1987.

————. *Missing Time.* New York: Richard Marek, 1981.

Jung, Carl G. *Flying Saucers: A Modern Myth of Things Seen in the Sky.* New York: Signet Books, 1969.

Keyhoe, Donald E. *The Flying Saucers Are Real!* New York: Fawcett Publications, 1950.

Kinder, Gary. *Light Years.* New York: The Atlantic Monthly Press, 1987.

Larsen, S. J. *Close Encounters: A Factual Report on UFOs.* Milwaukee: Raintree, 1978.

Lorenzen, J., and C. E. Lorenzen. *Abducted!* New York: Berkley, 1977.

Montgomery, Ruth. *Aliens Among Us.* New York: Putnam, 1985.

341

Puharich, Andrija. *URI: A Journal of the Mystery of Uri Geller.* Garden City, N.Y.: Anchor/Doubleday, 1974.

Rimmer, John. *The Evidence for Alien Abductions.* Northamptonshire: Aquarian Press, 1984.

Rogo, D. Scott, ed. *Alien Abductions.* New York: New American Library, 1980

Rutledge, H. D. *Project Identification: The First Scientific Field Study on UFO Phenomena.* Englewood Cliffs, N.J.: Prentice-Hall, 1981.

Sachs, Margaret. *The UFO Encyclopedia.* New York: Perigee/Putnam, 1980.

Sagan, Carl. *Cosmos.* New York: Ballantine, 1985.

Sprinkle, R. Leo. "Hypnotic and Psychic Implications in the Investigation of UFO Reports." In *Encounters with UFO Occupants,* edited by C. E. Lorenzen and J. Lorenzen, 256–329. New York: Berkley, 1976.

Steiger, Brad. *The UFO Abductors.* New York: Berkley, 1988.

Steiger, Brad, and Frances Steiger. *The Fellowship.* New York: Dolphin/Doubleday, 1988.

———. *The Star People.* New York: Berkley, 1981.

Strieber, Whitley. *Communion.* New York: Morrow, 1987.

———. *Transformation: The Breakthrough.* New York: Morrow, 1988.

Vallée, Jacques. *Dimensions: A Casebook of Alien Contact.* Chicago: Contemporary Books, 1988.

———. *The Messengers of Deception.* Berkeley, Calif.: And/Or Press, 1979.

———. *UFO Enigma: Challenge to Science.* New York: Ballantine, 1966.

Von Däniken, Erich. *Chariots of the Gods?* New York: Berkley, 1984.

———. *Gods From Outer Space.* New York: Bantam, 1972.

Walton, T. *The Walton Affair.* New York: Berkley, 1978.

Wilson, Clifford. *The Alien Agenda.* New York: Signet/New American Library, 1988.

ABOUT THE AUTHOR

EDITH FIORE, PH.D., graduated with a doctorate in clinical psychology from the University of Miami. She first became interested in hypnosis when she attended a workshop in self-hypnosis at the Esalen Institute, and she began to incorporate hypnosis into her therapy fourteen years ago. The author of *You Have Been Here Before: A Psychologist Looks at Past Lives* and *The Unquiet Dead: A Psychologist Treats Spirit Possession,* Dr. Fiore now practices psychology in Saratoga, California.

Printed in the United States
by Baker & Taylor Publisher Services